Life of Galileo

The Resistible Rise of Arturo Ui

The Caucasian Chalk Circle

D0170981

Works of Bertolt Brecht
published by
Arcade

The Good Person of Szechwan

The Good Person of Szechwan, Mother Courage and Her Children,
and *Fear and Misery of the Third Reich*

Life of Galileo, The Resistible Rise of Arturo Ui,
and *The Caucasian Chalk Circle*

Mother Courage and Her Children

The Threepenny Opera, Baal, and *The Mother*

BERTOLT BRECHT

Life of Galileo
Translated by John Willett

The Resistible Rise of Arturo Ui
Translated by Ralph Manheim

The Caucasian Chalk Circle
Translated by James and Tania Stern with W. H. Auden

Introduction by Hugh Rorrison

ARCADE PUBLISHING • NEW YORK

FIRST ARCADE PAPERBACK EDITION 1994

Life of Galileo was originally published in German under the title *Leben des Galilei* and was first published in 1980 in this translation, which was revised in 1986. *The Resistible Rise of Arturo Ui*, originally published in German under the title *Der aufhaltsame Aufstieg des Arturo Ui*, was first published in this translation in 1979. *The Caucasian Chalk Circle*, originally published in German under the title *Der kaukasische Kreiderkreis*, was first published in 1960 in this translation, which was revised in 1976 and 1984.

ISBN 1-55970-190-0
Library of Congress Catalog Card Number 93-24754
Library of Congress Cataloging-in-Publication information is available.

Published in the United States by Arcade Publishing, Inc., New York
Distributed by Little, Brown and Company

10 9 8 7 6 5 4 3 2 1

PRINTED IN THE UNITED STATES OF AMERICA

CAUTION

Contents

Bertolt Brecht
Chronology of life and work

Brecht's life falls into three distinct phases demarcated by his forced exile from his native Germany during the Hitler years. From 1898-1933 he is in Germany; from 1933-1947 he is in exile in various parts of the world; in 1947 he returns to Europe, first to Switzerland then to Berlin.

Germany

1898 Eugen Berthold Friedrich Brecht born on 10 February at Augsburg where his father was an employee and later director of the Haindl paper mill.

1908 Brecht goes to Augsburg Grammar School (Realgymnasium) where he is an indifferent pupil and a rebel in his quiet way, numbering among his friends Caspar Neher, later his designer. Brecht was almost expelled for taking a dismissive, anti-patriotic line when set an essay with the title 'It is a sweet and honourable thing to die for one's country'.

1917 Brecht enrols as a medical student at Munich University, where he also attends Arthur Kutscher's theatre seminar. He samples the bohemian literary life of the city.

1918 Brecht is conscripted and serves as a medical orderly, though he still lives at home. He writes *Baal*, a rumbustious, even outrageous dramatic tribute to natural drives and anarchic sexuality, and writes articles for the local newspaper, *Augsburger Neueste Nachrichten*.

1919 Brecht writes *Drums in the Night*. His Augsburg girlfriend, Paula Banholzer, bears him a son, Frank.

He meets the comedian Karl Valentin, the theatre director Erich Engel, and actresses Elisabeth Bergner, Blandine Ebinger, Carola Neher and the opera singer, Marianne Zoff. He writes theatre reviews for *Volkswillen*, a local Independent Socialist daily.

1920   Brecht visits Berlin.

1921   Brecht's registration at Munich University is cancelled. An attempt to make himself known in literary circles in Berlin ends with him in hospital suffering from malnutrition. His new friendship with Arnolt Bronnen, the playwright, leads him to change the spelling of his name to Bertolt, or Bert.

1922   Brecht marries Marianne Zoff. He writes *In the Jungle of Cities*.

1923   Brecht's daughter Hanne is born. The activities of Hitler's National Socialists are hotly discussed in Brecht's Munich circle. The first productions of *In the Jungle of Cities* and *Baal* take place in Munich and Leipzig respectively.

1924   Brecht directs Christopher Marlowe's *Edward II* which he and Lion Feuchtwanger had adapted. He was already using certain devices (plot summaries before scenes, white face make-up to indicate fear) to induce critical detachment in actors and audience. He finally settles in Berlin and is taken on as dramaturg (literary adviser) at Max Reinhardt's Deutsches Theater. Elisabeth Hauptmann becomes his secretary/assistant. The actress Helene Weigel bears him a son, Stefan.

1925   Klabund's *The Chalk Circle*, premiered at Frankfurt and Hanover in January, is directed in Berlin in October by Max Reinhardt with Elisabeth Bergner in the female lead.

1926   *Man Equals Man* premiered at Darmstadt and Düsseldorf. Brecht's work on a play (which he never finished) called *Joe Fleischhacker*, which was to deal with the Chicago Grain Exchange, leads him to the study of

Marx as the only adequate method of analysing the workings of capitalism.

1927 Brecht divorces Marianne Zoff. He works with Erwin Piscator, the pioneer of communist political theatre in Germany, on a dramatisation of Hasek's novel *The Good Soldier Schweik*. He publishes a volume of poems, the *Hauspostille* (Domestic Breviary).

1928 *The Threepenny Opera*, music by Kurt Weill, words by Brecht (based on a translation of John Gay's *Beggar's Opera* by Brecht's friend and collaborator Elisabeth Hauptmann) opens at the Theater am Schiffbauer- damm and becomes the hit of the season. Brecht had provocatively transferred bourgeois manners to a Soho criminal setting.

1929 Brecht works with Elisabeth Hauptmann and Weill on *Happy End*. He marries Helene Weigel. Elisabeth Hauptmann attempts suicide. *The Baden-Baden Cantata* is staged at the Baden-Baden Music Festival, music by Hindemith.

1930 Brecht's daughter Barbara born. His Lehrstück or didactic play, *The Measures Taken*, is given its first performance in Berlin. The communist didactic plays for amateur performance were intended to clarify the ideas of the performers as much as the audience. The first performance of *The Rise and Fall of the City of Mahagonny*, an opera with words by Brecht and music by Kurt Weill, causes a riot as the Nazis voice their criticism at Leipzig. In his notes on the opera Brecht tabulates the difference between the traditional *dramatic* (or Aristotelian) and the new *epic* (or non-Aristotelian) theatre at which he is aiming. Brecht objects to the *Threepenny Film*, sues Nero Films and loses, but accepts an ex gratia payment to refrain from an appeal.

1931 Brecht completes *St Joan of the Stockyards* (first per- formed in 1959).

1932   Brecht's only film, *Kuhle Wampe*, is held up by the censor. He visits Moscow when it opens there in May. His dramatisation of Maxim Gorky's novel *The Mother* is performed by a left-wing collective in Berlin, music by Hanns Eisler. It demonstrates the development of a worker's mother towards proletarian class-consciousness. Beginning of Brecht's relationship with Margarete Steffin. Brecht studies Marxism under the dissident communist Karl Korsch.

Exile

1933   The Nazis come to power. The night after the German parliament building (the Reichstag) is burnt down, Brecht flees with his family to Prague. He moves to Vienna, then Zurich, finally settling on the island of Fyn in Denmark. His relationship with Ruth Berlau begins. He visits Paris for the opening of *The Seven Deadly Sins*.

1934   Brecht visits London. The themes of flight and exile enter his poetry.

1935   Brecht is stripped of his German citizenship. He visits Moscow where he talks to the Soviet dramatist Sergei Tretiakov about the 'alienation effect'. He attends the International Writers' Conference in Paris. He visits New York to look in on a production of *The Mother*, which does not meet with his approval.

1936   Brecht attends the International Writers' Conference in London. He writes anti-fascist poetry.

1937   Brecht attends the International Writers' Conference in Paris with Ruth Berlau. *Senora Carrar's Rifles* is premiered in Paris.

1938   Franco's right-wing Falangists emerge as the likely victors in the Spanish Civil War and Chamberlain signs away the Sudetenland in the Munich Treaty in an effort to appease Hitler. *Fear and Misery of the Third Reich* is given its first performance in Paris. Brecht writes *The*

Earth Moves in three weeks ending on 23 November. He revises it with the assistance of Margarete Steffin, adds a fourteenth scene and retitles it *Life of Galileo*.

1939 In a radio interview with scientists of the Niels Bohr Institute he hears of the discovery of a great new source of energy, nuclear fission. His first response is positive. In April he moves to Stockholm with his family. He finishes writing *Mother Courage and her Children*.

1940 German forces march into Denmark. In Lidingo Brecht completes *The Augsburg Chalk Circle*, a short story set in the Thirty Years War. Brecht's household moves to Helsinki in Finland where his friendship with the writer Hella Wuolijoki begins.

1941 Brecht completes *Mr Puntila and his Man Matti*, *The Good Person of Szechwan* and *The Resistible Rise of Arturo Ui*. He writes war poetry and 'Finnish Epigrams'. Leaving Finland Brecht travels through the Soviet Union via Leningrad and Moscow (where Margarete Steffin dies) to Vladivostock and sails to the U.S.A. He arrives in Los Angeles in July and settles with his family in Santa Monica. He makes contact with other exiles (Heinrich Mann, Lion Feuchtwanger and Fritz Lang, the film director) and with the natives (Orson Welles). First performance of *Mother Courage and her Children* in neutral Switzerland.

1942 Brecht prepares his *Poems in Exile* for publication. He works on the screenplay for Fritz Lang's film, *Hangmen also Die*. He participates in the anti-war, anti-fascist activities of exile groups. He meets Charles Laughton.

1943 The first performances of *The Good Person of Szechwan* and of *Life of Galileo* take place in Zurich.

1944 Brecht becomes a member of the newly formed Council for a Democratic Germany. In April Jed Harris, an American producer and director, enquires about *Galileo*, and Brecht looks afresh at its 'moral'. He writes the first version of *The Caucasian Chalk Circle*, and almost immediately starts reworking it. He studies Arthur Waley's translations of Chinese poetry. In September he begins to revise *Galileo* with Charles Laughton. Ruth Berlau bears him a son who does not survive.

1945 *Fear and Misery of the Third Reich* is performed in New York under the title *The Private Life of the Master Race*. Brecht and Laughton complete the English version of *Galileo* but the dropping of the atomic bombs on Hiroshima and Nagasaki in August gives rise to another revision which stresses the social responsibility of the scientist.

1946 The first performance of Brecht's adaptation of Webster's *The Duchess of Malfi* takes place in Boston.

1947 Charles Laughton appears in the title role of *Life of Galileo* in Beverly Hills and New York. Brecht appears before the *House Committee on Unamerican Activities* and proves himself a master of ambiguity when cross-examined about his communist activities.

Return

Brecht and Helene Weigel go to Zurich, leaving their son Stefan, who is an American citizen, in the U.S.A. Brecht meets Max Frisch, his old friend and designer Caspar Neher, and the playwright Carl Zuckmayer.

1948 Brecht's adaptation of *Antigone of Sophocles* is performed in Chur, Switzerland, and *Mr Puntila and his Man Matti* is given its first performance in Zurich. He publishes the *Little Organum for the Theatre*. Brecht travels to Berlin and starts rehearsals of *Mother Courage* at the Deutsches Theater in the Soviet sector of the city. *The Caucasian Chalk Circle* is first performed in Eric and Maja Bentley's English translation by students at Northfield, Minnesota.

1949 *Mother Courage* opens at the Deutsches Theater with Helene Weigel in the title role. Brecht visits Zurich again before settling in Berlin. The Berliner Ensemble, Brecht and Helene Weigel's own state-subsidised company, is formed and opens with *Puntila*. Brecht adapts J.M.R. Lenz's *The Tutor*. At Gottfried von Einem's suggestion Brecht applies for an Austrian passport (H. Weigel is Austrian) as Caspar Neher had already done. He works with Neher on a play for the Salzburg Festival, which is to be an international showcase for his work.

1951   *The Mother* is performed by the Berliner Ensemble. Brecht finishes the first version of his adaptation of Shakespeare's *Coriolanus*. His opera with music by Paul Dessau, *The Trial of Lucullus*, is tried out and meets with official disfavour.

1953   Brecht writes *Turandot*, and the *Buckow Elegies*. Ethel and Julius Rosenberg are executed in the U.S.A. for betraying atomic secrets to the Russians. Brecht is elected President of the German section of the PEN Club, the international writers' association. On 17 June there are strikes and demonstrations protesting about working conditions in the German Democratic Republic. Brecht writes a letter to the Secretary of the Socialist Unity Party which is released to the press in a doctored form.

1954   The trial of atomic physicist Robert J. Oppenheimer begins in the U.S.A., and Albert Einstein writes an article inveighing against this modern 'inquisition', but the idea that science is subordinate to state security gains currency. Brecht is awarded the Stalin Peace Prize. The Berliner Ensemble moves into its own home, the Theater am Schiffbauerdamm (where he had triumphed with *The Threepenny Opera* in 1928), and performs *The Caucasian Chalk Circle*. The prologue, *The Struggle for the Valley*, is now designated as Act I. Brecht makes public his objections to the Paris Treaty (which incorporated the Federal Republic of Germany into NATO) and to re-armament in general. The Berliner Ensemble's productions of *Mother Courage* and Kleist's *The Broken Pitcher* are enthusiastically received as the highlights of the Paris Théâtre des Nations festival. *Mother Courage* is awarded the prizes for best play and best production.

1955   Brecht adapts Farquhar's *The Recruiting Officer* as *Drums and Trumpets*. He goes to Moscow to receive the Lenin Peace Prize. In December Brecht begins rehearsals of *Life of Galileo* using the third version of the play, a modified retranslation into German of Laughton's English version. Ernst Busch takes the title role. Harry Buckwitz, directing the West German premiere of *The Caucasian Chalk Circle* at Frankfurt, omits *The Struggle for the Valley* as politically inopportune.

1956   Brecht's health prevents him from carrying on with *Galileo* and he hands over the direction to Erich Engel. He visits Milan for Giorgio Strehler's production of *The Threepenny Opera* at the Piccolo Teatro. Brecht is preparing the Berliner Ensemble, which by this time has become generally recognised as the foremost progressive theatre in Europe, for a visit to London when he dies of a heart attack on 14 August. The visit goes ahead and *Mother Courage*, *The Caucasian Circle*, and *Trumpets and Drums* are presented at the Palace Theatre at the end of August for a short season – a landmark in Brecht's reception in the United Kingdom.

Introduction

Bertolt Brecht: 1898–1956

Brecht is an elusive figure, part Baal, part Schweyk, part Galileo – the list could go on. He could use people and yet command absolute loyalty, not least from the many women in his life. He was a dedicated survivor who learnt to co-exist with many masters. A Communist from the late twenties, he never joined the Party. Aware of the excesses of Stalinism (which devoured some of his friends), he never took a public stand against the Soviet Union, yet in 1941 he ended up in California rather than Moscow. Arraigned by McCarthy's House Committee on Unamerican Activities, he convinced his interrogators that he was not a Communist without prejudicing his long-held convictions. When he returned to Europe he chose to have an East German theatre, a West German publisher and an Austrian passport, all for the best of reasons.

His work can be as ambiguous as his behaviour. Try as he might to make plays like *Mother Courage and her Children* and *Life of Galileo* say one thing, they always ended up saying something else behind his back, and they are the better for it. The pragmatic British on first acquaintance took an overdose of Brecht's theories and made him seem dull. Brecht himself was too pragmatic to take his own theorising seriously when he had a stage in front of him; since the days in Berlin when, unathletic as he was, he consorted with boxers and racing cyclists and pointed to their fans as the kind of connoisseurs and enthusiasts he would like to see watching his plays, his aim had always been to entertain as well as inform.

Brecht was born in 1898 in the sleepy Bavarian provincial town of Augsburg, where his father managed a paper mill. He grew up in comfortable circumstances with an avenue of chestnut trees outside the door and a moat full of swans not far away. His mother was Protestant and his father Catholic but this seems to have caused no tension; indeed, being brought up in his mother's church produced the bonus of early familiarity with Luther's German Bible, which remained a fertile source of vocabulary and incident all his writing life. His schooling was also free from pressure, and he later claimed that if he had learned anything, it was in spite of his teachers. He certainly pitted his wits against the system: one anecdote tells how the young Brecht watched one of his friends erase some red pencil and claim, unsuccessfully, that his homework was undermarked. Brecht then added a few underlinings and asked for an explanation of the 'errors', forcing his embarrassed French teacher to raise his mark. Brecht was not very good at French.

Out of school ne pursued his own cultural interests, admiring, at one time or another, Napoleon, Nietzsche and Hauptmann, and developing a taste for literary outsiders. The bohemian lives of the French poets Villon, Rimbaud and Verlaine fascinated him, and in German he was drawn to the anti-classical tradition of Büchner and Wedekind and often sang the latter's saucy little songs to his friends, accompanying himself on the guitar.

Brecht was already gregarious and his circle included Caspar Neher, who would later be his designer, Georg Pfanzelt (nickname: Orge), Otto Müller (nickname: Müllereisert). Their adolescent discussions on life and art in Brecht's attic den or on the river bank were the germ of his later production teams. According to Brecht he had his first experience of sex at seventeen, and from then on he seems to have been something of a stud – an Americanism that would have appealed to him.

In 1917 Brecht enrolled as a medical student at Munich University, possibly to stave off conscription to the Great War, since he certainly was never committed to medicine. One course which interested him was Artur Kutscher's drama seminar. Professor Kutscher was a friend of Wedekind and his biographer, and he enjoyed a reputation as a theatrical pundit. But Brecht was unimpressed and did not hesitate to criticise one of Kutscher's favourites, the minor expressionist Hanns Johst, who later became a prominent Nazi. Johst's *The Lonely One*, a stage biography of the nineteenth-century dramatist, boor and misfit, C.D. Grabbe, was deemed by Brecht to be sentimental and nauseating, and he volunteered to write a better play on the subject himself. *Baal* was the result, and it was the professor's turn to be nauseated. They parted in mutual contempt.

Brecht sampled what Schwabing, Munich's artistic quarter, had to offer. He saw Wedekind play *The Marquis of Keith* and was impressed with the way, as the immoralist hero of his own play, he controlled his audience, despite his shortcomings as an actor. He met the eccentric popular comedian Karl Valentin, and his one-acter *Respectable Wedding* is his homage to Valentin's zany Bavarian sketches.

In 1919 Brecht wrote his second play, *Drums in the Night*, a cynical response to the post-war months. Its hero, Kragler returns late from the war to find his fiancée Anna pregnant and engaged to an 'upwardly mobile' war-profiteer of whom her family approves. Snubbed by her, Kragler repairs to a pub and mobilises support for a Communist rising in the newspaper quarter. It is 1919 and the 'German Revolution' is in progress. Then Anna comes after him and he cops out with the line, 'I am a swine, and swine go home'. Kragler's abandonment of the revolutionaries in favour of 'a big, broad, white bed' later embarrassed Brecht, and he tried to argue that Kragler was a negative, comic figure. His next play too, *In the Jungle of Cities*, is cynical: it is set in Chicago and shows an unmotivated rivalry between Schlink, a Malayan timber merchant, and Garga, an assistant librarian. Brecht wanted the audience to forget about meaning and sit back and admire the technique of the combatants. He was already trying to sharpen audience responses: for *Drums in the Night* he had festooned the auditorium with banners which instructed the audience to take an unromantic view of the proceedings.

The first of Brecht's plays to be performed was *Drums in the Night*, with which Otto Falckenberg opened the 1922/23 season at the Munich Kammerspiele. It received a rave notice from Herbert Ihering, one of the top two Berlin critics, who praised the imagery and power of the writing and claimed that Brecht had altered the literary landscape at a stroke. Ihering then gave Brecht's career a further boost by awarding him the Kleist Prize, Germany's premier dramatic award. 1923 saw productions of *The Jungle of Cities* at Munich and *Baal* at Leipzig, and in 1924 Brecht, whom Falckenberg had taken on as dramaturg, or literary advisor, directed an adaptation of Marlowe's *Edward II* on which he had collaborated with Lion Feuchtwanger, an established novelist who later became famous for *Jew Süss*. It was a strikingly unusual production. The story goes that Brecht asked Karl Valentin what soldiers going into battle looked like. 'They get the willies, go white' was the answer, so he put the soldiers in white-face, one of the first shock effects of the type later invested with ideological significance and canonized as 'alienation effects'. He was a rising star, and he was sedulously cultivating his career.

Berlin was the mecca of the German theatre in the Twenties, and Brecht visited it in 1920 and 1921 when the idealistic phase of Expressionism was giving way to Black Expressionism, which invested the new loose forms with a harsh and brutal pessimism. Brecht became friendly with one of the most combative of the new shockers, Arnolt Bronnen, and changed Bertold to the snappier Bertolt, just as his new friend had done. He persuaded Bronnen to let him direct his play *Parricide* but the matter ended in shambles when the two stars, Heinrich George and Agnes Straub, walked out quivering with rage and shock respectively at Brecht's requirements. It was only in 1924, when he had two plays accepted in Berlin, *The Jungle of Cities* at Max Reinhardt's Deutsches Theater and *Edward II* at the Prussian State Theatre, that he moved there permanently. He was put on a

salary as dramaturg at the Deutsches Theater, but according
to Carl Zuckmayer, another aspiring playwright Reinhardt
had on the payroll, Brecht only went into the office to pinch
coal in his briefcase. Germany was just recovering from the
hyper-inflation of 1923.

In Berlin Brecht met Elisabeth Hauptmann and persuaded
his publisher that manuscripts would come in faster if he
could have her as his secretary. More and more he was taking
to discussing work in progress with his friends and trying out
new pieces on anybody who dropped in, so frequent rewrites
became necessary. Elisabeth Hauptmann was always around
to make unobtrusive notes and prepare new drafts at all hours
for the next day's work. She had a hand in all of his plays
between 1924 and 1933, and it is from her records that we
know of Brecht's awakening interest in Marxism in 1926.

From 1924 one of the leading directors in Germany was
Erwin Piscator, who had returned from service on the
Western Front as a Communist and begun politicizing the
German theatre with agitprop plays in 1920. By 1926 he was
using film, documentation and constructivist sets to bring
out the political and economic context of the plays he staged.
Brecht knew him and tried to write a play called *Wheat* when
Piscator set up his own company, the Piscatorbühne, in 1927.
He abandoned the project when he realised that capitalist
commodity trading – the action was set in the Chicago Grain
Exchange – made no sense, except for a few speculators.
Marxism seemed to offer a means of coming to grips with
social processes which otherwise defied dramatic analysis.

Brecht also met Kurt Weill in Berlin. Weill had set plays by
Georg Kaiser and Yvan Goll to music, and he was interested
in working with Brecht. Elisabeth Hauptmann had begun to
translate John Gay's *The Beggar's Opera*, which had been
successfully revived in London. Then E.J. Aufricht chanced
on Brecht in a café one day when he was looking for a piece
with which to open a theatre he had just leased, and Brecht
offered to update Gay's ballad opera with Weill for him. His

offer was accepted and he and Weill put the opera together in
the South of France that summer. The rehearsals were
chaotic and dogged by accidents and it came as a surprise to
all concerned when *The Threepenny Opera* became the hit of the
season and a considerable money-spinner for its authors.
With its underworld setting, its police corruption, its
rapacious characters and its risqué songs the piece cocked a
snook at respectable society, and respectable society loved it.
Only later, when he was preparing a film version, did Brecht
seriously try to put political teeth into *The Threepenny Opera*,
for by that time his political views had hardened, not least
after seeing the police opening fire on a peaceful May Day
parade in 1929.

Brecht and Weill and Elisabeth Hauptmann tried unsuccessfully to repeat the formula with *Happy End*, but the real
sequel was in a sense *The Rise and Fall of the City of Mahagonny*
which took Brecht's unlovely modern subject matter and
Weill's jazzy, popular, unmistakably contemporary music
into the genteel confines of Germany's opera houses.

At the time of his biggest popular hit Brecht's attention was
however more and more turning to politics. He devised, for
amateur performance, a number of short *Lehrstücke*, or
teaching plays, as demonstration models of political commit-
ment in action. In the most radical and controversial of these,
The Measures Taken, a Soviet agitator in China has been
liquidated for sympathising openly, against orders, with the
coolies. The play reconstructs the events leading to his death
and makes it clear that the individual must submit absolutely
to Party directives. In *The Exception and the Rule* a bearer
travelling through the desert is shot by his master when he
reaches for his water bottle to share the last drops with him.
A court acquits the master on the grounds that masters can
normally assume that servants want to kill them. In deciding
where the original mistake lay in such an instance, audience
and actors would raise their political consciousness. The
biggest of these directly political pieces was *The Mother*, an

adaptation of Maxim Gorky's novel, which showed the title figure's progress from maternal quietism to socialist activism in pre-revolutionary Russia. Helene Weigel played the lead and Margarete Steffin, who was to be Brecht's next close collaborator, had a bit part. That was in 1932 and the political situation was tense when the play opened. The police eventually banned performances in working-class districts on the pretext that some of the venues were not licensed for theatrical performances, and the play was given as a reading, in which 'alienated' form Brecht found it even more effective.

He had by this time codified his ideas on the epic theatre that was to replace the traditional dramatic or Aristotelian theatre which he regarded as a dream factory that turned out comforting illusions. Epic theatre would be a stimulant rather than a narcotic, and would help change the world. It would tell stories, but in such a way that audiences would be forced to weigh up and judge the events they saw. Smooth, seamless plots would give way to strings of independent incidents moving in jumps and curves, and these 'montages' would keep the audience alert and critical of the way things developed. Brecht believed that characters could be dismantled and reconstructed – he had demonstrated this in *Man Equals Man* – so the classical fixed hero was to give way to figures conditioned by their social situation who changed when that situation changed. At the same time he saw the individual as the agent of social change, so there was to be a constant dialectic or process of reciprocal influence and change. Brecht modified and developed these ideas in later years, but the basic notion remained intact: that theatre had a part to play in bringing about a better, socialist world.

Hitler came to power on 30 January 1933, the Reichstag burnt down on 27 February, and Brecht went into exile the next day. He eventually bought a house in Skovbostrand on the Danish island of Fyn. For the next fourteen years he had neither a theatre nor a public that understood his language. After Hitler's annexation of Austria, only Switzerland, notably the Zurich Schauspielhaus, offered politically unfettered professional facilities for German-language plays.

Brecht now turned to the anti-fascist cause, attending conferences in Paris and London and co-editing a journal that was published in Moscow. He subscribed to the Party line that fascism was the final stage of capitalism, a conspiracy of the rich against the poor which would collapse of its own accord, and his writing in this phase is uninspired, with the happy exception of his poetry. That more private art seemed to prosper in those dark days. He and Kurt Weill wrote an off-beat ballet, *The Seven Deadly Sins*, for Weill's wife, Lotte Lenya. He turned to straight realism, first with *Fear and Misery of the Third Reich*, a string of scenes from life under Hitler, and then with *Senora Carrar's Rifles*, a morale-booster for the Spanish Civil War.

He was however gradually finding his feet in Denmark with his wife and family and Margarete Steffin at his side, eventually joined by Ruth Berlau, a Danish actress who took on the task of promoting his work in Denmark. He was out of Germany, and the working-class voters who were the target of the *Lehrstücke* were out of range, so the political message in his plays became more general and oblique. In 1938 he wrote *Life of Galileo*, the first of a series of masterpieces, which used historical and exotic subjects to deal with contemporary issues. Galileo's cunning, in the first version at least, offered intellectuals in Germany a seventeenth-century recipe for survival in an authoritarian state. *Mother Courage and her Children*, still in the seventeenth century, was a warning against war, which was directed in the first instance at the Danes, lest they should think they could fraternise with the Nazis and come off unscathed. *The Caucasian Chalk Circle* offered a parable on the equitable use of resources from ancient China as a model for what should happen in Europe after Hitler's defeat. The pared-down economy and the schematic figures of the *Lehrstücke* gave way in these plays to a wealth of colour and incident and a parade of some of the most memorable figures in modern theatre, Galileo, Courage, Grusha and Azdak.

Brecht moved to Stockholm in 1939 and to Finland in 1940 where he wrote *The Good Person of Szechwan*, as well as a comedy, *Mr Puntila and his Man Matti*, and a satire, *The Resistible Rise of Arturo Ui*. The last two were aimed at the U.S.A., but were too unconventional to stand much chance on the American commercial stage. In 1941, with Finland threatened by the Germans, he travelled to Moscow. Margarete Steffin had to stay behind there and died of tuberculosis, while the Brecht ménage moved on via Vladivostock to the United States.

In the United States Brecht settled in Santa Monica, close to Hollywood. It was his intention to break into films, but he found working conditions and the prevalent ethos uncongenial. Friends like Fritz Lang and Peter Lorre (whom Brecht had discovered) tried to help, but he could not adapt to the American scene which had been such a fertile source of inspiration in Berlin. His memories of the Theatre Union's efforts to produce *The Mother* in New York in 1935 made him cautious of small-time theatre, but he dreamed of success on Broadway. *The Caucasian Chalk Circle* was conceived as a Broadway vehicle for Luise Rainer, an Austrian who had won two Academy Awards for film roles, and when he revised *Life of Galileo* with Charles Laughton his hope was that Laughton would sweep New York off its feet. Nothing much came of these things, because the American theatre was geared to entertainment, and laughter and tears were not part of the Brecht formula: there, as in Britain, it was to take another ten years before the techniques and something of the spirit of Brecht's theatre began to be assimilated.

Besides being a devastated country, Germany was under military occupation when the war ended and Brecht did not leave the U.S.A. until 1947. By that time McCarthyism was at its height and he appeared before the Committee on Unamerican Activities. He outwitted his investigators with ironic half-truths and skilful innuendo. The Committee thanked him for being an exemplary witness.

Brecht went to Switzerland in 1947, and then, because of visa problems – he had been stateless since 1938 – he returned to Berlin, as he had escaped in 1933, via Prague. He arrived in the Eastern Sector on 22 October 1948 to a warm welcome from the Communist cultural establishment. Brecht needed a German audience and his decision to settle in East Berlin was a natural one, given his unswerving conviction that Communism was the future, its warts necessary but temporary. He was no sycophant though, and observed, when the government announced that the people had let it down in 1953, that perhaps the government should elect another people.

East Berlin treated Brecht lavishly. He was given facilities to direct *Mother Courage* at the Deutsches Theater in 1948, then his own company, the Berliner Ensemble in 1949, and finally his own theatre, the Theater am Schiffbauerdamm in 1954. Brecht was now mainly a director, and it was in these years that he directed the meticulously rehearsed model productions of *Puntila*, *The Mother*, *The Caucasian Chalk Circle* among others, introducing techniques and effects that have since become standard – revealed lighting, uncluttered, spartan sets with a few solid, workmanlike props, well-worn costumes, visible scene-changes, demonstrative, unhistrionic acting, banner captions between scenes, songs – all of which in his hands added up to productions of startling freshness and conviction. Some of these were known as alienation effects designed to make the familiar seem odd and thus stimulate critical appraisal. Stepping out of the action to sing a song could do this in the fifties when plays mainly tried to sustain a consistent illusion, but in the theatre today's innovations are standard practice tomorrow, so new ways constantly have to be found of keeping Brecht's plays sharp and fresh. His reputation has suffered, not least in Britain, from leaden productions which tried so hard to be Brechtian that they forgot the wily old pragmatist's favourite English proverb, the proof of the pudding is in the eating. He spiced his plays to suit the audience's palate, and foreign directors should do so too, with discretion.

In Berlin with Helene Weigel managing the Ensemble, with the assistance of Elisabeth Hauptmann (scripts) and Ruth Berlau (photographic records), and with a bevy of young actresses around him, Brecht should have been happy, but he was under constant strain – from work, conflicting relationships and political irritation (the German Democratic Republic was not quite his kind of Communism). By 1954 his work in Berlin was internationally acclaimed, even in England where Kenneth Tynan was campaigning vigorously for him in the *Observer*. He was preparing the company for a visit to London when he died of a heart attack on 14 August 1956. The visit went ahead and left an unmistakeable mark on the British theatre which, with the Royal Court and the Royal Shakespeare Company in the vanguard, was to change radically under Brecht's posthumous influence.

Life of Galileo

Life of Galileo was the first major play conceived and written in exile. The first version was written in three weeks in November 1939, though Brecht had clearly researched the subject earlier, possibly in 1933 for a projected series of dramatisations of the great trials of history. 1938 had seen Britain and France cave in and sacrifice Czechoslovakia to Hitler at Munich, and the Spanish Civil War was going badly for the Republican side, so the theme of retrenchment and resistance was topical. At this stage the play was called *The Earth Moves* and showed Galileo outwitting the Inquisition by recanting only in order to continue his research clandestinely and smuggle the results abroad. This Galileo was a positive anti-hero. Brecht's musical collaborator Hanns Eisler saw him as the incarnation of 'low cunning for survival', so his behaviour could be construed as a model to encourage

intellectuals trapped in the Third Reich to work underground
while they waited for the overthrow of the regime.

There is of course something of Brecht's own plight too in
Galileo's situation. His emigration put him out of circulation
so that he was reduced to indirect opposition from abroad.
He and Galileo had the common problem of deciding how to
respond to political oppression, though Galileo was much
nearer the centre of the storm. It was a play with great
relevance at the time.

However when Brecht came back to it in the USA in 1944
he became aware of a moral that had slipped in unnoticed as
he tried to 'follow history'. His play implied that scientific
research took precedence over social responsibility. When he
first heard of nuclear fission on Danish radio in 1939 Brecht
did not react negatively: he felt he was himself something of a
scientist and his plays social experiments. By 1944 however
Nazi science, not least experiments on concentration camp
inmates, had changed his whole perspective and he began to
revise his picture of Galileo. The bomb dropped on
Hiroshima in August, 1945 came as ghastly confirmation
after he and Charles Laughton had completed their new
version of the play. Brecht wrote:

> The 'atomic' age made its debut at Hiroshima ...
> Overnight the biography of the founder of the new system
> of physics read differently.

The revised version put a new construction on Galileo's
behaviour and made Galileo himself a party to his own
re-interpretation. In scene 14, when he is given the *Discorsi*,
Andrea, like the earlier Brecht, sees Galileo as a cunning
old fox. Not so, Galileo insists. He recanted out of sheer
cowardice at a time when he had enough popular support to
resist the Church. Instead of establishing the principle that
the scientist had a duty to mankind, he had sold science out to
the ruling classes in what Brecht called the 'original sin' of the
modern natural sciences. It was eventually to lead to
Mengele's experiments at Auschwitz, and to Hiroshima.

Making Galileo the scapegoat for the aberrations of science puts considerable strain on the characterisation, and even in the revised version of the play he is a positive figure for the first nine scenes. His stage demonstration of the state of astronomy for Andrea in the opening scene reveals him as a lucid and passionate teacher as he expounds not only the principles of the Copernican system, but also its social implications. He expands on the latter when he explains the church's vested interest in the status quo to the Little Monk in scene 8, and he almost permits himself to criticise the plight of the peasants in conversation with Bellarmin and Barberini, but his real outburst against the landowners is reserved for Ludovico in scene 9. Galileo's analogy between the Ptolemaic system and hierarchical rule of the feudal landowners, aided and abetted by the Church seems a natural one, but it is based on Karl Marx's theory of history as a class struggle, which was only formulated in the nineteenth century, so Brecht's Galileo looks at events around him with the benefit of considerable hindsight. In this respect he is in fact Brecht's spokesman, and if we bear this in mind his final revision of his self-estimate may seem less implausible.

Galileo believes in reason, he has a Gargantuan appetite for life, he is a connoisseur of wine and something of a gourmet, appalled at the thought that anyone might eat an olive without due application of the critical faculties, he is the antithesis of the academic stuffed shirts at the court of Florence, and all of this makes it hard to see his exchange with Vanni in scene 11 as social treachery. When Vanni offers Galileo a lift, Brecht would have us believe that he is actually inviting him to join the bourgeois, capitalist manufacturers (who were in the end to replace the landowning aristocracy as the new ruling class) and participate in the exploitation of his own work for the benefit of humanity. It is however hard to see his casual refusal, worried as he is at being kept waiting by the Grand Duke, as an historic decision.

Galileo is visibly broken by his interrogation in scene 13,

and by the end of the play he is almost blind. Ernst Busch
who played Galileo at the Berliner Ensemble rejected the
author's view,

> What do I see on the stage? . . . A man who has ruined his
> eyes at the telescope and almost gone blind by working in
> the light of the moon – making an illegal copy of a
> manuscript that will benefit mankind. We are not told this
> – we see it . . . And I am supposed to hate this man?
> Condemn him? I can't, no matter how many commentaries
> they offer me. Not while I am watching it, not in the
> theatre. Reading is another matter.

The contradiction between Brecht's intention and his
achievement is not a fault, certainly not in performance, and
the character he created is richer in poetic possibilities than
his obsessively restricted view of it admitted.

Life of Galileo is the only play which Brecht based directly on
a famous historical figure. In contrast to *Mother Courage and her
Children* it takes a turning point of history and shows how it
was handled at the top level. The Church's quarrel with
Galileo at the time was largely theological. His theory that
the sun is the centre of the known universe challenged the
accepted dogma that placed the earth at the centre of
creation. Brecht as a materialist ignores this aspect of the
situation and represents the Church solely as a power
structure, the spiritual arm of the ruling class.

Life of Galileo, although it covers twenty-six years and leaves
long gaps as it traces Galileo's tussle with the Papacy, uses
conventional techniques of dramatic concentration rather
than epic curves and jumps. The action moves from Padua to
Venice, Florence, Rome, then back to the vicinity of Florence
and on to the Italian border, but there is no loose-knit
rambling action, no real sense of movement, no need for the
revolving stage which gave *Mother Courage and her Children* and
The Caucasian Chalk Circle their characteristic epic openness.
Life of Galileo is an indoor play. There is no commentator in

the play, and the characters never step out of their roles and never have their feelings expressed through a third party, so formally it has almost no epic features. What it does have in scene 1 are brilliant epic demonstrations of the revolutions of the earth with a chair and a washstand, and of its rotation with an apple and a splinter of wood. These are theatrical inventions of the first order that set a pattern of visible experiment which runs through this play. The principles of the Ptolemaic and Copernican systems are the premises on which the intellectual structure of the play stands, and Brecht clarifies them at the outset in terms a child can understand, and he does so with images as much as words.

Galileo's journey from bright optimism to despairing cynicism under the constraints of an authoritarian regime still has the power to move an audience, but it is the cynicism and despair that Brecht found so despicable which touch a contemporary nerve. Brecht's analysis simplifies the issue when it implies that Galileo could have changed the course of history by entering an alliance with progressive social forces. Scientific ethics in the USSR are not noticeably different from those in the USA. Yet Galileo's crisis of conscience and moral collapse, precisely because their presentation is contradictory, leave the audience with a problem and a challenge to relate them to contemporary experience in the best epic tradition.

Brecht wrote *Life of Galileo* to make a topical point. The Nazis and the development of military science gave it a new point when he revised it in 1944/45, and when he made the final revision for the Berliner Ensemble in 1955 the Cold War and general re-armament made it pertinent again. Now Chernobyl and the Reagan Star Wars programme make it a play for today.

The Resistible Rise of Arturo Ui
At the end of 1935 the left-wing Theatre Union decided to

stage *The Mother* in New York and Brecht sailed to the USA to supervise what he hoped would be a bridgehead for him in the American theatre. He failed to establish any rapport with the young production team and was finally thrown bodily out of rehearsals. *The Mother* flopped. Brecht, at a loose end, spent much of his time at the cinema under the pretext (according to Hanns Eisler who was his companion at the time) of 'social studies'. It was the heyday of the gangster film which glamorised the underworld of the Prohibition era (1919–1933), and Brecht became a fan, particularly of James Cagney. One critic detects the influence of Howard Hawks' violent classic of the genre, *Scarface*, in *Ui*.

Brecht was fascinated by the whole subject of gangsterdom and collected cuttings, among them 'The Gang Wars of New York' by Fred Pasley. Gang battles were reported in the papers on a heroic scale, and commentators had already identified gang bosses like Al Capone as perverted variants of the great American 'self-made man', different only in degree from the old industrial barons like Rockefeller, Ford and J.P. Morgan. In the career of Dutch Schulz, whose killing made headlines at the time, Brecht saw the elements of the Hitler story: police corruption, tie-ups with legitimate business, venal politicians rigging the law to suit the gangsters, and finally the thugs able to operate in open defiance of the authorities. At some point Brecht read Louis Adamic's *The Story of Class Violence in America* and Pasley's *Al Capone*, and it was Capone's career with its intriguing parallels to the rise of the Nazis that provided the plot of *The Resistible Rise of Arturo Ui* when Brecht came back to the subject in 1941. He was then in Finland waiting for a US visa and saw the piece as one for the American stage.

The play was neither published nor produced in Brecht's lifetime. It was unacceptable in 1941 in an America that was about to enter the war, and the post-war Germany to which Brecht returned was understandably sensitive on the subject of the Nazis. Brecht had written a satire on their progress up to 1935, but he anticipated that its perspective, fullness and accuracy would be scrutinised more than rigorously, and the subsequent critical response has vindicated his reservations. Instead of looking at the play as a parable of power and corruption, critics have tended to view it as an allegory of Hitler's rise and to fault it for not touching on the Jews, or mentioning the support for Hitler among the unemployed proletariat, or giving a full picture of Hitler's personality, and so on. This is a mistake. It assumes that the play is a definitive analysis of the rise of Hitler – a tall order in 1941 – whereas what Brecht really did was to take the gangster formula and the facts of Capone's career and structure them as a comic parallel to the rise of the Nazis. The result is a conflation of US gangster history and German history, and an American historian might equally well object that Brecht had not covered all the angles on Capone. That said, however, one does well to remember that behind the farcical treatment is an important subject. As Ekkehard Schall at the Berliner Ensemble in 1959 amply demonstrated, Ui is a bravura role, and the play can be a scintillating spectacle. The danger is that the spectacle may swamp the message. This is why Brecht thought that audiences should have digested *Fear and Misery of the Third Reich* so that they would know what he was talking about, before being exposed to *The Resistible Rise of Arturo Ui*.

Brecht's method is to develop the action in self-contained scenes, each of them ending with a projected text indicating the historical event to which it alludes. The Dogsborough affair which occupies the first five scenes works as a demonstration of corruption in American public life and at the same time charts Ui's rise from cheap hoodlum to city boss. It alludes to the 'Osthilfe scandal' when Prussian land-owners pressed an estate on President Hindenburg in return for political favours, and is tangential to the rise of Hitler. This leads up to the burning of the warehouse in scene 7 which alludes to the Reichstag fire in 1933 which was probably, though it has never been proved beyond doubt, started by the Nazis themselves. The warehouse fire persuades the greengrocers to accept Ui's protection, the Reichstag fire made Germany accept Hitler's 'enabling laws', which set aside the constitution so that Hitler could fight the 'red menace' with any methods he chose. Germany became a police state. The rigged trial of the hapless Fish corresponds to the trial of the unemployed Dutchman, Van der Lübbe. The murder of Roma combines the St Valentine's Day Massacre, when Capone wiped out a rival bootlegging gang, with the 'handshake murder' of another rival, O'Banion, and alludes to Hitler's elimination of the leaders of the paramilitary S.A., notably Ernst Röhm, who had helped him to power but by 1934 were a political embarrassment. The *Sunday Express* on July 1 ran the headline 'Hitler stamps out a mutiny like a gangster – Seven of his commanders executed . . . His prisoners slaughtered without trial.' O'Banion who had a limp and ran a flower shop as a front for his racket, became Givola, who stands for Goebbels who had a similar impediment. The murder of Dullfeet corresponds to the assassination of the Austrian Chancellor Dollfuss in 1935 and Ui's designs on Cicero correspond to the annexation of Austria in 1938. The allusions would have been clear enough in 1941 to a German audience, but the projections which were presumably for America are helpful today, though they do give ammunition to those who carp that the historical parallel is incomplete.

Part of the fun is that the play is written in verse, using broken hexameters which parody the high style of German historical drama. In contrast to the heroics of the gangster movie, this cuts Brecht's criminals down to size. Formal parody is not limited to the deliberate mismatching of elevated metre with low-life subject. The classic German quotation about the transience of theatrical performance, 'Posterity plaits no laurels for the actor' (from Schiller's *Wallenstein*) is re-attributed in scene 3 to the gangster, and Ui's scene with Dullfeet in Givola's flower shop with its ambulatory dialogue composed of intercalated, single, rhyming lines is a formal reprise of the seduction of Gretchen in Martha's garden from Goethe's *Faust*. Ui's abrupt approach to Dullfeet's widow is a parody of Gloucester's wooing of Lady Anne in *Richard III*, and the apparition of Roma could derive either from *Richard III* or from *Julius Caesar*. Finally, as the text for Ui's voice and movement lesson from The Actor, Brecht uses Shakespeare's classic exercise in forensic rhetoric, Mark Antony's subtly modulated obituary from *Julius Caesar* (III, 2). Brecht was not the first to point out how close politics are to showmanship: in Germany a character in C.D. Grabbe's *Napoleon* (1831) observes of the hero that it is becoming difficult to distinguish the generals from the actors. But it was the Nazis with their massed rallies in open-air arenas, with Hitler swooping down from the clouds in silver planes to address the faithful, and, not least, with Goebbels's manipulation of the media who paved the way for modern mass politics. Stalin of course perfected his own method of information management, with consequences under which Brecht's chosen home, the German Democratic Republic, among others, still silently groans today.

Brecht saw Ui's approach to mass communication with its deliberate deception of the little man as a specifically fascist phenomenon, but the 'selling' of presidents, and the professional restructuring of the abrasive TV personas of prime ministers is a familiar part of the communications industry. In unmasking the empty pathos of the Nazis' public style Brecht exposed an even bigger subject.

The Caucasian Chalk Circle

The Caucasian Chalk Circle was the last of the great plays of Brecht's exile, and the first to look beyond the Nazis and the Second World War to the future. He wrote it for Luise Rainer, an Austrian actress who had won two Academy Awards, one of them for the film of Pearl S. Buck's novel, *The Good Earth*, set in China. Like the American version of *Life of Galileo* it was conceived as a star vehicle with an eye on Broadway, and the heroine Grusha turned out to be too appealing, causing Brecht to revise the role straight away. It was the 'Mother-Courage-problem' all over again; audiences had to be prevented from empathising too freely with Grusha's adopted maternity, and made to view her like Breughel's *Dulle Griet* as a drab, stubborn beast of burden, with, according to Brecht, an appealing combination of quixotic audacity and gormlessness. Luise Rainer did not take the part.

The play has three separate parts. In the first scene, which Brecht initially called the prologue and which some productions omit, two rival collective farms in Soviet Georgia come to an amicable agreement about the utilisation of a disputed valley in 1945. The peasants then act a play set in ancient Grusinia, first the story of how Grusha mothers the Governor's son after a bloody revolt, and then the story of how Azdak unwittingly shelters the fugitive Grand Duke and is made judge as a reward for his disrespectful wit when he goes to the capital to turn himself in for his crime. The two stories converge when the Governor's widow after a counter-revolt reclaims her son and Azdak has to judge between the real and the foster mother.

The Caucasian Chalk Circle is a refined and complex example of epic theatre. It does not develop an integrated conflict in terms of character, but tells two separate exotic tales to illuminate a problem posed in a prologue. There are large jumps between the separate narrative blocks which make up this 'montage'. The Grusha and Azdak components are themselves built up from short episodes which demonstrate aspects of their respective interaction with society, and the episodes are linked by the Singer, who functions as narrator and commentator. The constant alternation between two modes of presentation, the multi-character episodes and the solo narrative, forces the audience to retune at regular intervals and inhibits the suspension of disbelief which Brecht considered to be death to the critical faculties.

The first abrupt shift, from a scene which has distinct features of Socialist Realism with its Girl Tractor Driver and its good-natured 'shop-floor' argument about future policy, to a scene in which the collective farmers appear as their own feudal forebears, some of them opulently dressed and masked, is anti-illusionistic. Even in the television age, when the flashback has become a standard feature of our visual syntax, the way the Azdak story reverts back at the start of scene five to the very Easter Day on which Grusha's story began in scene two can confuse readers and audiences.

The use of the Singer as a narrator in *The Caucasian Chalk Circle* merits close attention as the most consistent and at the same time the most varied use of this epic device in all Brecht's plays. We know at the start of the Grusha story that the Singer is the celebrated folk-singer, Arkady Cheidze, who is staging the play within the play. He indicates his status as prompter and stage-manager by leafing through a dog-eared script to refresh his memory before launching into his verse description of 'the city of the damned', and he stands outside the action from then on, interrupting to link the episodes, to fill in relevant information, and keep the audience's assessment on the right lines, to clarify in his own terms what is going through Grusha's mind, and sum up the message at the end. After he has focused our attention on the Governor's visit to the church on Easter Sunday, a crowd of beggars and petitioners followed by the Governor's retinue issues from the palace gate and, in a tableau with dialogue, illustrates and expands the narrator's introduction.

This establishes the pattern of epic introduction and dramatic illustration which runs through the play. The audience is told what is going to happen and then left to watch and judge as it unfolds.

The Singer's commentary, which is prominent in the Grusha story, is from the beginning sympathetic to the underdog. Grusha's decision to save the Governor's baby son is taken without words. The Singer mediates her feelings.

This avoids sentimentality and enables Brecht to present her action as natural human behaviour, like feeling love, or feeling at one with nature, or feeling the simple satisfaction of a task well done. To counteract any notion that maternal feelings might come into it at this stage, the baby's appeal is framed in a series of questions that clarify the implications for Grusha if she ignores them. Using the Singer Brecht can explore a decision-making process that could only otherwise be revealed by means of a potentially more emotive soliloquy. He can also bring out the dialectic of Grusha's position, for she loses whatever way she chooses to act, as is indicated by the paradoxical line, 'Terrible is the temptation to do good.'

The Singer's function is reduced in the Azdak scenes, because Azdak is articulate enough to speak for himself, though he does have songs which put Azdak's constructive subversion of the legal system into perspective as a brief interlude of justice for the underdog in an age of exploitation. The songs, involving as they do a change in presentation, are often seen as alienation effects, but Angelika Hurwicz, who played the original Grusha in the Berliner Ensemble production, warns against over-emphasising this. She cites the song which provides the backing for the reunion of Simon and Grusha in scene four as an example:

> Brecht wanted the actors to accompany the text sung by the Singer with finely modulated facial expressions. Mistrust, reproach, disappointment, were to be reflected in their faces. The song is a poetic interpretation of their silence. At the same time as he expressed Simon Chachava's reproachful thoughts the Singer was not to sing in a detached narrative fashion, but was to be angry and accusing. This moment cannot be categorized under any stylistic principle, but is simply a poetic, autonomous, artistically beautiful moment.

At points like this it is apparent that any attempt to codify the principles of epic theatre and to claim that at a given point they will operate in a given way fails to take account of Brecht's personal style and his feeling for the theatre, and these ultimately determined how a scene was best interpreted to preserve the overall artistic integrity of the production. Brecht's favourite English saying was, 'The proof of the pudding is in the eating'. The proof of a play lies in the audience response, and Brecht was not above a little culinary redisposition to get the spicing right.

In one sense the meaning of *The Caucasian Chalk Circle* is contained in the last four lines:

That what there is shall belong to those who are good
    for it, thus
The children to the maternal, that they thrive;
The carriages to the good drivers, that they drive well;
And the valley to the waterers, that it shall bear fruit.

But in this, the only major play written for the post-war world, Brecht was also affirming his faith in a future which, he remained convinced, belonged to Communism, in spite of Stalin (whom he called 'the necessary one'), and more pertinently in relation to this play, in spite of the atrocities associated with the collectivisation of agriculture in the USSR. The play is about change, about laws having to be scrutinized to ensure they have retained their validity. The collective farmers do this in the form of grass-roots consulta-tion in a scene of idealised communism. 'The Chalk Circle' shows that in feudal (and by extension capitalist) times it takes Azdak's ingenious subversion of the law to achieve the same end.

Both Grusha who develops from wooden stubbornness to aggressive class-consciousness in the course of the action, and Azdak, the unconventional judge, are Brecht's own magnifi-cent creations: they appear neither in Li Hsing Dao's thirteenth-century Chinese play nor in Klabund's 1925 adaptation, *The Chalk Circle*. Brecht saw Azdak as a covert utopian socialist, a Shakespearian jester licensed by circumstance to take personal revenge on the regime of the Fat Prince. His trials are farces, but there is a method in them as the cases of the Invalid and the Blackmailer demonstrate. The Invalid is fined 1000 piastres and the Doctor is not punished for his 'inexcusable professional mistake.' This paradoxical verdict becomes clear when Azdak tells the Blackmailer, who forfeits only half his take because he blackmails the landowning classes, he should study medicine. His only aptitude is for extracting money, precisely what the Doctor failed to do (his inexcusable mistake). The professional man like the blackmailer is an extortionist (just as the bourgeoisie in *The Threepenny Opera* are robbers). So in the knockabout farce, the monied classes (Landowner and Invalid) end up poorer, while the haphazard, generous Doctor gets off free. Behind the apparent whimsy of the action is a vision of a world where medicine will be a service to the community and not a marketable product, which in Britain in the eighties again seems like a remote vision.

Azdak is another in Brecht's line of anti-heroes. He is a cynic when it comes to heroism, a tactician who will grovel for his life because self-preservation overrides all else. In this vital, anarchic individualist from whom justice briefly flows, Brecht has produced the antithesis, if not the anathema of the faceless bureaucrats who, since he wrote, have come to seem characteristic of the new ruling classes in east and west in the post-war era.

It might be said that a scene in which the collective peasants make their own reasoned decision which is then reported back to the capital in good faith by the strikingly docile Expert is the work of a dreamer unversed in the realities of modern society. But Brecht was aware of these realities, so perhaps he is telling his audience that they, the people, are the final arbiters of the validity of the law and of their own destiny, and it is for them to ensure that their rights are not usurped by judges, or bureaucrats acting in their name.

Life of Galileo

Collaborator: M. STEFFIN

Translator: JOHN WILLETT

Characters

GALILEO GALILEI
ANDREA SARTI
MRS SARTI, *Galileo's housekeeper, Andrea's mother*
LUDOVICO MARSILI, *a rich young man*
THE PROCURATOR OF PADUA UNIVERSITY, *Mr Priuli*
SAGREDO, *Galileo's friend*
VIRGINIA, *Galileo's daughter*
FEDERZONI, *a lens-grinder, Galileo's assistant*
THE DOGE
SENATORS
COSIMO DE MEDICI, *Grand Duke of Florence*
THE COURT CHAMBERLAIN
THE THEOLOGIAN
THE PHILOSOPHER
THE MATHEMATICIAN
THE OLDER COURT LADY
THE YOUNGER COURT LADY
GRAND-DUCAL FOOTMAN
TWO NUNS
TWO SOLDIERS
THE OLD WOMAN
A FAT PRELATE
TWO SCHOLARS
TWO MONKS
TWO ASTRONOMERS
A VERY THIN MONK

THE VERY OLD CARDINAL
FATHER CHRISTOPHER CLAVIUS, *astronomer*
THE LITTLE MONK
THE CARDINAL INQUISITOR
CARDINAL BARBERINI, *subsequently Pope Urban VIII*
CARDINAL BELLARMIN
TWO CLERICAL SECRETARIES
TWO YOUNG LADIES
FILIPPO MUCIUS, *a scholar*
MR GAFFONE, *Rector of the University of Pisa*
THE BALLAD-SINGER
HIS WIFE
VANNI, *an ironfounder*
AN OFFICIAL
A HIGH OFFICIAL
AN INDIVIDUAL
A MONK
A PEASANT
A FRONTIER GUARD
A CLERK
Men, women, children

1

Galileo Galilei, a teacher of mathematics at Padua, sets out to prove Copernicus's new cosmogony

In the year sixteen hundred and nine
Science's light began to shine.
At Padua city in a modest house
Galileo Galilei set out to prove
The sun is still, the earth is on the move.

Galileo's rather wretched study in Padua. It is morning. A boy, Andrea, the housekeeper's soñ, brings in a glass of milk and a roll.

GALILEO *washing down to the waist, puffing and cheerful:* Put that milk on the table, and don't you shut any of those books.

ANDREA: Mother says we must pay the milkman. Or he'll start making a circle round our house, Mr Galilei.

GALILEO: Describing a circle, you mean, Andrea.

ANDREA: Whichever you like. If we don't pay the bill he'll start describing a circle round us, Mr Galilei.

GALILEO: Whereas when Mr Cambione the bailiff comes straight for us what sort of distance between two points is he going to pick?

ANDREA *grinning:* The shortest.

GALILEO: Right. I've got something for you. Look behind the star charts.

Andrea rummages behind the star charts and brings out a big wooden model of the Ptolemaic system.

ANDREA: What is it?

GALILEO: That's an armillary sphere. It's a contraption to show how the planets move around the earth, according to our forefathers.

ANDREA: How?

GALILEO: Let's examine it. Start at the beginning. Description?

ANDREA: In the middle there's a small stone.

GALILEO: That's the earth.

ANDREA: Round it there are rings, one inside another.

GALILEO: How many?

ANDREA: Eight.

GALILEO: That's the crystal spheres.

ANDREA: Stuck to the rings are little balls.

GALILEO: The stars.

ANDREA: Then there are bands with words painted on them.

GALILEO: What sort of words?

ANDREA: Names of stars.

GALILEO: Such as . . .

ANDREA: The lowest ball is the moon, it says. Above that's the sun.

GALILEO: Now start the sun moving.

ANDREA *moves the rings*: That's great. But we're so shut in.

GALILEO *drying himself*: Yes, I felt that first time I saw one of those. We're not the only ones to feel it. *He tosses the towel to Andrea, for him to dry his back with.* Walls and spheres and immobility! For two thousand years people have believed that the sun and all the stars of heaven rotate around mankind. Pope, cardinals, princes, professors, captains, merchants, fishwives and schoolkids thought they were sitting motionless inside this crystal sphere. But now we are breaking out of it, Andrea, at full speed. Because the old days are over and this is a new time. For the last hundred years mankind has seemed to be expecting something.

Our cities are cramped, and so are men's minds. Superstition and the plague. But now the word is 'that's how things are, but they won't stay like that'. Because everything is in motion, my friend.

I like to think that it began with the ships. As far as men could remember they had always hugged the coast, then suddenly they abandoned the coast line and ventured out across the seas. On our old continent a rumour sprang up: there might be new ones. And since our ships began sailing to them the laughing continents have got the message: the great ocean they feared, is a little puddle. And a vast desire has sprung up to know the reasons for everything: why a stone falls when you let it go and why it rises when you toss it up. Each day something fresh is discovered. Men of a hundred, even, are getting the young people to bawl the latest example into their ear. There have been a lot of discoveries, but there is still plenty to be found out. So future generations should have enough to do.

As a young man in Siena I watched a group of building workers argue for five minutes, then abandon a thousand-year old method of shifting granite blocks in favour of a new and more efficient arrangement of the ropes. Then and there I knew, the old days are over and this is a new time. Soon humanity is going to understand its abode, the heavenly body on which it dwells. What is written in the old books is no longer good enough. For where faith has been enthroned for a thousand years doubt now sits. Everyone says: right, that's what it says in the books, but let's have a look for ourselves. That most solemn truths are being familiarly nudged; what was never doubted before is doubted now.

This has created a draught which is blowing up the gold-embroidered skirts of the prelates and princes, revealing the fat and skinny legs underneath, legs like our own. The heavens, it turns out, are empty. Cheerful laughter is our response. But the waters of the earth drive the new spinning machines, while in the shipyards, the ropewalks and sail-lofts five hundred hands are moving together in a new system.

It is my prophecy that our own lifetime will see astronomy being discussed in the marketplaces. Even the fishwives' sons will hasten off to school. For these novelty-seeking people in our cities will be delighted with a new astronomy that sets the earth moving too. The old idea was always that the stars were fixed to a crystal vault to stop them falling down. Today we have found the courage to let them soar through space without support; and they are travelling at full speed just like our ships, at full speed and without support.

And the earth is rolling cheerfully around the sun, and the fishwives, merchants, princes, cardinals and even the Pope are rolling with it.

The universe has lost its centre overnight, and woken up to find it has countless centres. So that each one can now be seen as the centre, or none at all. Suddenly there is a lot of room.

Our ships sail far overseas, our planets move far out into space, in chess too the rooks have begun sweeping far across the board.

What does the poet say? O early morning of beginnings . . .

ANDREA:
O early morning of beginnings
O breath of wind that
Cometh from new shores!

And you'd better drink up your milk, because people are sure to start arriving soon.

GALILEO: Have you understood what I told you yesterday?

ANDREA: What? All that about Copper Knickers and turning?

GALILEO: Yes.

ANDREA: No. What d'you want me to understand that for? It's very difficult, and I'm not even eleven till October.

GALILEO: I particularly want you to understand it. Getting

people to understand it is the reason why I go on working and buying expensive books instead of paying the milkman.

ANDREA: But I can see with my own eyes that the sun goes down in a different place from where it rises. So how can it stay still? Of course it can't.

GALILEO: You can see, indeed! What can you see? Nothing at all. You just gawp. Gawping isn't seeing. *He puts the iron washstand in the middle of the room.* Right: this is the sun. Sit down. *Andrea sits on one of the chairs, Galileo stands behind him.* Where's the sun, right or left of you?

ANDREA: Left.

GALILEO: And how does it get to be on your right?

ANDREA: By you carrying it to my right, of course.

GALILEO: Isn't there any other way? *He picks him up along with the chair and makes an about-turn.* Now where's the sun?

ANDREA: On my right.

GALILEO: Did it move?

ANDREA: Not really.

GALILEO: So what did move?

ANDREA: Me.

GALILEO *bellows*: Wrong! You idiot! The chair!

ANDREA: But me with it!

GALILEO: Of course. The chair's the earth. You're sitting on it.

MRS SARTI *has entered in order to make the bed. She has been watching*: Just what are you up to with my boy, Mr Galilei?

GALILEO: Teaching him to see, Mrs Sarti.

MRS SARTI: What, by lugging him round the room?

ANDREA: Lay off, mother. You don't understand.

MRS SARTI: Oh, don't I? And you do: is that it? There's a young gentleman wants some lessons. Very well dressed, got a letter of introduction too. *Hands it over.* You'll have Andrea believing two and two makes five any minute now, Mr Galilei. As if he didn't already muddle up everything you tell him. Only last night he was arguing that the earth goes round the sun. He's got it into his head that some gentleman called Copper Knickers worked that one out.

ANDREA: Didn't Copper Knickers work it out, Mr Galilei? You tell her.

MRS SARTI: You surely can't tell him such stories? Making him trot it all out at school so the priests come and see me because he keeps on coming out with blasphemies. You should be ashamed of yourself, Mr Galilei.

GALILEO *eating his breakfast*: In consequence of our researches, Mrs Sarti, and as a result of intensive argument, Andrea and I have made discoveries which we can no longer hold back from the world. A new time has begun, a time it's a pleasure to live in.

MRS SARTI: Well. Let's hope your new time will allow us to pay the milkman, Mr Galilei. *Indicating the letter of introduction.* Just do me a favour and don't send this man away. I'm thinking of the milk bill. *Exit.*

GALILEO *laughing*: Let me at least finish my milk! *To Andrea:* So you did understand something yesterday?

ANDREA: I only told her to wake her up a bit. But it isn't true. All you did with me and that chair was turn it sideways, not like this. *He makes a looping motion with his arm.* Or I'd have fallen off, and that's a fact. Why didn't you turn the chair over? Because it would have proved I'd fall off if you turned it that way. So there.

GALILEO: Look, I proved to you . . .

ANDREA: But last night I realised that if the earth turned that way I'd be hanging head downwards every night, and that's a fact.

GALILEO *takes an apple from the table*: Right, now this is the earth.

ANDREA: Don't keep on taking that sort of example, Mr Galilei. They always work.

GALILEO *putting back the apple*: Very well.

ANDREA: Examples always work if you're clever. Only I can't lug my mother round in a chair like you did me. So you see it's a rotten example really. And suppose your apple is the earth like you say? Nothing follows.

GALILEO *laughing*: You just don't want to know.

ANDREA: Pick it up again. Why don't I hang head downwards at night, then?

GALILEO: Right: here's the earth and here's you standing on it. *He takes a splinter from a piece of firewood and sticks it into the apple.* Now the earth's turning round.

ANDREA: And now I'm hanging head downwards.

GALILEO: What d'you mean? Look at it carefully. Where's your head?

ANDREA *pointing*: There. Underneath.

GALILEO: Really? *He turns it back*: Isn't it in precisely the same position? Aren't your feet still underneath? You don't stand like this when I turn it, do you? *He takes out the splinter and puts it in upside down.*

ANDREA: No. Then why don't I notice it's turning?

GALILEO: Because you're turning with it. You and the air above you and everything else on this ball.

ANDREA: Then why does it look as if the sun's moving?

GALILEO *turns the apple and the splinter round again*: Right: you're seeing the earth below you; that doesn't change, it's always underneath you and so far as you're concerned it doesn't move. But then look what's above you. At present the lamp's over your head, but once I've turned the apple what's over it now; what's above?

ANDREA *turns his head similarly*: The stove.

GALILEO: And where's the lamp?

ANDREA: Underneath.

GALILEO: Ha.

ANDREA: That's great: that'll give her something to think about. *Enter Ludovico Marsili, a rich young man.*

GALILEO: This place is getting like a pigeon loft.

LUDOVICO: Good morning, sir. My name is Ludovico Marsili.

GALILEO *reading his letter of introduction*: So you've been in Holland?

LUDOVICO: Where they were all speaking about you, Mr Galilei.

GALILEO: Your family owns estates in the Campagna?

LUDOVICO: Mother wanted me to have a look-see, find out what's cooking in the world and all that.

GALILEO: And in Holland they told you that in Italy, for instance, I was cooking?

LUDOVICO: And since Mother also wanted me to have a look-see in the sciences . . .

GALILEO: Private tuition: ten scudi a month.

LUDOVICO: Very well, sir.

GALILEO: What are your main interests?

LUDOVICO: Horses.

GALILEO: Ha.

LUDOVICO: I've not got the brains for science, Mr Galilei.

GALILEO: Ha. In that case we'll make it fifteen scudi a month.

LUDOVICO: Very well. Mr Galilei.

GALILEO: I'll have to take you first thing in the morning. That'll be your loss, Andrea. You'll have to drop out of course. You don't pay, see?

ANDREA: I'm off. Can I have the apple?

GALILEO: Yes.

Exit Andrea.

LUDOVICO: You'll have to be patient with me. You see, everything in the sciences goes against a fellow's good sound commonsense. I mean, look at that queer tube thing they're selling in Amsterdam. I gave it a good looking-over. A green leather casing and a couple of lenses, one this way – *he indicates a concave lens* – and the other that way – *he indicates a convex lens*. One of them's supposed to magnify and the other reduces. Anyone in his right mind would expect them to cancel out. They don't. The thing makes everything appear five times the size. That's science for you.

GALILEO : What appears five time the size?

LUDOVOCI : Church spires, pigeons, anything that's a long way off.

GALILEO : Did you yourself see church spires magnified in this way?

LUDOVICO : Yes sir.

GALILEO : And this tube has two lenses? *He makes a sketch on a piece of paper.* Did it look like that? *Ludovico nods.* How old's this invention?

LUDOVICO : Not more than a couple of days, I'd say, when I left Holland; at least that's how long it had been on the market.

GALILEO *almost friendly*: And why does it have to be physics? Why not horsebreeding?
Enter Mrs Sarti unobserved by Galileo.

LUDOVOCI : Mother thinks you can't do without a bit of science. Nobody can drink a glass of wine without science these days, you know.

GALILEO : Why didn't you pick a dead language or theology? That's easier. *Sees Mrs Sarti.* Right, come along on Tuesday morning. *Ludovico leaves.*

GALILEO : Don't give me that look. I accepted him.

MRS SARTI : Because I caught your eye in time. The procurrator of the university is out there.

GALILEO : Show him in, he matters. There may be 500 scudi in this. I wouldn't have to bother with pupils.
Mrs Sarti shows in the procurator. Galileo has finished dressing, meanwhile jotting down figures on a piece of paper.

GALILEO : Good morning. Lend us half a scudo. *The procurator digs a coin out of his purse and Galileo gives it to Sarti.* Sarti, tell Andrea to go to the spectacle-maker's and get two lenses: there's the prescription.

Exit Mrs Sarti with the paper.

PROCURATOR: I have come in connection with your application for a rise in salary to 1000 scudi. I regret that I cannot recommend it to the university. As you know, courses in mathematics do not attract new students. Mathematics, so to speak, is an unproductive art. Not that our Republic doesn't esteem it most highly. It may not be so essential as philosophy or so useful as theology, but it nonetheless offers infinite pleasures to its adepts.

GALILEO *busy with his papers*: My dear fellow, I can't manage on 500 scudi.

PROCURATOR: But, Mr Galilei, your week consists of two two-hour lectures. Given your outstanding reputation you can certainly get plenty of pupils who can afford private lessons. Haven't you got private pupils?

GALILEO: Too many, sir. I teach and I teach, and when am I supposed to learn? God help us, I'm not half as sharp as those gentlemen in the philosophy department. I'm stupid. I understand absolutely nothing. So I'm compelled to fill the gaps in my knowledge. And when am I supposed to do that? When am I to get on with my research? Sir, my branch of knowledge is still avid to know. The greatest problems still find us with nothing but hypotheses to go on. Yet we keep asking ourselves for proofs. How am I to provide them if I can only maintain my home by having to take any thickhead who can afford the money and din it into him that parallel lines meet at infinity?

PROCURATOR: Don't forget that even if the Republic pays less well than certain princes it does guarantee freedom of research. In Padua we even admit Protestants to our lectures. And give them doctors' degrees too. In Mr Cremonini's case we not only failed to hand him over to the Inquisition when he was proved, proved, Mr Galilei – to have made irreligious remarks, but actually granted him a rise in salary. As far as Holland Venice is known as the republic where the Inquisition has no say. That should mean something to you, being an astronomer, that's to say operating in a field where for some time now the doctrines of the church have hardly been treated with proper respect.

GALILEO: You people handed Mr Giordano Bruno over to Rome. Because he was propagating the ideas of Copernicus.

PROCURATOR: Not because he was propagating the ideas of Mr Copernicus, which anyway are wrong, but because he was not a Venetian citizen and had no regular position here. So you needn't drag in the man they burned. Incidentally, however free we are, I wouldn't go around openly citing a name like his, which is subject to the express anathema of the church: not even here, not even here.

GALILEO: Your protection of freedom of thought is pretty good business, isn't it? By showing how everywhere else the Inquisition prevails and burns people, you get good teachers cheap for this place. You make up for your attitude to the Inquisition by paying lower salaries than anyone.

PROCURATOR: That's most unfair. What use would it be to you to have limitless spare time for research if any ignorant monk in the Inquisition could just put a ban on your thoughts? Every rose has its thorn, Mr Galilei, and every ruler has his monks.

GALILEO: So what's the good of free research without free time to research in? What happens to its results? Perhaps you'd kindly show this paper about falling bodies to the gentlemen at the Signoria – *he indicates a bundle of manuscript* – and ask them if it isn't worth a few extra scudi.

PROCURATOR: It's worth infinitely more than that, Mr Galilei.

GALILEO: Sir, not infinitely more, a mere 500 scudi more.

PROCURATOR: What is worth scudi is what brings scudi in.

If you want money you'll have to produce something else. When you're selling knowledge you can't ask more than the buyer is likely to make from it. Philosophy, for instance, as taught by Mr Colombe in Florence, nets the prince at least 10,000 scudi a year. I know your laws on falling bodies have made a stir. They've applauded you in Prague and Paris. But the people who applaud don't pay Padua University what you cost it. You made an unfortunate choice of subject, Mr Galilei.

GALILEO: I see. Freedom of trade, freedom of research. Free trading in research, is that it?

PROCURATOR: Really, Mr Galilei, what a way of looking at it! Allow me to tell you that I don't quite understand your flippant remarks. Our Republic's thriving foreign trade hardly strikes me as a matter to be sneered at. And speaking from many years of experience as procurator of this university I would be even more disinclined to speak of scientific research in what I would term with respect, so frivolous a manner. *While Galileo glances longingly at his work table*: Consider the conditions that surround us. The slavery under whose whips the sciences in certain places are groaning. Whips cut from old leather bindings. Nobody there needs to know how a stone falls, merely what Aristotle wrote about it. Eyes are only for reading with. Why investigate falling bodies, when it's the laws governing grovelling bodies that count? Contrast the infinite joy with which our Republic welcomes your ideas, however daring they may be. Here you have a chance to research, to work. Nobody supervises you, nobody suppresses you. Our merchants know the value of better linen in their struggle with their competitors in Florence; they listen with interest to your cry for better physics, and physics in turn owes much to their cry for better looms. Our most prominent citizens take an interest in your researches, call on you, get you to demonstrate your findings: men whose time is precious. Don't underrate trade, Mr Galilei. Nobody here would stand for the slightest interference with your work or let outsiders make difficulties for you. This is a place where you can work, Mr Galilei, you have to admit it.

GALILEO *in despair*: Yes.

PROCURATOR: As for the material aspects: why can't you give us another nice piece of work like those famous proportional compasses of yours, the ones that allow complete mathematical dunces to trace lines, reckon compound interest on capital, reproduce a land survey on varying scales and determine the weight of cannon balls?

GALILEO: Kids' stuff.

PROCURATOR: Here's something that fascinated and astonished our top people and brought in good money, and you call it kids' stuff. I'm told even General Stefano Gritti can work out square roots with your instrument.

GALILEO: A real miracle. – All the same, Priuli, you've given me something to think about. Priuli, I think I might be able to let you have something of the kind you want. *He picks up the paper with the sketch.*

PROCURATOR: Could you? That would be the answer. *Gets up*: Mr Galilei, we realise that you are a great man. A great but dissatisfied man, if I may say so.

GALILEO: Yes, I am dissatisfied, and that's what you'd be paying me for if you had any brains. Because I'm dissatisfied with myself. But instead of doing that you force me to be dissatisfied with you. I admit I enjoy doing my stuff for you gentlemen of Venice in your famous arsenal and in the shipyards and cannon foundries. But you never give me the time to follow up the hunches which come to me there and which are important for my branch of science. That way you muzzle the threshing ox. I am 46 years old and have achieved nothing that satisfies me.

PROCURATOR: I mustn't interrupt you any longer.

GALILEO: Thank you.

Exit the Procurator.
Galileo is left alone for a moment or two and begins to work. Then
Andrea hurries in.

GALILEO *working*: Why didn't you eat the apple?

ANDREA: I need it to convince her that it turns.

GALILEO: Listen to me, Andrea: don't talk to other people about our ideas.

ANDREA: Why not?

GALILEO: The big shots won't allow it.

ANDREA: But it's the truth.

GALILEO: But they're forbidding it. – And there's something more. We physicists may think we have the answer, but that doesn't mean we can prove it. Even the ideas of a great man like Copernicus still need proving. They are only hypotheses. Give me those lenses.

ANDREA: Your half scudo wasn't enough. I had to leave my coat. As security.

GALILEO: How will you manage without a coat this winter?
Pause. Galileo arranges the lenses on the sheet with the sketch on it.

ANDREA: What's a hypothesis?

GALILEO: It's when you assume that something's likely, but haven't any facts. Look at Felicia down there outside the basket-maker's shop breastfeeding her child: it remains a hypothesis that she's giving it milk and not getting milk from it, till one actually goes and sees and proves it. Faced with the stars we are like dull-eyed worms that can hardly see at all. Those old constructions people have believed in for the last thousand years are hopelessly rickety: vast buildings most of whose wood is in the buttresses propping them up. Lots of laws that explain very little, whereas our new hypothesis has very few laws that explain a lot.

ANDREA: But you proved it all to me.

GALILEO: No, only that that's how it could be. I'm not saying it isn't a beautiful hypothesis; what's more there's nothing against it.

ANDREA: I'd like to be a physicist too, Mr Galilei.

GALILEO: That's understandable, given the million and one questions in our field still waiting to be cleared up. *He has gone to the window and looked through the lenses. Mildly interested*: Have a look through that, Andrea.

ANDREA: Holy Mary, it's all quite close. The bells in the campanile very close indeed. I can even read the copper letters: GRACIA DEI.

GALILEO: That'll get us 500 scudi.

2

Galileo presents the Venetian Republic with a new invention

No one's virtue is complete:
Great Galileo liked to eat.
You will not resent, we hope
The truth about his telescope.

The great arsenal of Venice, alongside the harbour.

Senators, headed by the Doge. To one side, Galileo's friend Sagredo and the fifteen-year-old Virginia Galilei with a velvet cushion on which rests a two-foot-long telescope in a crimson leather case. On a dais, Galileo. Behind him the telescope's stand, supervised by Federzoni the lens-grinder.

GALILEO: Your Excellency; august Signoria! In my capacity as mathematics teacher at your university in Padua and director of your great arsenal here in Venice I have always seen it as my job not merely to fulfil my exalted task as a teacher but also to provide useful inventions that would be of exceptional advantage to the Venetian Republic. Today it is with deep joy and all due deference that I find myself able to demonstrate and hand over to you a completely new instrument, namely my spyglass or telescope, fabricated in your world-famous Great Arsenal on the loftiest Christian and scientific principles, the product of seventeen years of patient research by your humble servant. *Galileo leaves the dais and stands alongside Sagredo. Applause. Galileo bows.*

GALILEO *softly to Sagredo*: Waste of time.

SAGREDO *softly*: You'll be able to pay the butcher, old boy.

GALILEO: Yes, they'll make money on this. *He bows again.*

PROCURATOR *steps on to the dais*: Your Excellency, august Signoria! Once again a glorious page in the great book of the arts is inscribed in a Venetian hand. *Polite applause*: Today a world-famous scholar is offering you, and you alone, a highly marketable tube, for you to manufacture and sell as and how you wish. *Louder applause.* What is more, has it struck you that in wartime this instrument will allow us to distinguish the number and types of the enemy's ships at least two hours before he does ours, with the result that we shall know how strong he is and be able to choose whether to pursue, join battle or run away? *Very loud applause.* And now, your Excellency, august Signoria, Mr Galileo invites you to accept this instrument which he has invented, this testimonial to his intuition, at the hand of his enchanting daughter.

Music. Virginia steps forward, bows and hands the telescope to the Procurator, who passes it to Federzoni. Federzoni puts it on the stand and focusses it. Doge and Senators mount the dais and look through the tube.

GALILEO *softly*: I'm not sure how long I'll be able to stick this circus. These people think they're getting a lucrative plaything, but it's a lot more than that. Last night I turned it on the moon.

SAGREDO: What did you see?

GALILEO: The moon doesn't generate its own light.

SAGREDO: What?

SENATORS: I can make out the fortifications of Santa Rosita, Mr Galilei. – They're having their dinner on that boat. Fried fish. Makes me feel peckish.

GALILEO: I'm telling you astronomy has stagnated for the last thousand years because they had no telescope.

SENATOR: Mr Galilei!

SAGREDO: They want you.

SENATOR: That contraption lets you see too much. I'll have to tell my women they can't take baths on the roof any longer.

GALILEO: Know what the Milky Way consists of?

SAGREDO: No.

GALILEO: I do.

SENATOR: One should be able to ask 10 scudi for a thing like that, Mr Galilei. *Galileo bows.*

VIRGINIA *leading Ludovico up to her father:* Ludovico wants to congratulate you, Father.

LUDOVICO *embarrassed:* I congratulate you, sir.

GALILEO: I've improved it.

LUDOVICO: Yes, sir. I see you've made the casing red. In Holland it was green.

GALILEO *turning to Sagredo:* I've even begun to wonder if I couldn't use it to prove a certain theory.

SAGREDO: Watch your step.

PROCURATOR: Your 500 scudi are in the bag, Galileo.

GALILEO *disregarding him:* Of course I'm sceptical about jumping to conclusions.

The Doge, a fat unassuming man, has come up to Galileo and is trying to address him with a kind of dignified awkwardness.

PROCURATOR: Mr Galilei, His Excellency the Doge.

The Doge shakes Galileo's hand.

GALILEO: Of course, the 500! Are you satisfied, your Excellency?

DOGE: I'm afraid our republic always has to have some pretext before the city fathers can do anything for our scholars.

PROCURATOR: But what other incentive can there be, Mr Galilei?

DOGE *smiling*: We need that pretext.

The Doge and the Procurator lead Galileo towards the Senators, who gather round him. Virginia and Ludovico slowly go away.

VIRGINIA: Did I do all right?

LUDOVICO: Seemed all right to me.

VIRGINIA: What's the matter?

LUDOVICO: Nothing, really. I suppose a green casing would have been just as good.

VIRGINIA: It strikes me they're all very pleased with Father.

LUDOVICO: And it strikes me I'm starting to learn a thing or two about science.

3

10 January 1610. Using the telescope, Galileo discovers celestial phenomena that confirm the Copernican system. Warned by his friend of the possible consequences of his research, Galileo proclaims his belief in human reason

> January ten, sixteen ten:
> Galileo Galilei abolishes heaven.

Galileo's study in Padua. Night. Galileo and Sagredo at the telescope, wrapped in heavy overcoats.

SAGREDO *looking through the telescope, half to himself*: The crescent's edge is quite irregular, jagged and rough. In the dark area, close to the luminous edge, there are bright spots.

They come up one after the other. The light starts from the
spots and flows outwards over bigger and bigger surfaces,
where it merges into the larger luminous part.

GALILEO: What's your explanation of these bright spots?

SAGREDO: It's not possible.

GALILEO: It is. They're mountains.

SAGREDO: On a star?

GALILEO: Huge mountains. Whose peaks are gilded by the
rising sun while the surrounding slopes are still covered by
night. What you're seeing is the light spreading down into
the valleys from the topmost peaks.

SAGREDO: But this goes against two thousand years of
astronomy.

GALILEO: It does. What you are seeing has been seen by no
mortal except myself. You are the second.

SAGREDO: But the moon can't be an earth complete with
mountains and valleys, any more than the earth can be a
star.

GALILEO: The moon can be an earth complete with mountains and valleys, and the earth can be a star. An ordinary
celestial body, one of thousands. Take another look. Does
the dark part of the moon look completely dark to you?

SAGREDO: No. Now that I look at it, I can see a feeble ashy-
grey light all over it.

GALILEO: What sort of light might that be?

SAGREDO: ?

GALILEO: It comes from the earth.

SAGREDO: You're talking through your hat. How can the
earth give off light, with all its mountains and forests and
waters; it's a cold body.

GALILEO: The same way the moon gives off light. Both
of them are lit by the sun, and so they give off light. What
the moon is to us, we are to the moon. It sees us sometimes
as a crescent, sometimes as a half-moon, sometimes full and
sometimes not at all.

SAGREDO: In other words, there's no difference between the moon and earth.

GALILEO: Apparently not.

SAGREDO: Ten years ago in Rome they burnt a man at the stake for that. His name was Giordano Bruno, and that is what he said.

GALILEO: Exactly. And that's what we can see. Keep your eye glued to the telescope, Sagredo, my friend. What you're seeing is the fact that there is no difference between heaven and earth. Today is 10 January 1610. Today mankind can write in its diary: Got rid of Heaven.

SAGREDO: That's frightful.

GALILEO: There is another thing I discovered. Perhaps it's more appalling still.

MRS SARTI *quietly*: Mr Procurator.

The Procurator rushes in.

PROCURATOR: I'm sorry to come so late. Do you mind if I speak to you alone?

GALILEO: Mr Sagredo can listen to anything I can, Mr Priuli.

PROCURATOR: But you may not exactly be pleased if the gentleman hears what has happened. Unhappily it is something quite unbelievable.

GALILEO: Mr Sagredo is quite used to encountering unbelievable when I am around, let me tell you.

PROCURATOR: No doubt, no doubt. *Pointing at the telescope*: Yes, that's the famous contraption. You might just as well throw it away. It's useless, utterly useless.

SAGREDO, *who has been walking around impatiently*: Why's that?

PROCURATOR: Are you aware that this invention of yours which you said was the fruit of seventeen years of research can be bought on any street corner in Italy for a few scudi? Made in Holland, what's more. There is a Dutch merchantman unloading 500 telescopes down at the harbour at this very moment.

GALILEO: Really?

PROCURATOR: I find your equanimity hard to understand, sir.

SAGREDO: What are you worrying about? Thanks to this instrument, let me tell you, Mr Galilei has just made some revolutionary discoveries about the universe.

GALILEO *laughing*: Have a look, Priuli.

PROCURATOR: And let me tell you it's quite enough for me to have made my particular discovery, after getting Galileo's salary doubled for that piece of rubbish. It's a pure stroke of luck that the gentlemen of the signoria, in their confidence that they had secured the republic a monopoly of this instrument, didn't look through it and instantly see an ordinary streetseller at the nearest corner, magnified to the power of seven and hawking an identical tube for twice nothing. *Galileo laughs resoundingly.*

SAGREDO: My dear Mr Priuli. I may not be competent to judge this instrument's value for commerce but its value for philosophy is so boundless that . . .

PROCURATOR: For philosophy indeed. What's a mathematician like Mr Galilei got to do with philosophy? Mr Galilei, you did once invent a very decent water pump for the city and your irrigation system works well. The weavers too report favourably on your machine. So how was I to expect something like this?

GALILEO: Not so fast, Priuli. Sea passages are still long, hazardous and expensive. We need a clock in the sky we can rely on. A guide for navigation, right? Well, I have reason to believe that the telescope will allow us to make clear sightings of certain stars that execute extremely regular movements. New star charts might save our shipping several million scudi, Priuli.

PROCURATOR: Don't bother. I've listened too long already. In return for my help you've made me the laughing-stock of the city. I'll go down to history as the procurator who fell for a worthless telescope. It's all very well for you to laugh. You've got your 500 scudi. But I'm an honourable man, and I tell you this world turns my stomach.

He leaves, slamming the door.

GALILEO: He's really quite likeable when he's angry. Did you hear that? A world where one can't do business turns his stomach.

SAGREDO: Did you know about these Dutch instruments?

GALILEO: Of course, by hearsay. But the one I made these skinflints in the Signoria was twice as good. How am I supposed to work with the bailiffs in the house? And Virginia will soon have to have a dowry: she's not bright. Then I like buying books about other things besides physics, and I like a decent meal. Good meals are when I get most of my ideas. A degraded age! They were paying me less than the carter who drives their wine barrels. Four cords of firewood for two courses on mathematics. Now I've managed to squeeze 500 scudi out of them, but I've still got debts, including some dating from twenty years back. Give me five years off to research, and I'd have proved it all. I'm going to show you another thing.

SAGREDO *is reluctant to go to the telescope*: I feel something not all that remote from fear, Galileo.

GALILEO: I'm about to show you one of the shining milk-white clouds in the Milky Way. Tell me what it's made up of.

SAGREDO: They're stars, an infinite number.

GALILEO: In Orion alone there are 500 fixed stars. Those are the countless other worlds, the remote stars the man they burned talked about. He never saw them, he just expected them to be there.

SAGREDO: But even supposing our earth is a star, that's still a long way from Copernicus's view that it goes round the sun. There's not a star in the sky that has another star going round it. But the moon does go round the earth.

GALILEO: Sagredo, I wonder. I've been wondering since

the day before yesterday. Here we have Jupiter. *He focusses on it.* Round it we have four smaller neighbouring stars that are invisible except through the tube. I saw them on Monday but without bothering to note their position. Yesterday I looked again. I could swear the position of all four had changed. I noted them down. They've changed again. What's this? I saw four. *Agitated:* Have a look.

SAGREDO: I can see three.

GALILEO: Where's the fourth? There are the tables. We must work out what movements they might have performed. *Excited, they sit down to work. The stage darkens, but Jupiter and its accompanying stars can be seen on the cyclorama. As it grows light once more they are still sitting there in their winter coats.*

GALILEO: That's the proof. The fourth one can only have gone behind Jupiter, where it can't be seen. So here you've a star with another one going round it.

SAGREDO: What about the crystal sphere Jupiter is attached to?

GALILEO: Yes, where has it got to? How can Jupiter be attached if other stars circle round it? It's not some kind of prop in the sky, some base in the universe. It's another sun.

SAGREDO: Calm down. You're thinking too quickly.

GALILEO: What d'you mean, quickly? Wake up, man! You're seeing something nobody has ever seen before. They were right.

SAGREDO: Who, Copernicus and his lot?

GALILEO: And the other fellow. The whole world was against them, and they were right. Andrea must see this! *In great excitement he hurries to the door and shouts:* Mrs Sarti! Mrs Sarti!

SAGREDO: Don't get worked up, Galileo!

GALILEO: Get worked up, Sagredo! Mrs Sarti!

SAGREDO *turns the telescope away:* Stop bellowing like an idiot.

GALILEO: Stop standing there like a stuffed dummy when the truth has been found.

SAGREDO: I'm not standing like a stuffed dummy; I'm trembling with fear that it may be the truth.

GALILEO: Uh?

SAGREDO: Have you completely lost your head? Don't you realise what you'll be getting into if what you see there is true? And if you go round telling all and sundry that the earth is a planet and not the centre of the universe?

GALILEO: Right, and that the entire universe full of stars isn't turning around our tiny little earth, anyone could guess.

SAGREDO: In other words that it's just a lot of stars. Then where's God?

GALILEO: What d'you mean?

SAGREDO: God! Where is God?

GALILEO *angrily*: Not there anyway. Any more than he'd be here on earth, suppose there were creatures out there wanting to come and look for him.

SAGREDO: So where is God?

GALILEO: I'm not a theologian. I'm a mathematician.

SAGREDO: First and foremost you're a human being. And I'm asking: where is God in your cosmography?

GALILEO: Within ourselves or nowhere.

SAGREDO *shouting*: Like the man they burned said?

GALILEO: Like the man they burned said.

SAGREDO: That's what they burned him for. Less than ten years back.

GALILEO: Because he couldn't prove it. Because it was just a hypothesis. Mrs Sarti!

SAGREDO: Galileo, ever since I've known you you've known how to cover yourself. For seventeen years here in Padua and three more in Pisa you have been patiently teaching the Ptolemaic system proclaimed by the Church and confirmed by the writings the Church is based on. Like Copernicus you thought it was wrong but you taught it just the same.

GALILEO: Because I couldn't prove anything.

SAGREDO *incredulously*: And do you imagine that makes any difference!

GALILEO: A tremendous difference. Look, Sagredo, I believe in Humanity, which means to say I believe in human reason. If it weren't for that belief each morning I wouldn't have the power to get out of bed.

SAGREDO: Then let me tell you something. I don't. Forty years spent among human beings has again and again brought it home to me that they are not open to reason. Show them a comet with a red tail, scare them out of their wits, and they'll rush out of their houses and break their legs. But try making one rational statement to them, and back it up with seven proofs, and they'll just laugh at you.

GALILEO: That's quite untrue, and it's a slander. I don't see how you can love science if that's what you believe. Nobody who isn't dead can fail to be convinced by proof.

SAGREDO: How can you imagine their pathetic shrewdness has anything to do with reason?

GALILEO: I'm not talking about their shrewdness. I know they call a donkey a horse when they want to sell it and a horse a donkey when they want to buy. That's the kind of shrewdness you mean. But the horny-handed old woman who gives her mule an extra bundle of hay on the eve of a journey, the sea captain who allows for storms and doldrums when laying in stores, the child who puts on his cap once they have convinced him that it may rain: these are the people I pin my hopes to, because they all accept proof. Yes, I believe in reason's gentle tyranny over people. Sooner or later they have to give in to it. Nobody can go on indefinitely watching me – *he drops a pebble on the ground* – drop a pebble, then say it doesn't fall. No human being is capable of that. The lure of a proof is too great. Nearly everyone succumbs to it; sooner or later we all do. Thinking is one of the chief pleasures of the human race.

MRS SARTI *enters:* Do you want something, Mr Galilei?

GALILEO *who is back at his telescope making notes; in a very friendly voice:* Yes, I want Andrea.

MRS SARTI: Andrea? He's asleep in bed.

GALILEO: Can't you wake him up?

MRS SARTI: Why d'you want him?

GALILEO: I want to show him something he'll appreciate. He's to see something nobody but us two has seen since the earth was made.

MRS SARTI: Something more through your tube?

GALILEO: Something through my tube, Mrs Sarti.

MRS SARTI: And I'm to wake him up in the middle of the night for that? Are you out of your mind? He's got to have his sleep. I wouldn't think of waking him.

GALILEO: Definitely not?

MRS SARTI: Definitely not.

GALILEO: In that case, Mrs Sarti, perhaps you can help me. You see, a question has arisen where we can't agree, probably because both of us have read too many books. It's a question about the heavens, something to do with the stars. This is it: are we to take it that the greater goes round the smaller, or does the smaller go round the greater?

MRS SARTI *cautiously:* I never know where I am with you. Mr Galilei. Is that a serious question, or are you pulling my leg again?

GALILEO: A serious question.

MRS SARTI: Then I'll give you a quick answer. Do I serve your dinner or do you serve mine?

GALILEO: You serve mine. Yesterday it was burnt.

MRS SARTI: And why was it burnt? Because I had to fetch you your shoes in the middle of my cooking. Didn't I fetch you your shoes?

GALILEO: I suppose so.

MRS SARTI: You see, you're the one who has studied and is able to pay.

GALILEO: I see. I see there's no problem. Good night Mrs Sarti.

Mrs Sarti, amused, goes off.

GALILEO: Don't tell me people like that can't grasp the truth. They grab at it.

The bell has begun sounding for early morning Mass. Enter Virginia in a cloak, carrying a shielded light.

VIRGINIA: Good morning, Father.

GALILEO: Why are you up at this hour?

VIRGINIA: Mrs Sarti and I are going to early mass. Ludovico's coming too. What sort of night was it, Father?

GALILEO: Clear.

VIRGINIA: Can I have a look?

GALILEO: What for? *Virginia does not know what to say.* It's not a toy.

VIRGINIA: No, Father.

GALILEO: Anyhow the tube is a flop, so everybody will soon be telling you. You can get it for 3 scudi all over the place and the Dutch invented it ages ago.

VIRGINIA: Hasn't it helped you see anything fresh in the sky?

GALILEO: Nothing in your line. Just a few dim little spots to the left of a large planet; I'll have to do something to draw attention to them. *Talking past his daughter to Sagredo*: I might christen them 'the Medicean Stars' after the Grand-Duke of Florence. *Again to Virginia*: You'll be interested to hear, Virginia, that we'll probably be moving to Florence. I've written to them to ask if the Grand Duke can use me as his court mathematician.

VIRGINIA *radiant*: At Court?

SAGREDO: Galileo!

GALILEO: My dear fellow, I'll need time off. I need proofs. And I want the fleshpots. And here's a job where I won't have to take private pupils and din the Ptolemaic system into them, but shall have the time, time, time, time, time –

to work out my proofs; because what I've got so far isn't enough. It's nothing, just wretched odds and ends. I can't take on the whole world with that. There's not a single shred of proof to show that any heavenly body whatever goes round the sun. But I am going to produce the proofs, proofs for everyone, from Mrs Sarti right up to the Pope. The only thing that worries me is whether the court will have me.

VIRGINIA: Of course they'll have you, Father, with your new stars and all that.

GALILEO: Run along to your mass.

Exit Virginia.

GALILEO: I'm not used to writing to important people. *He hands Sagredo a letter.* Do you think this is well expressed?

SAGREDO *reads out the end of the letter*: 'My most ardent desire is to be closer to you, the rising sun that will illuminate this age.' The grand duke of Florence is aged nine.

GALILEO: That's it. I see; you think my letter is too submissive. I'm wondering if it is submissive enough – not too formal, lacking in authentic servility. A reticent letter would be all right for someone whose distinction it is to have proved Aristotle correct, but not for me. A man like me can only get a halfway decent job by crawling on his belly. And you know what I think of people whose brains aren't capable of filling their stomachs.

Mrs Sarti and Virginia pass the men on their way to mass.

SAGREDO: Don't go to Florence, Galileo.

GALILEO: Why not?

SAGREDO: Because it's run by monks.

GALILEO: The Florentine Court includes eminent scholars.

SAGREDO: Flunkeys.

GALILEO: I'll take them by the scruff of the neck and I'll drag them to the telescope. Even monks are human beings, Sagredo. Even they are subject to the seduction of proof. Copernicus, don't forget, wanted them to believe his figures;

but I only want them to believe their eyes. If the truth is too feeble to stick up for itself then it must go over to the attack. I'm going to take them by the scruff of the neck and force them to look through this telescope.

SAGREDO: Galileo, I see you embarking on a frightful road. It is a disastrous night when mankind sees the truth. And a delusive hour when it believes in human reason. What kind of person is said to go into things with his eyes open? One who is going to his doom. How could the people in power give free rein to somebody who knows the truth, even if it concerns the remotest stars? Do you imagine the Pope will hear the truth when you tell him he's wrong, and not just hear that he's wrong? Do you imagine he will merely note in his diary: January 10th 1610 – got rid of heaven? How can you propose to leave the Republic with the truth in your pocket, risking the traps set by monks and princes and brandishing your tube. You may be a sceptic in science, but you're childishly credulous as soon as anything seems likely to help you to pursue it. You don't believe in Aristotle, but you do believe in the Grand Duke of Florence. Just now, when I was watching you at the telescope and you were watching those new stars, it seemed to me I was watching you stand on blazing faggots; and when you said you believed in proof I smelt burnt flesh. I am fond of science, my friend, but I am fonder of you. Don't go to Florence, Galileo.

GALILEO: If they'll have me I shall go.

On a curtain appears the last page of his letter:

In giving the noble name of the house of Medici to the new stars which I have discovered I realise that whereas the old gods and heroes were immortalised by being raised to the realm of the stars in this case the noble name of Medici will ensure that these stars are remembered for ever. For my own part I commend myself to you as one of your loyalest and most humble servants who considers it the height of privilege to have been born as your subject.

There is nothing for which I long more ardently than to be closer to you, the rising sun which will illuminate this epoch.

Galileo Galilei.

4

Galileo has exchanged the Venetian Republic for the Court of Florence. His discoveries with the telescope are not believed by the court scholars

The old says: What I've always done I'll always do.
The new says: If you're useless you must go.

Galileo's house in Florence. Mrs Sarti is preparing Galileo's study for the reception of guests. Her son Andrea is sitting tidying the star charts.

MRS SARTI: There has been nothing but bowing and scraping ever since we arrived safe and sound in this marvellous Florence. The whole city files past the tube, with me mopping the floor after them. If there was anything to all these discoveries the clergy would be the first to know. I spent four years in service with Monsignor Filippo without every managing to get all his library dusted. Leather bound books up to the ceiling – and no slim volumes of poetry either. And that good Monsignor had a whole cluster of sores on his bottom from sitting and poring over all that learning; d'you imagine a man like that doesn't know the answers? And today's grand visit will be such a disaster that I'll never be able to meet the milkman's eye tomorrow. I knew what I was about when I advised him to give the gentlemen a good supper first, a proper joint of lamb, before they

inspect his tube. But no: *she imitates Galileo*: 'I've got some-
thing else for them.'
There is knocking downstairs.
MRS SARTI *looks through the spyhole in the window*: My goodness,
the Grand Duke's arrived. And Galileo is still at the
University.
*She hurries down the stairs and admits the Grand Duke of
Tuscany, Cosimo de Medici, together with his chamberlain and two
court ladies.*
COSIMO: I want to see that tube.
CHAMBERLAIN: Perhaps your Highness will possess himself
until Mr Galilei and the other university gentlemen have
arrived. *To Mrs Sarti*: Mr Galileo was going to ask our
astronomers to test his newly discovered so-called Medicean
stars.
COSIMO: They don't believe in the tube, not for one moment.
So where is it?
MRS SARTI: Upstairs in the study.
*The boy nods, points up the staircase and runs up it at a nod from
Mrs Sarti.*
CHAMBERLAIN *a very old man*: Your Highness! *To Mrs Sarti*:
Have we *got* to go up there? I wouldn't have come at all if
his tutor had not been indisposed.
MRS SARTI: The young gentleman will be all right. My own
boy is up there.
COSIMO *entering above*: Good evening!
*The two boys bow ceremoniously to each other. Pause. Then Andrea
turns back to his work.*
ANDREA *very like his master*: This place is getting like a pigeon
loft.
COSIMO: Plenty of visitors?
ANDREA: Stump around here staring, and don't know the
first thing.
COSIMO: I get it. That the . . .? *Pointing to the telescope.*
ANDREA: Yes, that's it. Hands off, though.

COSIMO: And what's that? *He points to the wooden model of the Ptolemaic system.*

ANDREA: That's Ptolemy's thing.

COSIMO: Showing how the sun goes round, is that it?

ANDREA: So they say.

COSIMO *sitting down on a chair, takes the model on his lap*: My tutor's got a cold. I got off early. It's all right here.

ANDREA *shambles around restlessly and irresolutely shooting doubtful looks at the unknown boy, then finds that he cannot hold out any longer, and brings out a second model from behind the maps, one representing the Copernican system*: But really it's like this.

COSIMO: What's like this?

ANDREA *pointing at Cosimo's model*: That's how people think it is and – *pointing at his own* – this is how it is really. The earth turns round the sun, get it?

COSIMO: D'you really mean that?

ANDREA: Sure, it's been proved.

COSIMO: Indeed? I'd like to know why I'm never allowed to see the old man now. Yesterday he came to supper again.

ANDREA: They don't believe it, do they?

COSIMO: Of course they do.

ANDREA *suddenly pointing at the model on Cosimo's lap*: Give it back: you can't even understand that one.

COSIMO: Why should you have two?

ANDREA: Just you hand it over. It's not a toy for kids.

COSIMO: No reason why I shouldn't give it to you, but you need to learn some manners, you know.

ANDREA: You're an idiot, and to hell with manners, just give it over or you'll start something.

COSIMO: Hands off, I tell you.

They start brawling and are soon tangled up on the floor.

ANDREA: I'll teach you to handle a model properly! Say 'pax'.

COSIMO: It's broken. You're twisting my hand.

ANDREA: We'll see who's right. Say it turns or I'll bash you.

COSIMO: Shan't. Stop it, Ginger. I'll teach you manners.

ANDREA: Ginger: who are you calling Ginger?

They go on brawling in silence. Enter Galileo and a group of university professors downstairs. Federzoni follows.

CHAMBERLAIN: Gentlemen, his highness's tutor Mr Suri has a slight indisposition and was therefore unable to accompany his highness.

THEOLOGIAN: I hope it's nothing serious.

CHAMBERLAIN: Not in the least.

GALILEO *disappointed*: Isn't his highness here?

CHAMBERLAIN: His highness is upstairs. Please don't let me detain you. The court is so very eager to know what our distinguished university thinks about Mr Galileo's remarkable instrument and these amazing new stars.

They go upstairs.

The boys are now lying quiet, having heard the noise downstairs.

COSIMO: Here they are. Let me get up.

They stand up quickly.

THE GENTLEMEN *on their way upstairs*: No, there's nothing whatever to worry about. – Those cases in the old city: our faculty of medicine says there's no question of it being plague. Any miasmas would freeze at this temperature. – The worst possible thing in such a situation is to panic. – It's just the usual incidence of colds for this time of year. – Every suspicion has been eliminated. – Nothing whatever to worry about.

Greetings upstairs.

GALILEO: Your highness, I am glad to be able to introduce the gentlemen of your university to these new discoveries in your presence.

Cosimo bows formally in all directions, including Andrea's.

THEOLOGIAN *noticing the broken Ptolemaic model on the floor*: Something seems to have got broken here.

Cosimo quickly stoops down and politely hands Andrea the model.
Meantime Galileo unobtrusively shifts the other model to one side.

GALILEO *at the telescope*: As your highness no doubt realises, we astronomers have been running into great difficulties in our calculations for some while. We have been using a very ancient system which is apparently consistent with our philosophy but not, alas, with the facts. Under this ancient, Ptolemaic system the motions of the stars are presumed to be extremely complex. The planet Venus, for instance, is supposed to have an orbit like this. *On a board he draws the epicyclical orbit of Venus according to the Ptolemaic hypothesis.* But even if we accept the awkwardness of such motions we are still unable to predict the position of the stars accurately. We do not find them where in principle they ought to be. What is more, some stars perform motions which the Ptolemaic system just cannot explain. Such motions, it seems to me, are performed by certain small stars which I have recently discovered around the planet Jupiter. Would you gentlemen care to start by observing these satellites of Jupiter, the Medicean stars?

ANDREA *indicating the stool by the telescope*: Kindly sit here.

PHILOSOPHER: Thank you, my boy. I fear things are not quite so simple. Mr Galileo, before turning to your famous tube, I wonder if we might have the pleasure of a disputation? Its subject to be: Can such planets exist?

MATHEMATICIAN: A formal dispute.

GALILEO: I was thinking you could just look through the telescope and convince yourselves?

ANDREA: This way, please.

MATHEMATICIAN: Of course, of course. I take it you are familiar with the opinion of the ancients that there can be no stars which turn round centres other than the earth, nor any which lack support in the sky?

GALILEO: I am.

PHILOSOPHER: Moreover, quite apart from the very possibility of such stars, which our mathematician – *he turns towards the mathematician* – would appear to doubt, I would like in all humility to pose the philosophical question: are such stars necessary? Aristotelis divini universum . . .

GALILEO: Shouldn't we go on using the vernacular? My colleague Mr Federzoni doesn't understand Latin.

PHILOSOPHER: Does it matter if he understands us or not?

GALILEO: Yes.

PHILOSOPHER: I am so sorry. I thought he was your lens-grinder.

ANDREA: Mr Federzoni is a lens-grinder and a scholar.

PHILOSOPHER: Thank you, my boy. Well, if Mr Federzoni insists . . .

GALILEO: I insist.

PHILOSOPHER: The argument will be less brilliant, but it's your house. The universe of the divine Aristotle, with the mystical music of its spheres and its crystal vaults, the orbits of its heavenly bodies, the slanting angle of the sun's course, the secrets of the moon tables, the starry richness catalogued in the southern hemisphere and the transparent structure of the celestial globe add up to an edifice of such exquisite proportions that we should think twice before disrupting its harmony.

GALILEO: How about your highness now taking a look at his impossible and unnecessary stars through this telescope?

MATHEMATICIAN: One might be tempted to answer that, if your tube shows something which cannot be there, it cannot be an entirely reliable tube, wouldn't you say?

GALILEO: What d'you mean by that?

MATHEMATICIAN: It would be rather more appropriate, Mr Galileo, if you were to name your reasons for assuming that there could be free-floating stars moving about in the highest sphere of the unalterable heavens.

PHILOSOPHER: Your reasons, Mr Galileo, your reasons.

GALILEO: My reasons! When a single glance at the stars

themselves and my own notes makes the phenomenon evident? Sir, your disputation is becoming absurd.

MATHEMATICIAN: If one could be sure of not over-exciting you one might say that what is in your tube and what is in the skies is not necessarily the same thing.

PHILOSOPHER: That couldn't be more courteously put.

FEDERZONI: They think we painted the Medicean stars on the lens.

GALILEO: Are you saying I'm a fraud?

PHILOSOPHER: How could we? In his highness's presence too.

MATHEMATICIAN: Your instrument – I don't know whether to call it your brainchild or your adopted brainchild – is most ingeniously made, no doubt of that.

PHILOSOPHER: And we are utterly convinced, Mr Galilei, that neither you nor anyone else would bestow the illustrious name of our ruling family on stars whose existence was not above all doubt. *All bow deeply to the grand duke.*

COSIMO *turns to the ladies of the court*: Is something the matter with my stars?

THE OLDER COURT LADY: There is nothing the matter with your highness's stars. It's just that the gentlemen are wondering if they are really and truly there.
Pause.

THE YOUNGER COURT LADY: I'm told you can actually see the wheels on the Plough.

FEDERZONI: Yes, and all kinds of things on the Bull.

GALILEO: Well, are you gentlemen going to look through it or not?

PHILOSOPHER: Of course, of course.

MATHEMATICIAN: Of course.
Pause. Suddenly Andrea turns and walks stiffly out across the whole length of the room. His mother stops him.

MRS SARTI: What's the matter with you?

ANDREA: They're stupid. *He tears himself away and runs off.*

PHILOSOPHER: A lamentable boy.

CHAMBERLAIN: Your highness: gentlemen: may I remind you that the state ball is due to start in three quarters of an hour.

MATHEMATICIAN: Let's not beat about the bush. Sooner or later Mr Galilei will have to reconcile himself to the facts. Those Jupiter satellites of his would penetrate the crystal spheres. It is as simple as that.

FEDERZONI: You'll be surprised: the crystal spheres don't exist.

PHILOSOPHER: Any textbook will tell you that they do, my good man.

FEDERZONI: Right, then let's have new textbooks.

PHILOSOPHER: Your highness, my distinguished colleague and I are supported by none less than the divine Aristotle himself.

GALILEO *almost obsequiously*: Gentlemen, to believe in the authority of Aristotle is one thing, tangible facts are another. You are saying that according to Aristotle there are crystal spheres up there, so certain motions just cannot take place because the stars would penetrate them. But suppose those motions could be established? Mightn't that suggest to you that those crystal spheres don't exist? Gentlemen, in all humility I ask you to go by the evidence of your eyes.

MATHEMATICIAN: My dear Galileo, I may strike you as very old-fashioned, but I'm in the habit of reading Aristotle now and again, and there, I can assure you, I trust the evidence of my eyes.

GALILEO: I am used to seeing the gentlemen of the various faculties shutting their eyes to every fact and pretending that nothing has happened. I produce my observations and everyone laughs: I offer my telescope so they can see for themselves, and everyone quotes Aristotle.

FEDERZONI: The fellow had no telescope.

MATHEMATICIAN: That's just it.

PHILOSOPHER *grandly*: If Aristotle is going to be dragged in the mud – that's to say an authority recognized not only by every classical scientist but also by the chief fathers of the church – then any prolonging of this discussion is in my view a waste of time. I have no use for discussions which are not objective. Basta.

GALILEO: Truth is born of the times, not of authority. Our ignorance is limitless: let us lop one cubic millimeter off it. Why try to be clever now that we at last have a chance of being just a little less stupid? I have had the unimaginable luck to get my hands on a new instrument that lets us observe one tiny corner of the universe a little, but not all that much, more exactly. Make use of it.

PHILOSOPHER: Your highness, ladies and gentlemen, I just wonder where all this is leading?

GALILEO: I should say our duty as scientists is not to ask where truth is leading.

PHILOSOPHER *agitatedly*: Mr Galilei, truth might lead us anywhere!

GALILEO: Your highness. At night nowadays telescopes are being pointed at the sky all over Italy. Jupiter's moons may not bring down the price of milk. But they have never been seen before, and yet all the same they exist. From this the man in the street concludes that a lot else might exist if only he opened his eyes. It is your duty to confirm this. What has made Italy prick up its ears is not the movements of a few distant stars but the news that hitherto unquestioned dogmas have begun to totter – and we all know that there are too many of those. Gentlemen, don't let us fight for questionable truths.

FEDERZONI: You people are teachers: you should be stimulating the questions.

PHILOSOPHER: I would rather your man didn't tell us how to conduct a scholarly disputation.

GALILEO: Your highness! My work in the Great Arsenal in Venice brought me into daily contact with draughtsmen, builders and instrument mechanics. Such people showed me a lot of new approaches. They don't read much, but rely on the evidence of their five senses, without all that much fear as to where such evidence is going to lead them...

PHILOSOPHER: Oho!

GALILEO: Very much like our mariners who a hundred years ago abandoned our coasts without knowing what other coasts they would encounter, if any. It looks as if the only way today to find that supreme curiosity which was the real glory of classical Greece is to go down to the docks.

PHILOSOPHER: After what we've heard so far I've no doubt that Mr Galilei will find admirers at the docks.

CHAMBERLAIN: Your highness, I am dismayed to note that this exceptionally instructive conversation has become a trifle prolonged. His highness must have some repose before the court ball.

At a sign, the grand duke bows to Galileo. The court quickly gets ready to leave.

MRS SARTI *blocks the grand duke's way and offers him a plate of biscuits*: A biscuit, your highness? *The Older court lady leads the grand duke out.*

GALILEO *hurrying after them*: But all you gentlemen need do is look through the telescope!

CHAMBERLAIN: His highness will not fail to submit your ideas to our greatest living astronomer: Father Christopher Clavius, chief astronomer at the papal college in Rome.

5

Undeterred even by the plague, Galileo carries on with his researches

(a)

Early morning. Galileo at the telescope, bent over his notes. Enter Virginia with a travelling bag.

GALILEO: Virginia! Has something happened?

VIRGINIA: The convent's shut; they sent us straight home. Arcetri has had five cases of plague.

GALILEO *calls*: Sarti!

VIRGINIA: Market Street was barricaded off last night. Two people have died in the old town, they say, and there are three more dying in hospital.

GALILEO: As usual they hushed it all up till it was too late.

MRS SARTI *entering*: What are you doing here?

VIRGINIA: The plague.

MRS SARTI: God alive! I'll pack. *Sits down.*

GALILEO: Pack nothing. Take Virginia and Andrea. I'll get my notes.

He hurries to his table and hurriedly gathers up papers. Mrs Sarti puts Andrea's coat on him as he runs up, then collects some food and bed linen. Enter a grand-ducal footman.

FOOTMAN: In view of the spread of the disease his highness has left the city for Bologna. However, he insisted that Mr Galilei too should be offered a chance to get to safety. The carriage will be outside your door in two minutes.

MRS SARTI *to Virginia and Andrea*: Go outside at once. Here, take this.

ANDREA: What for? If you don't tell me why I shan't go.

MRS SARTI: It's the plague, my boy.

VIRGINIA: We'll wait for Father.

MRS SARTI: Mr Galilei, are you ready?

GALILEO *wrapping the telescope in the tablecloth*: Put Virginia and Andrea in the carriage. I won't be a moment.

VIRGINIA: No, we're not going without you. Once you start packing up your books you'll never finish.

MRS SARTI: The coach is there.

GALILEO: Have some sense, Virginia, if you don't take your seats the coachman will drive off. Plague is no joking matter.

VIRGINIA *protesting, as Mrs Sarti and Andrea escort her out*: Help him with his books, or he won't come.

MRS SARTI *from the main door*: Mr Galilei, the coachman says he can't wait.

GALILEO: Mrs Sarti, I don't think I should go. It's all such a mess, you see: three months' worth of notes which I might as well throw away if I can't spend another night or two on them. Anyway this plague is all over the place.

MRS SARTI: Mr Galilei! You must come now! You're crazy.

GALILEO: You'll have to go off with Virginia and Andrea. I'll follow.

MRS SARTI: Another hour, and nobody will be able to get away. You must come. *Listens*. He's driving off. I'll have to stop him.

Exit.

Galileo walks up and down. Mrs Sarti re-enters, very pale, without her bundle.

GALILEO: What are you still here for? You'll miss the children's carriage.

MRS SARTI: They've gone. Virginia had to be held in. The children will get looked after in Bologna. But who's going to see you get your meals?

GALILEO: You're crazy. Staying in this city in order to cook! *Picking up his notes*: Don't think I'm a complete fool, Mrs

Sarti. I can't abandon these observations. I have powerful enemies and I must collect proofs for certain hypotheses.

MRS SARTI: You don't have to justify yourself. But it's not exactly sensible.

(b)

Outside Galileo's house in Florence. Galileo steps out and looks down the street. Two nuns pass by.

GALILEO *addresses them*: Could you tell me, sisters, where I can buy some milk? The milk woman didn't come this morning, and my housekeeper has left.

ONE NUN: The only shops open are in the lower town.

THE OTHER NUN: Did you come from here? *Galileo nods.* This is the street!

The two nuns cross themselves, mumble a Hail Mary and hurry away. A man goes by.

GALILEO *addresses him*: Aren't you the baker that delivers our bread to us? *The man nods.* Have you seen my housekeeper? She must have left last night. She hasn't been around all day. *The man shakes his head. A window is opened across the way and a woman looks out.*

WOMAN *yelling*: Hurry! They've got the plague opposite! *The man runs off horrified.*

GALILEO: Have you heard anything about my housekeeper?

WOMAN: Your housekeeper collapsed in the street up there. She must have realised. That's why she went. So inconsiderate!

She slams the window shut.

Children come down the street. They see Galileo and run away screaming. Galileo turns round; two soldiers hurry up, encased in armour.

SOLDIERS: Get right back indoors!

They push Galileo back into his house with their long pikes. They bolt the door behind him.

GALILEO *at the window*: Can you tell me what happened to the woman?

SOLDIERS: They throw them on the heap.

WOMAN *reappears at the window*: That whole street back there is infected. Why can't you close it off?
The soldiers rope the street off.

WOMAN: But that way nobody can get into our house. This part doesn't have to be closed off. This part's all right. Stop it! Stop! Can't you listen? My husband's still in town, he won't be able to get through to us. You animals! *She can be heard inside weeping and screaming. The soldiers leave. At another window an old woman appears.*

GALILEO: That must be a fire back there.

THE OLD WOMAN: They've stopped putting them out where there's any risk of infection. All they can think about is the plague.

GALILEO: Just like them. It's their whole system of government. Chopping us off like the diseased branch of some barren figtree.

THE OLD WOMAN: That's not fair. It's just that they're powerless.

GALILEO: Are you the only one in your house?

THE OLD WOMAN: Yes. My son sent me a note. Thank God he got a message last night to say somebody back there had died, so he didn't come home. There were eleven cases in our district during the night.

GALILEO: I blame myself for not making my housekeeper leave in time. I had some urgent work, but she had no call to stay.

THE OLD WOMAN: We can't leave either. Who's to take us in? No need for you to blame yourself. I saw her. She left early this morning, around seven o'clock. She must have been ill; when she saw me coming out to fetch in the bread she deliberately kept away from me. She didn't want them to close off your house. But they're bound to find out.

A rattling sound is heard.

GALILEO: What's that?

THE OLD WOMAN: They're trying to make noises to drive away the clouds with the plague seeds in them.

Galileo roars with laughter.

THE OLD WOMAN: Fancy being able to laugh now.

A man comes down the street and finds it roped off.

GALILEO: Hey, you! This street's closed off and I've nothing to eat. Hey! Hey!

The man has quickly hurried away.

THE OLD WOMAN: They may bring something. If not I can leave a jug of milk outside your door tonight, if you're not scared.

GALILEO: Hey! Hey! Can't anybody hear us?

All of a sudden Andrea is standing by the rope. He has been crying.

GALILEO: Andrea! How did you get here?

ANDREA: I was here first thing. I knocked but you didn't open your door. They told me you . . .

GALILEO: Didn't you go off in the carriage?

ANDREA: Yes. But I managed to jump out. Virginia went on. Can't I come in?

THE OLD WOMAN: No, you can't. You'll have to go to the Ursulines. Your mother may be there.

ANDREA: I've been. But they wouldn't let me see her. She's too ill.

GALILEO: Did you walk the whole way back? It's three days since you left, you know.

ANDREA: It took all that time. Don't be cross with me. They arrested me once.

GALILEO *helplessly*: Don't cry. You know, I've found out lots of things since you went. Shall I tell you? *Andrea nods between his sobs.* Listen carefully or you won't understand. You remember me showing you the planet Venus? Don't bother about that noise, it's nothing. Can you remember? You know what I saw? It's like the moon! I've seen it as a half-circle and I've seen it as a sickle. What d'you say to that? I can demonstrate the whole thing to you with a lamp and a small ball. That proves it's yet another planet with no light of its own. And it turns round the sun in a simple circle; isn't that marvellous?

ANDREA *sobbing*: Yes, and that's a fact.

GALILEO *quietly*: I never asked her to stay.

Andrea says nothing

GALILEO: But of course if I hadn't stayed myself it wouldn't have happened.

ANDREA: They'll have to believe you now, won't they?

GALILEO: I've got all the proofs I need now. Once this is over, I tell you, I shall go to Rome and show them.

Down the street come two masked men with long poles and buckets. They use these to pass bread through the window to Galileo and the old woman.

THE OLD WOMAN: And there's a woman across there with three children. Leave something for her too.

GALILEO: But I've got nothing to drink. There's no water left in the house. *The two shrug their shoulders.* Will you be coming back tomorrow?

ONE MAN *in a muffled voice, since he has a rag over his mouth*: Who knows what'll happen tomorrow?

GALILEO: If you do come, could you bring me a small book I need for my work?

THE MAN *gives a stifled laugh*: As if a book could make any difference. You'll be lucky if you get bread.

GALILEO: But this boy is my pupil, and he'll be there and can give it you for me. It's the chart giving the periodicity of Mercury, Andrea: I've mislaid it. Can you get me one from the school?

The men have gone on.

ANDREA: Of course. I'll get it, Mr Galilei. *Exit. Galileo likewise goes in. The old woman comes out of the house opposite and puts a jug outside Galileo's door.*

6

1616. The Vatican research institute, the Collegium Romanum, confirms Galileo's findings

Things take indeed a wondrous turn
When learned men do stoop to learn.
Clavius, we are pleased to say
Upheld Galileo Galilei.

Hall of the Collegium Romanum in Rome. It is night-time. High ecclesiastics, monks and scholars in groups. On his own, to one side, Galileo. The atmosphere is extremely hilarious. Before the beginning of the scene a great wave of laughter is heard.

A FAT PRELATE *clasps his belly with laughing*: Stupidity! Stupidity! I'd like to hear a proposition that people won't believe.

A SCHOLAR: For instance: that you have an incurable aversion to meals, Monsignor.

A FAT PRELATE: They'd believe it; they'd believe it. Things have to make sense to be disbelieved. That Satan exists: that's something they doubt. But that the earth spins round like a marble in the gutter; that's believed all right. O sancta simplicatas!

A MONK *play-acting*: I'm getting giddy. The earth's spinning round too fast. Permit me to hold on to you, professor. *He pretends to lurch and clutches one of the scholars.*

THE SCHOLAR *following suit*: Yes, the old girl has been on the bottle again.
He clutches another.

THE MONK: Stop, stop! We're skidding off. Stop, I said!

A SECOND SCHOLAR: Venus is all askew. I can only see one half of her backside. Help!

A group of laughing monks forms, acting as if they were doing their best not to be swept off a ship's deck in a storm.

A SECOND MONK : As long as we aren't flung on to the moon! It's said to have terribly sharp peaks, my brethren.

THE FIRST SCHOLAR : Dig your heels in and resist.

THE FIRST MONK : And don't look down. I'm losing my balance.

THE FAT PRELATE *intentionally loudly, aiming at Galileo*: Oh, that's impossible. Nobody is unbalanced in the Collegium Romanum.

Much laughter. Two of the Collegium astronomers enter from a door. There is a silence.

A MONK : Are you still going over it? That's scandalous.

THE FIRST ASTRONOMER *angrily*: Not us.

THE SECOND ASTRONOMER : What's this meant to lead to? I don't understand Clavius's attitude ... One can't treat everything as gospel that has been put forward in the past fifty years. In 1572 a new star appeared in the eighth and highest sphere, the sphere of the fixed stars, which seemed larger and more brilliant than all the stars round it, and within eighteen months it had gone out and been annihilated. Does that mean we must question the eternity and immutability of the heavens?

PHILOSOPHER : Give them half a chance and they'll smash up our whole starry sky.

THE FIRST ASTRONOMER : Yes, what are we coming to? Five years later Tycho Brahe in Denmark established the course of a comet. It started above the moon and broke through one crystal sphere after another, the solid supports on which all the moving of the heavenly bodies depend. It encountered no obstacles, there was no deflection of its light. Does that mean we must doubt the existence of the spheres?

THE PHILOSOPHER : It's out of the question. As Italy's and

the Church's greatest astronomer, how can Christopher Clavius stoop to examine such a proposition?

THE FAT PRELATE: Outrageous.

THE FIRST ASTRONOMER: He is examining it, though. He's sitting in there staring through that diabolical tube.

THE SECOND ASTRONOMER: Principiis obsta! It all started when we began reckoning so many things – the length of the solar year, the dates of solar and lunar eclipses, the position of the heavenly bodies – according to the tables established by Copernicus, who was a heretic.

A MONK: Which is better, I ask you: to have an eclipse of the moon happen three days later than the calendar says, or never to have eternal salvation at all?

A VERY THIN MONK *comes forward with an open bible, fanatically thrusting his finger at a certain passage*: What do the Scriptures say? "Sun, stand thou still on Gibeon and thou, moon, in the valley of Ajalon." How can the sun stand still if it never moves at all as suggested by this heretic? Are the Scriptures lying?

THE FIRST ASTRONOMER: No, and that's why we walked out.

THE SECOND ASTRONOMER: There *are* phenomena that present difficulties for us astronomers, but does mankind have to understand everything? *Both go out.*

THE VERY THIN MONK: They degrade humanity's dwelling place to a wandering star. Men, animals, plants and the kingdoms of the earth get packed on a cart and driven in a circle round an empty sky. Heaven and earth are no longer distinct, according to them. Heaven because it is made of earth, and earth because it is just one more heavenly body. There is no more difference between top and bottom, between eternal and ephemeral. That we are short-lived we know. Now they tell us that heaven is short-lived too. There are sun, moon and stars, and we live on the earth, it used to be said, and so the Book has it; but now these people are saying the earth is another star. Wait till they say man and animal are not distinct either, man himself is an animal, there's nothing but animals!

THE FIRST SCHOLAR *to Galileo*: Mr Galilei, you've let something fall.

GALILEO *who had meanwhile taken his stone from his pocket, played with it and finally allowed it to drop on the floor, bending to pick it up*: Rise, monsignor; I let it rise.

THE FAT PRELATE *turning round*: An arrogant fellow.

Enter a very old cardinal supported by a monk. They respectfully make way for him.

THE VERY OLD CARDINAL: Are they still in there? Can't they settle such a trivial matter more quickly? Clavius must surely know his astronomy. I am told that this Mr Galilei moves mankind away from the centre of the universe and dumps it somewhere on the edge. Clearly this makes him an enemy of the human race. We must treat him as such. Mankind is the crown of creation, as every child knows, God's highest and dearest creature. How could He take something so miraculous, the fruit of so much effort, and lodge it on a remote, minor, constantly elusive star? Would he send His Son to such a place? How can there be people so perverse as to pin their faith to these slaves of the multiplication table! Which of God's creatures would stand for anything like that?

THE FAT PRELATE *murmurs*: The gentleman is present.

THE VERY OLD CARDINAL *to Galileo*: It's you, is it? You know, my eyesight is not what it was, but I can still see one thing: that you bear a remarkable likeness to what's-his-name, you know, that man we burned.

THE MONK: Your Eminence should avoid excitement. The doctor . . .

THE VERY OLD CARDINAL *shakes him off. To Galileo*: You want to debase the earth even though you live on it and derive everything from it. You are fouling your own nest.

But I for one am not going to stand for that. *He pushes the monk away and begins proudly striding to and fro.* I am not just any old creature on any insignificant star briefly circling in no particular place. I am walking, with a firm step, on a fixed earth, it is motionless, it is the centre of the universe, I am at the centre and the eye of the Creator falls upon me and me alone. Round about me, attached to eight crystal spheres, revolve the fixed stars and the mighty sun which has been created to light my surroundings. And myself too, that God may see me. In this way everything comes visibly and incontrovertibly to depend on me, mankind, God's great effort, the creature on whom it all centres, made in God's own image, indestructible and . . . *He collapses.*

THE MONK: Your Eminence has overstrained himself.

At this moment the door at the back opens and the great Clavius enters at the head of his astronomers. Swiftly and in silence he crosses the hall without looking to one side or the other and addresses a monk as he is on the way out.

CLAVIUS: He's right. *He leaves, followed by the astronomers. The door at the back remains open. Deadly silence. The very old Cardinal recovers consciousness.*

THE VERY OLD CARDINAL: What's that? Have they reached a conclusion?

Nobody dares tell him.

THE MONK: Your Eminence must be taken home. *The old man is assisted out. All leave the hall, worried. A little monk from Clavius's committee of experts pauses beside Galileo.*

THE LITTLE MONK *confidentially*: Mr Galilei, before he left Father Clavius said: Now it's up to the theologians to see how they can straighten out the movements of the heavens once more. You've won. *Exit*

GALILEO *tries to hold him back*: It has won. Not me: reason has won.

The little monk has already left. Galileo too starts to go. In the doorway he encounters a tall cleric, the Cardinal Inquisitor, who is accompanied by an astronomer. Galileo bows. Before going out he whispers a question to the guard at the door.

GUARD *whispers back*: His Eminence the Cardinal Inquisitor. *The astronomer leads the Cardinal Inquisitor up to the telescope.*

7

But the Inquisition puts Copernicus's teachings on the Index (March 5th, 1616)

When Galileo was in Rome
A cardinal asked him to his home.
He wined and dined him as his guest
And only made one small request.

Cardinal Bellarmin's house in Rome. A ball is in progress. In the vestibule, where two clerical secretaries are playing chess and making notes about the guests, Galileo is received with applause by a small group of masked ladies and gentlemen. He arrives accompanied by his daughter Virginia and her fiancé Ludovico Marsili.

VIRGINIA: I'm not dancing with anybody else, Ludovico.
LUDOVICO: Your shoulder-strap's undone.
GALILEO:
    Fret not, daughter, if perchance
    You attract a wanton glance.
    The eyes that catch a trembling lace
    Will guess the heartbeat's quickened pace.
    Lovely woman still may be
    Careless with felicity.
VIRGINIA: Feel my heart.
GALILEO *puts his hand on her heart*: It's thumping.
VIRGINIA: I'd like to look beautiful.

GALILEO: You'd better, or they'll go back to wondering whether it turns or not.

LUDOVICO: Of course it doesn't turn. *Galileo laughs.* Rome is talking only of you. But after tonight, sir, they will be talking about your daughter.

GALILEO: It's supposed to be easy to look beautiful in the Roman spring. Even I shall start looking like an overweight Adonis. *To the secretaries*: I am to wait here for his Eminence the Cardinal. *To the couple*: Go off and enjoy yourselves. *Before they leave for the ball offstage Virginia again comes running back.*

VIRGINIA: Father, the hairdresser in the Via del Trionfo took me first, and he made four other ladies wait. He knew your name right away. *Exit.*

GALILEO *to the secretaries as they play chess*: How can you go on playing old-style chess? Cramped, cramped. Nowadays the play is to let the chief pieces roam across the whole board. The rooks like this – *he demonstrates* – and the bishops like that and the Queen like this and that. That way you have enough space and can plan ahead.

FIRST SECRETARY: It wouldn't go with our small salaries, you know. We can only do moves like this. *He makes a small move.*

GALILEO: You've got it wrong, my friend, quite wrong. If you live grandly enough you can afford to sweep the board. One has to move with the times, gentlemen. Not just hugging the coasts; sooner or later one has to venture out. *The very old cardinal from the previous scene crosses the stage, led by his monk. He notices Galileo, walks past him, turns round hesitantly and greets him. Galileo sits down. From the ballroom boys' voices are heard singing Lorenzo di Medici's famous poem on transience,*

I who have seen the summer's roses die
And all their petals pale and shrivelled lie

Upon the chilly ground, I know the truth:
How evanescent is the flower of youth.

GALILEO: Rome – A large party?

THE FIRST SECRETARY: The first carnival since the plague
years. All Italy's great families are represented here tonight.
The Orsinis, the Villanis, the Nuccolis, the Soldanieris, the
Canes, the Lecchis, the d'Estes, the Colombinis ...

SECOND SECRETARY *interrupting*: Their Eminences Cardinals Bellarmin and Barberini.

*Enter Cardinal Bellarmin and Cardinal Barberini. They are
holding sticks with the masks of a lamb and a dove over their faces.*

BARBERINI *pointing at Galileo*: 'The sun also ariseth, and the
sun goeth down, and hasteth to his place where he arose.' So
says Solomon, and what does Galileo say?

GALILEO: When I was so high – *he indicates with his hand* –
your Eminence, I stood on a ship and called out 'The shore
is moving away.' Today I realise that the shore was standing
still and the ship moving away.

BARBERINI: Ingenious, ingenious – what our eyes see,
Bellarmin, in other words the rotation of the starry heavens,
is not necessarily true – witness the ship and the shore. But
what is true – i.e. the rotation of the earth – cannot be
perceived. Ingenious. But his moons of Jupiter are a tough
nut for our astronomers to crack. Unfortunately I once
studied some astronomy, Bellarmin. It sticks to you like the
itch.

BELLARMIN: We must move with the times, Barberini. If
new star charts based on a new hypothesis help our mariners to navigate, then they should make use of them. We
only disapprove of such doctrines as run counter to the
Scriptures.

He waves toward the ballroom in greeting.

GALILEO: The Scriptures ... 'He that withholdeth corn, the
people shall curse him.' Proverbs of Solomon.

BARBERINI: 'A prudent man concealeth knowledge.' Proverbs of Solomon.

GALILEO: 'Where no oxen are the crib is clean: but much increase is by the strength of the ox.'

BARBERINI: 'He that ruleth his spirit is better than he that taketh a city.'

GALILEO: 'But a broken spirit drieth the bones.' *Pause.* 'Doth not wisdom cry?'

BARBERINI: 'Can one go upon hot coals, and his feet not be burned?' – Welcome to Rome, Galileo my friend. You know its origins? Two little boys, so runs the legend, were given milk and shelter by a she-wolf. Since that time all her children have had to pay for their milk. The she-wolf makes up for it by providing every kind of pleasure, earthly and heavenly, ranging from conversations with my friend Bellarmin to three or four ladies of international repute; let me point them out to you . . .

He takes Galileo upstage to show him the ballroom. Galileo follows reluctantly.

BARBERINI: No? He would rather have a serious discussion. Right. Are you sure, Galileo my friend, that you astronomers aren't merely out to make astronomy simpler for yourselves? *He leads him forward once more.* You think in circles and ellipses and constant velocities, simple motions such as are adapted to your brains. Suppose it had pleased God to make his stars move like this? *With his finger he traces an extremely complicated course at an uneven speed.* What would that do to your calculations?

GALILEO: Your Eminence, if God had constructed the world like that – *he imitates Barberini's course* – then he would have gone on to construct our brains like that, so that they would regard such motions as the simplest. I believe in men's reason.

BARBERINI: I think men's reason is not up to the job.

Silence. He's too polite to go on and say he thinks mine is not up to the job.

Laughs and walks back to the balustrade.

BELLARMIN: Men's reason, my friend, does not take us very far. All around us we see nothing but crookedness, crime and weakness. Where is truth?

GALILEO *angrily*: I believe in men's reason.

BARBERINI *to the secretaries*: You needn't take this down; it's a scientific discussion among friends.

BELLARMIN: Think for an instant how much thought and effort it cost the Fathers of the Church and their countless successors to put some sense into this appalling world of ours. Think of the brutality of the landowners in the Campagna who have their half-naked peasants flogged to work, and of the stupidity of those poor people who kiss their feet in return.

GALILEO: Horrifying. As I was driving here I saw . . .

BELLARMIN: We have shifted the responsibility for such occurrences as we cannot understand – life is made up of them – to a higher Being, and argued that all of them contribute to the fulfilment of certain intentions, that the whole thing is taking place according to a great plan. Admittedly this hasn't satisfied everybody, but now you come along and accuse this higher Being of not being quite clear how the stars move, whereas you yourself are. Is that sensible?

GALILEO *starts to make a statement*: I am a faithful son of the Church . . .

BARBERINI: He's a terrible man. He cheerfully sets out to convict God of the most elementary errors in astronomy. I suppose God hadn't got far enough in his studies before he wrote the bible; is that it? My *dear* fellow . . .

BELLARMIN: Wouldn't you also think it possible that the Creator had a better idea of what he was making than those he has created?

GALILEO: But surely, gentlemen, mankind may not only get the motions of the stars wrong but the Bible too?

BELLARMIN: But isn't interpreting the Bible the business of Holy Church and her theologians, wouldn't you say? *Galileo is silent.*

BELLARMIN: You have no answer to that, have you? *He makes a sign to the secretaries:* Mr Galilei, tonight the Holy Office decided that the doctrine of Copernicus, according to which the sun is motionless and at the centre of the cosmos, while the earth moves and is not at the centre of the cosmos, is foolish, absurd, heretical and contrary to our faith. I have been charged to warn you that you must abandon this view.

GALILEO: What does this mean?

From the ballroom boys can be heard singing a further verse of the madrigal:

> I said: This lovely springtime cannot last
> So pluck your roses before May is past.

Barberini gestures Galileo not to speak till the song is finished. They listen.

GALILEO: And the facts? I understand that the Collegium Romanum had approved my observations.

BELLARMIN: And expressed their complete satisfaction, in terms very flattering to you.

GALILEO: But the moons of Jupiter, the phases of Venus . . .

BELLARMIN: The Holy Congregation took its decision without going into such details.

GALILEO: In other words, all further scientific research . . .

BELLARMIN: Is explicitly guaranteed, Mr Galilei. In line with the Church's view that it is impossible for us to know, but legitimate for us to explore. *He again greets a guest in the ballroom.* You are also at liberty to treat the doctrine in question mathematically, in the form of a hypothesis. Science is the rightful and much-loved daughter of the

Church, Mr Galilei. None of us seriously believes that you want to shake men's faith in the Church.

GALILEO *angrily*: What destroys faith is invoking it.

BARBERINI: Really? *He slaps him on the shoulder with a roar of laughter. Then he gives him a keen look and says in a not unfriendly manner*: Don't tip the baby out with the bathwater, Galileo my friend. *We* shan't. We need you more than you need us.

BELLARMIN: I cannot wait to introduce Italy's greatest mathematician to the Commissioner of the Holy Office, who has the highest possible esteem for you.

BARBERINI *taking Galileo's other arm..* At which he turns himself back into a lamb. You too, my dear fellow, ought really to have come disguised as a good orthodox thinker. It's my own mask that permits me certain freedoms today. Dressed like this I might be heard to murmur: If God didn't exist we should have to invent him. Right, let's put on our masks once more. Poor old Galileo hasn't got one. *They put Galileo between them and escort him into the ballroom.*

FIRST SECRETARY: Did you get that last sentence?

SECOND SECRETARY: Just doing it. *They write rapidly.* Have you got that bit where he said he believes in men's reason? *Enter the Cardinal Inquisitor.*

THE INQUISITOR: Did the conversation take place?

FIRST SECRETARY *mechanically*: To start with Mr Galilei arrived with his daughter. She has become engaged today to Mr . . . *The Inquisitor gestures him not to go on.* Mr Galilei then told us about the new way of playing chess in which, contrary to all the rules, the pieces are moved right across the board.

THE INQUISITOR *with a similar gesture*: The transcript. *A secretary hands him the transcripts and the cardinal sits down and skims through it. Two young ladies in masks cross the stage; they curtsey to the cardinal.*

ONE YOUNG LADY: Who's that?

THE OTHER: The Cardinal Inquisitor.

They giggle and go off. Enter Virginia, looking around for something.

THE INQUISITOR *from his corner*: Well, my daughter?

VIRGINIA *gives a slight start, not having seen him*: Oh, your Eminence . . .

Without looking up, the Inquisitor holds out his right hand to her. She approaches, kneels and kisses his ring.

THE INQUISITOR: A splendid night. Permit me to congratulate you on your engagement. Your future husband comes from a distinguished family. Are you staying long in Rome?

VIRGINIA: Not this time, your Eminence. A wedding takes so much preparing.

THE INQUISITOR: Ah, then you'll be returning to Florence like your father. I am glad of that. I expect that your father needs you. Mathematics is not the warmest of companions in the home, is it? Having a creature of flesh and blood around makes all the difference. It's easy to get lost in the world of the stars, with its immense distances, if one is a great man.

VIRGINIA *breathlessly*: You are very kind, your Eminence. I really understand practically nothing about such things.

THE INQUISITOR: Indeed? *He laughs.* In the fisherman's house no one eats fish, eh? It will tickle your father to hear that almost all your knowledge about the world of the stars comes ultimately from me, my child. *Leafing through the transcript*: It says here that our innovators, whose acknowledged leader is your father – a great man, one of the greatest – consider our present ideas about the significance of the dear old earth to be a little exaggerated. Well, from Ptolemy's time – and he was a wise man of antiquity – up to the present day we used to reckon that the whole of creation – in other words the entire crystal ball at whose centre the earth lies – measured about twenty thousand diametres of the earth across. Nice and roomy, but not large enough for innovators. Apparently they feel that it is unimaginably far-flung and that the earth's distance from the sun – quite a respectable distance, we always found it – is so minute compared with its distance from the fixed stars on the outermost sphere that our calculations can simply ignore it. Yes, our innovators are living on a very grand scale.

Virginia laughs. So does the Inquisitor.

THE INQUISITOR: True enough, there are a few gentlemen of the Holy Office who have started objecting, as it were, to such a view of the world, compared with which our picture so far has been a little miniature such as one might hang round the neck of certain young ladies. What worries them is that a prelate or even a cardinal might get lost in such vast distances and the Almighty might lose sight of the Pope himself. Yes, it's very amusing, but I am glad to know that you will remain close to your great father whom we all esteem so highly, my dear child. By the way, do I know your Father Confessor . . .?

VIRGINIA: Father Christophorus of Saint Ursula.

THE INQUISITOR: Ah yes, I am glad that you will be going with your father. He will need you; perhaps you cannot imagine this, but the time will come. You are still so young and so very much flesh and blood, and greatness is occasionally a difficult burden for those on whom God has bestowed it; it can be. No mortal is so great that he cannot be contained in a prayer. But I am keeping you, my dear child, and I'll be making your fiancé jealous and maybe your father too by telling you something about the stars which is possibly out of date. Run off and dance; only mind you remember me to Father Christophorus.

Virginia makes a deep bow and goes.

8

A conversation

> Galileo, feeling grim,
> A young monk came to visit him.
> The monk was born of common folk.
> It was of science that they spoke.

*In the Florentine Ambassador's palace in Rome Galileo is listening to
the little monk who whispered the papal astronomer's remark to him
after the meeting of the Collegium Romanum.*

GALILEO: Go on, go on. The habit you're wearing gives you
the right to say whatever you want.

THE LITTLE MONK: I studied mathematics, Mr Galilei.

GALILEO: That might come in handy if it led you to admit
that two and two sometimes makes four.

THE LITTLE MONK: Mr Galilei, I have been unable to sleep
for three days. I couldn't see how to reconcile the decree I
had read with the moons of Jupiter which I had observed.
Today I decided to say an early mass and come to you.

GALILEO: In order to tell me Jupiter has no moons?

THE LITTLE MONK: No. I have managed to see the wisdom
of the decree. It has drawn my attention to the potential
dangers for humanity in wholly unrestricted research, and
I have decided to give astronomy up. But I also wanted to
explain to you the motives which can make even an
astronomer renounce pursuing that doctrine any further.

GALILEO: I can assure you that such motives are familiar to
me.

THE LITTLE MONK: I understand your bitterness. You have
in mind certain exceptional powers of enforcement at the
Church's disposal.

GALILEO: Just call them instruments of torture.

THE LITTLE MONK: But I am referring to other motives.
Let me speak about myself. My parents were peasants in the
Campagna, and I grew up there. They are simple people.
They know all about olive trees, but not much else. As I
study the phases of Venus I can visualise my parents sitting
round the fire with my sister, eating their curded cheese. I
see the beams above them, blackened by hundreds of years
of smoke, and I see every detail of their old worn hands and
the little spoons they are holding. They are badly off, but
even their misfortunes imply a certain order. There are so
many cycles, ranging from washing the floor, through the
seasons of the olive crop to the paying of taxes. There is a
regularity about the disasters that befall them. My father's
back does not get bent all at once, but more and more each
spring he spends in the olive groves; just as the successive
childbirths that have made my mother increasingly sexless
have followed well-defined intervals. They draw the
strength they need to carry their baskets sweating up the
stony tracks, to bear children and even to eat, from the
feeling of stability and necessity that comes of looking at
the soil, at the annual greening of the trees and at the little
church, and of listening to the bible passages read there
every Sunday. They have been assured that God's eye
is always on them – probingly, even anxiously –: that
the whole drama of the world is constructed around them
so that they, the performers, may prove themselves in their
greater or lesser roles. What would my people say if I told
them that they happen to be on a small knob of stone twisting endlessly through the void round a second-rate star,
just one among myriads? What would be the value or
necessity then of so much patience, such understanding of
their own poverty? What would be the use of Holy
Scripture, which has explained and justified it all – the sweat,
the patience, the hunger, the submissiveness – and now

turns out to be full of errors? No: I can see their eyes
wavering, I can see them letting their spoons drop, I can
see how betrayed and deceived they will feel. So nobody's
eye is on us, they'll say. Have we got to look after ourselves, old, uneducated and worn-out as we are? The
only part anybody has devised for us is this wretched,
earthly one, to be played out on a tiny star wholly dependent on others, with nothing revolving round it. Our
poverty has no meaning: hunger is no trial of strength, it's
merely not having eaten: effort is no virtue, it's just bending
and carrying. Can you see now why I read into the Holy
Congregations decree a noble motherly compassion; a vast
goodness of soul?

GALILEO: Goodness of soul! Aren't you really saying that
there's nothing for them, the wine has all been drunk, their
lips are parched, so they had better kiss the cassock? Why is
there nothing for them? Why does order in this country
mean the orderliness of a bare cupboard, and necessity
nothing but the need to work oneself to death? When there
are teeming vineyards and cornfields on every side? Your
Campagna peasants are paying for the wars which the
representative of gentle Jesus is waging in Germany and
Spain. Why does he make the earth the centre of the
universe? So that the See of St Peter can be the centre of the
earth! That's what it is all about. You're right, it's not about
the planets, it's about the peasants of the Campagna. And
don't talk to me about the beauty given to phenomena by
the patina of age! You know how the Margaritifera oyster
produces its pearl? By a mortally dangerous disease which
involves taking some unassimilable foreign body, like a
grain of sand, and wrapping it in a slimy ball. The process
all but kills it. To hell with the pearl, give me the healthy
oyster. Virtues are not an offshoot of poverty, my dear
fellow. If your people were happy and prosperous they
could develop the virtues of happiness and prosperity. At

present the virtues of exhaustion derive from exhausted fields, and I reject them. Sir, my new pumps will perform more miracles in that direction than all your ridiculous superhuman slaving. – 'Be fruitful and multiply', since your fields are not fruitful and you are being decimated by wars. Am I supposed to tell your people lies?

THE LITTLE MONK *much agitated*: We have the highest of all motives for keeping our mouths shut – the peace of mind of the less fortunate.

GALILEO: Would you like me to show you a Cellini clock that Cardinal Bellarmin's coachman brought round this morning? My dear fellow, authority is rewarding me for not disturbing the peace of mind of people like your parents, by offering me the wine they press in the sweat of their countenance which we all know to have been made in God's image. If I were to agree to keep my mouth shut my motives would be thoroughly low ones: an easy life, freedom from persecution, and so on.

THE LITTLE MONK: Mr Galilei, I am a priest.

GALILEO: You're also a physicist. And you can see that Venus has phases. Here, look out there! *He points at the window.* Can you see the little Priapus on the fountain next the laurel bush? The god of gardens, birds and thieves, rich in two thousand years of bucolic indecency. Even he was less of a liar. All right, let's drop it. I too am a son of the Church. But do you know the eighth Satire of Horace? I've been rereading it again lately, it acts as a kind of counterweight. *He picks up a small book.* He makes his Priapus speak – a little statue which was then in the Esquiline gardens. Starting:

Stump of a figtree, useless kind of wood
Was I once; then the carpenter, not sure
Whether to make a Priapus or a stool
Opted for the god . . .

Can you imagine Horace being told not to mention stools and agreeing to put a table in the poem instead? Sir, it offends my sense of beauty if my cosmogony has a Venus without phases. We cannot invent mechanisms to pump water up from rivers if we are not to be allowed to study the greatest of all mechanisms right under our nose, that of the heavenly bodies. The sum of the angles in a triangle cannot be varied to suit the Vatican's convenience. I can't calculate the courses of flying bodies in such a way as also to explain witches taking trips on broomsticks.

THE LITTLE MONK: But don't you think that the truth will get through without us, so long as it's true?

GALILEO: No, no, no. The only truth that gets through will be what we force through: the victory of reason will be the victory of people who are prepared to reason, nothing else. Your picture of the Campagna peasants makes them look like the moss on their own huts. How can anyone imagine that the sum of the angles in a triangle conflicts with *their* needs? But unless they get moving and learn how to think, they will find even the finest irrigation systems won't help them. Oh, to hell with it: I see your people's divine patience, but where is their divine anger?

THE LITTLE MONK: They are tired.

GALILEO *tosses him a bundle of manuscripts*: Are you a physicist, my son? Here you have the reasons why the ocean moves, ebbing and flowing. But you're not supposed to read it, d'you hear? Oh, you've already started. You are a physicist, then? *The little monk is absorbed in the papers.*

GALILEO: An apple from the tree of knowledge! He's wolfing it down. He is damned for ever, but he has got to wolf it down, the poor glutton. I sometimes think I'll have myself shut up in a dungeon ten fathoms below ground in complete darkness if only it will help me to find out what light is. And the worst thing is that what I know I have to tell people, like a lover, like a drunkard, like a traitor. It is

an absolute vice and leads to disaster. How long can I go on
shouting it into the void, that's the question.

THE LITTLE MONK *indicating a passage in the papers*: I don't
understand this sentence.

GALILEO: I'll explain it you, I'll explain it to you.

9

After keeping silent for eight years, Galileo is en-
couraged by the accession of a new pope, himself
a scientist, to resume his researches into the for-
bidden area: the sunspots

> Eight long years with tongue in cheek
> Of what he knew he did not speak.
> Then temptation grew too great
> And Galileo challenged fate.

*Galileo's house in Florence. Galileo's pupils – Federzoni, the little
monk and Andrea Sarti, a young man now – have gathered to see an
experiment demonstrated. Galileo himself is standing reading a book.
Virginia and Mrs Sarti are sewing her trousseau.*

VIRGINIA: Sewing one's trousseau is fun. That one's for
entertaining at the long table; Ludovico likes entertaining.
It's got to be neat, though; his mother can spot every loose
thread. She doesn't like Father's books. Nor does Father
Christophorus.

MRS SARTI: He hasn't written a book for years.

VIRGINIA: I think he realises he was wrong. A very high
church person in Rome told me a lot about astronomy. The
distances are too great.

ANDREA *writing the day's programme on the board*: 'Thursday
p.m. Floating bodies' – as before, ice, bucket of water,
balance, iron needle, Aristotle.

He fetches these things. The others are reading books.
Enter Filippo Mucius, a scholar in middle age. He appears some-
what distraught.

MUCIUS: Could you tell Mr Galilei that he has got to see me? He is condemning me unheard.

MRS SARTI: But he won't receive you.

MUCIUS: God will recompense you if you will only ask. I must speak to him.

VIRGINIA *goes to the stairs*: Father!

GALILEO: What is it?

VIRGINIA: Mr Mucius.

GALILEO *looking up sharply, goes to the head of the stairs, followed by his pupils*: What do you want?

MUCIUS: Mr Galilei, may I be allowed to explain those passages from my book which seem to contain a condemnation of Copernicus's theories about the rotation of the earth? I have . . .

GALILEO: What do you want to explain? You are fully in line with the Holy Congregation's decree of 1616. You cannot be faulted. You did of course study mathematics here, but that's no reason why we should need to hear you say that two and two makes four. You are quite within your rights in saying that this stone – *he takes a little stone from his pocket and throws it down to the hall* – has just flown up to the ceiling.

MUCIUS: Mr Galilei, I . . .

GALILEO: Don't talk to me about difficulties. I didn't let the plague stop me from recording my observations.

MUCIUS: Mr Galilei, there are worse things than the plague.

GALILEO: Listen to me: someone who doesn't know the truth is just thick-headed. But someone who does know it and calls it a lie is a crook. Get out of my house.

MUCIUS *tonelessly*: You're quite right.

He goes out.
Galileo goes back into his work room.

FEDERZONI: Too bad. He's not a great man and no one would take him seriously for one moment if he hadn't been your pupil. Now of course people are saying 'he's heard everything Galileo had to teach and he's forced to admit that it's all nonsense'.

MRS SARTI: I'm sorry for the poor gentleman.

VIRGINIA: Father was too good to him.

MRS SARTI: I really wanted to talk to you about your marriage, Virginia. You're such a child still, and got no mother, and your father keeps putting those little bits of ice on water. Anyhow I wouldn't ask him anything to do with your marriage if I were you. He'd keep on for days saying the most dreadful things, preferably at meals and when the young people are there, because he hasn't got half a scudo's worth of shame in his make-up, and never had. But I'm not talking about that kind of thing, just about how the future will turn out. Not that I'm in a position to know anything myself. I'm not educated. But nobody goes blindly into a serious affair like this. I really think you ought to go to a proper astronomer at the university and get him to cast your horoscope so you know what you're in for. Why are you laughing?

VIRGINIA: Because I've been.

MRS SARTI *very inquisitive*: What did he say?

VIRGINIA: For three months I'll have to be careful, because the sun will be in Aries, but then I shall get a particularly favourable ascendant and the clouds will part. So long as I keep my eye on Jupiter I can travel as much as I like, because I'm an Aries.

MRS SARTI: And Ludovico?

VIRGINIA: He's a Leo. *After a little pause*: That's supposed to be sensual. *Pause*

VIRGINIA: I know whose step that is. It's Mr Gaffone, the Rector.

Enter Mr Gaffone, Rector of the University.

GAFFONE: I'm just bringing a book which I think might interest your father. For heaven's sake please don't disturb him. I can't help it; I always feel that every moment stolen from that great man is a moment stolen from Italy. I'll lay it neatly and daintily in your hands and slip away, on tiptoe. *He goes. Virginia gives the book to Federzoni.*

GALILEO: What's it about?

FEDERZONI: I don't know. *Spelling out*: 'De maculis in sole'.

ANDREA: About sunspots. Yet another.
Federzoni irritably passes it on to him.

ANDREA: Listen to the dedication. 'To the greatest living authority on physics, Galileo Galilei.'
Galileo is once more deep in his book.

ANDREA: I've read the treatise on sunspots which Fabricius has written in Holland. He thinks they are clusters of stars passing between the earth and the sun.

THE LITTLE MONK: Doubtful, don't you think, Mr Galilei?
Galileo does not answer.

ANDREA: In Paris and in Prague they think they are vapours from the sun.

FEDERZONI: Hm.

ANDREA: Federzoni doubts it.

FEDERZONI: Leave me out of it, would you? I said 'Hm', that's all. I'm your lensgrinder, I grind lenses and you make observations of the sky through them and what you see isn't spots but 'maculis'. How am I to doubt anything? How often do I have to tell you I can't read the books, they're in Latin? *In his anger he gesticulates with the scales. One of the pans falls to the floor. Galileo goes over and picks it up without saying anything.*

THE LITTLE MONK: There's happiness in doubting: I wonder why.

ANDREA: Every sunny day for the past two weeks I've gone up to the attic, under the roof. The narrow chinks between the shingles let just a thin ray of light through. If you take a sheet of paper you can catch the sun's image upside down. I saw a spot as big as a fly, as smudged as a cloud. It was moving. Why aren't we investigating those spots, Mr Galilei?

GALILEO: Because we're working on floating bodies.

ANDREA: Mother's got great baskets full of letters. The whole of Europe wants to know what you think, you've such a reputation now, you can't just say nothing.

GALILEO: Rome allowed me to get a reputation because I said nothing.

FEDERZONI: But you can't afford to go on saying nothing now.

GALILEO: Nor can I afford to be roasted over a wood fire like a ham.

ANDREA: Does that mean you think the sunspots are part of this business?

Galileo does not answer.

ANDREA: All right, let's stick to our bits of ice, they can't hurt you.

GALILEO: Correct. – Our proposition, Andrea?

ANDREA: As for floating, we assume that it depends not on a body's form but on whether it is lighter or heavier than water.

GALILEO: What does Aristotle say?

THE LITTLE MONK: 'Discus latus platique . . .'

GALILEO: For God's sake translate it.

THE LITTLE MONK: 'A broad flat piece of ice will float on water whereas an iron needle will sink.'

GALILEO: Why does the ice not sink, in Aristotle's view?

THE LITTLE MONK: Because it is broad and flat and therefore cannot divide the water.

GALILEO: Right. *He takes a piece of ice and places it in the bucket.* Now I am pressing the ice hard against the bottom of the bucket. I release the pressure of my hands. What happens?

THE LITTLE MONK: It shoots up to the top again.

GALILEO: Correct. Apparently it can divide the water all right as it rises. Fulganzio!

THE LITTLE MONK: But why can it float in the first place? It's heavier than water, because it is concentrated water.

GALILEO: Suppose it were thinned-down water?

ANDREA: It has to be lighter than water, or it wouldn't float.

GALILEO: Aha.

ANDREA: Any more than an iron needle can float. Everything lighter than water floats and everything heavier sinks. QED.

GALILEO: Andrea, you must learn to think cautiously. Hand me the needle. A sheet of paper. Is iron heavier than water?

ANDREA: Yes.

Galileo lays the needle on a piece of paper and launches it on the water. A pause.

GALILEO: What happens?

FEDERZONI: The needle's floating. Holy Aristotle, they never checked up on him!

They laugh.

GALILEO: One of the main reasons why the sciences are so poor is that they imagine they are so rich. It isn't their job to throw open the door to infinite wisdom but to put a limit to infinite error. Make your notes.

VIRGINIA: What is it?

MRS SARTI: Whenever they laugh it gives me a turn. What are they laughing about, I ask myself.

VIRGINIA: Father says theologians have their bells to ring: physicists have their laughter.

MRS SARTI: Anyway I'm glad he isn't looking through his tube so often these days. That was even worse.

VIRGINIA: All he's doing now is put bits of ice in water: that can't do much harm.

MRS SARTI: I don't know.

Enter Ludovico Marsili in travelling clothes, followed by a servant carrying items of luggage. Virginia runs up and throws her arms round him.

VIRGINIA: Why didn't you write and say you were coming?

LUDOVICO: I happened to be in the area, inspecting our vineyards at Buccioli, and couldn't resist the chance.

GALILEO *as though short-sighted*: Who is it?

VIRGINIA: Ludovico.

THE LITTLE MONK: Can't you see him?

GALILEO: Ah yes, Ludovico. *Goes towards him.* How are the horses?

LUDOVICO: Doing fine, sir.

GALILEO: Sarti, we're celebrating. Get us a jug of that Sicilian wine, the old sort.

Exit Mrs Sarti with Andrea.

LUDOVICO *to Virginia*: You look pale. Country life will suit you. My mother is expecting you in September.

VIRGINIA: Wait a moment, I'll show you my wedding dress. *Runs out.*

GALILEO: Sit down.

LUDOVICO: I'm told there are over a thousand students going to your lectures at the university, sir. What are you working at just now?

GALILEO: Routine stuff. Did you come through Rome?

LUDOVICO: Yes. – Before I forget: my mother congratulates you on your remarkable tact in connection with those sun-sport orgies the Dutch have been going in for lately.

GALILEO *drily*: Very kind of her.

Mrs Sarti and Andrea bring wine and glasses. Everyone gathers round the table.

LUDOVICO: I can tell you what all the gossip will be about in Rome this February. Christopher Clavius said he's afraid the whole earth-round-the-sun act will start up again because of these sunspots.

ANDREA: No chance.

GALILEO: Any other news from the Holy City, aside from hopes of fresh lapses on my part?

LUDOVICO: I suppose you know that His Holiness is dying?

THE LITTLE MONK: Oh.

GALILEO: Who do they think will succeed him?

LUDOVICO: The favourite is Barberini.

GALILEO: Barberini.

ANDREA: Mr Galilei knows Barberini.

THE LITTLE MONK: Cardinal Barberini is a mathematician.

FEDERZONI: A scientist at the Holy See!

Pause.

GALILEO: Well: so now they need people like Barberini who have read a bit of mathematics! Things are beginning to move. Federzoni, we may yet see the day when we no longer have to look over our shoulder like criminals every time we say two and two equals four. *To Ludovico*: I like this wine, Ludovico. What do you think of it?

LUDOVICO: It's good.

GALILEO: I know the vineyard. The hillside is steep and stony, the grapes almost blue. I love this wine.

LUDOVOCI: Yes, sir.

GALILEO: It has got little shadows in it. And it is almost sweet but just stops short of it. – Andrea, clear all that stuff away, the ice, needle and bucket. – I value the consolations of the flesh. I've no use for those chicken-hearts who see them as weaknesses. Pleasure takes some achieving, I'd say.

THE LITTLE MONK: What have you in mind?

FEDERZONI: We're starting up the earth-round-the-sun act again.

ANDREA *hums*:

It's fixed, the Scriptures say. And so
Orthodox science proves.
The Holy Father grabs its ears, to show
It's firmly held. And yet it moves.

Andrea, Federzoni and the little monk hurry to the work table and clear it.

ANDREA: We might find that the sun goes round too. How would that suit you, Marsili?

LUDOVICO: What's the excitement about?

MRS SARTI: You're not going to start up that devilish business again, surely, Mr Galilei?

GALILEO: Now I know why your mother sent you to me. Barberini in the ascendant! Knowledge will become a passion and research an ecstasy. Clavius is right, those sunspots interest me. Do you like my wine, Ludovico?

LUDOVICO: I told you I did, Sir.

GALILEO: You really like it?

LUDOVICO *stiffly*: I like it.

GALILEO: Would you go so far as to accept a man's wine or his daughter without asking him to give up his profession? What has my astronomy got to do with my daughter? The phases of Venus can't alter my daughter's backside.

MRS SARTI: Don't be so vulgar. I am going to fetch Virginia.

LUDOVICO *holding her back*: Marriages in families like ours are not based on purely sexual considerations.

GALILEO: Did they stop you from marrying my daughter for eight years because I had a term of probation to serve?

LUDOVICO: My wife will also have to take her place in our pew in the village church.

GALILEO: You think your peasants will go by the saintliness of their mistress in deciding whether to pay rent or not?

LUDOVICO: In a sense, yes.

GALILEO: Andrea, Fulganzio, get out the brass reflector and the screen! We will project the sun's image on it so as to protect our eyes; that's your method, Andrea.
Andrea and the little monk fetch reflector and screen.

LUDOVICO: You did sign a declaration in Rome, you know, Sir, saying you would have nothing more to do with this earth-round-the-sun business.

GALILEO: Oh that. In those days we had a reactionary pope.

MRS SARTI: Had! And his Holiness not even dead yet!

GALILEO: Almost. Put a grid of squares on the screen. We will do this methodically. And then we'll be able to answer their letters, won't we, Andrea?

MRS SARTI: 'Almost' indeed. The man'll weigh his pieces of ice fifty times over, but as soon as it's something that suits his book he believes it blindly.

The screen is set up.

LUDOVICO: If His Holiness does die, Mr Galilei, irrespective who the next pope is and how intense his devotion to the sciences, he will also have to take into account the devotion felt for him by the most respected families in the land.

THE LITTLE MONK: God made the physical world, Ludovico; God made the human brain; God will permit physics.

MRS SARTI: Galileo, I am going to say something to you. I have watched my son slipping into sin with all those 'experiments' and 'theories' and 'observations' and there was nothing I could do about it. You set yourself up against the authorities and they have already warned you once. The highest cardinals spoke to you like to a sick horse. That worked for a time, but then two months ago, just after the Feast of the Immaculate Conception, I caught you secretly starting your 'observations' again. In the attic. I didn't say much but I knew what to do. I ran and lit a candle to St Joseph. It's more than I can cope with. When I get you on your own you show vestiges of sense and tell me you know you've got to behave or else it'll be dangerous; but two days of experiments and you're just as bad as before. If I choose to forfeit eternal bliss by sticking with a heretic that's my business, but you have no right to trample all over your daughter's happiness with your great feet.

GALILEO *gruffly*: Bring the telescope.

LUDOVICO: Giuseppe, take our luggage back to the coach.

The servant goes out.

MRS SARTI: She'll never get over this. You can tell her yourself.

Hurries off, still carrying the jug.

LUDOVICO: I see you have made your preparations. Mr Galileo, my mother and I spend three quarters of each year on our estate in the Campagna, and we can assure you that our peasants are not disturbed by your papers on Jupiter and its moons. They are kept too busy in the fields. But they could be upset if they heard that frivolous attacks on the church's sacred doctrines were in future to go unpunished. Don't forget that the poor things are little better than animals and get everything muddled up. They are like beasts really, you can hardly imagine it. If rumour says a pear has been seen on an apple tree they will drop their work and hurry off to gossip about it.

GALILEO *interested*: Really?

LUDOVICO: Beasts. If they come up to the house to make some minor complaint or other, my mother is forced to have a dog whipped before their eyes, as the only way to recall them to discipline and order and a proper respect. You, Mr Galileo, may see rich cornfields from your coach as you pass, you eat our olives and our cheese, without a thought, and you have no idea how much trouble it takes to produce them, how much supervision.

GALILEO: Young man, I do not eat my olives without a thought. *Roughly*: You're holding me up. *Calls through the door*: Got the screen?

ANDREA: Yes. Are you coming?

GALILEO: Dogs aren't the only thing you whip to keep them in line, are they Marsili?

LUDOVICO: Mr Galileo. You have a marvellous brain. Pity.

THE LITTLE MONK *amazed*: He's threatening you.

GALILEO: Yes, I might stir up his peasants to think new thoughts. And his servants and his stewards.

FEDERZONI: How? None of them can read Latin.

GALILEO: I might write in the language of the people, for the many, rather than in Latin for the few. Our new thoughts call for people who work with their hands. Who else cares about knowing the causes of things? People who only see bread on their table don't want to know how it got baked; that lot would sooner thank God than thank the baker. But the people who make the bread will understand that nothing moves unless it has been made to move. Your sister pressing olives, Fulganzio, won't be astounded but will probably laugh when she hears that the sun isn't a golden coat of arms but a motor: that the earth moves because the sun sets it moving.

LUDOVICO: You will always be the slave of your passions. Make my excuses to Virginia; I think it will be better if I don't see her.

GALILEO: Her dowry will remain available to you, at any time.

LUDOVICO: Good day. *He goes.*

ANDREA: And our kindest regards to all the Marsilis.

FEDERZONI: Who command the earth to stand still so their castles shan't tumble down.

ANDREA: And the Cenzis and the Villanis!

FEDERZONI: The Cervillis!

ANDREA: The Lecchis!

FEDERZONI: The Pirleonis!

ANDREA: Who are prepared to kiss the pope's toe only if he uses it to kick the people with!

THE LITTLE MONK *likewise at the instruments*: The new pope is going to be an enlightened man.

GALILEO: So let us embark on the examination of those spots on the sun in which we are interested, at our own risk and without banking too much on the protection of a new pope.

ANDREA *interrupting*: But fully convinced that we shall dispel Mr Fabricius's star shadows along with the sun vapours of Paris and Prague, and establish the rotation of the sun.

GALILEO: Somewhat convinced that we shall establish the rotation of the sun. My object is not to establish that I was right but to find out if I am. Abandon hope, I say, all ye who enter on observation. They may be vapours, they may be spots, but before we assume that they are spots – which is what would suit us best – we should assume that they are fried fish. In fact we shall question everything all over again. And we shall go forward not in seven-league boots but at a snail's pace. And what we discover today we shall wipe off the slate tomorrow and only write it up again once we have again discovered it. And whatever we wish to find we shall regard, once found, with particular mistrust. So we shall approach the observation of the sun with an irrevocable determination to establish that the earth does *not* move. Only when we have failed, have been utterly and hopelessly beaten and are licking our wounds in the profoundest depression, shall we start asking if we weren't right after all, and the earth does go round. *With a twinkle*: But once every other hypothesis has crumbled in our hands then there will be no mercy for those who failed to research, and who go on talking all the same. Take the cloth off the telescope and point it at the sun!

He adjusts the brass reflector

THE LITTLE MONK: I knew you had begun working on this. I knew when you failed to recognise Mr Marsili.

In silence they begin their observations. As the sun's flaming image appears on the screen Virginia comes running in in her wedding dress.

VIRGINIA: You sent him away, father.

She faints. Andrea and the little monk hurry to her side.

GALILEO: I've got to know.

10

During the next decade Galileo's doctrine spreads among the common people. Ballad-singers and pamphleteers everywhere take up the new ideas. In the carnival of 1632 many Italian cities choose astronomy as the theme for their guilds' carnival processions

A half-starved couple of fairground people with a baby and a five-year old girl enter a market place where a partly masked crowd is awaiting the carnival procession. The two of them are carrying bundles, a drum and other utensils.

THE BALLAD SINGER *drumming*: Honoured inhabitants, ladies and gentlemen! To introduce the great carnival procession of the guilds we are going to perform the latest song from Florence which is now being sung all over north Italy and has been imported by us at vast expense. It is called: Ye horrible doctrine and opinions of Messer Galileo Galilei, physicist to the court, or A Foretaste of ye Future. *He sings*:

> When the Almighty made the universe
> He made the earth and then he made the sun.
> Then round the earth he bade the sun to turn –
> That's in the Bible, Genesis, Chapter One.
> And from that time all creatures here below
> Were in obedient circles meant to go.
>
> So the circles were all woven:
> Around the greater went the smaller
> Around the pace-setter the crawler
> On earth as it is in heaven.
> Around the pope the cardinals
> Around the cardinals the bishops

Around the bishops the secretaries
Around the secretaries the aldermen
Around the aldermen the craftsmen
Around the craftsmen the servants
Around the servants the dogs, the chickens and the
  beggars.

That, good people, is the Great Order of things, ordo
ordinum as the theologians call it, regula aeternis, the rule
of rules; but what, dear people, happened?
Sings:

Up stood the learned Galilei
(Chucked away the Bible, whipped out his telescope, took a
quick look at the universe.)
  And told the sun 'Stop there.
  From now the whole creatio dei
  Will turn as I think fair:
  The boss starts turning from today
  His servants stand and stare'.

  Now that's no joke, my friends, it is no matter small.
  Each day our servants' insolence increases
  But one thing's true, pleasures are few. I ask you all:
  Who wouldn't like to say and do just as he pleases?

Honourable inhabitants, such doctrines are utterly impossible.
He sings:

  The serf stays sitting on his arse.
  This turning's turned his head.
  The altar boy won't serve the mass
  The apprentice lies in bed.

  No, no, my friends, the Bible is no matter small
  Once let them off the lead indeed all loyalty ceases
  For one thing's true, pleasures are few. I ask you all:
  Who wouldn't like to say and do just as he pleases?

Good people all, kindly take a glance at the future as fore-
told by the learned Doctor Galileo Galilei:

Two housewives standing buying fish
Don't like the fish they're shown
The fishwife takes a hunk of bread
And eats them up alone.
The mason clears the building site
And hauls the builders' stone.
And when the house is finished quite
He keeps it as his own.

Can such things be my friends? It is no matter small
For independent spirit spreads like foul diseases.
But one thing's true, pleasures are few. I ask you all:
Who wouldn't like to say and do just as he pleases?

The tenant gives his landlord hell
Not caring in the least.
His wife now feeds her children well
On the milk she fed the priest.

No, no, my friends, the Bible is no matter small
Once let them off the lead indeed all loyalty ceases.
But one thing's true, pleasures are few. I ask you all:
Who wouldn't like to say and do just as he pleases?

THE SINGER'S WIFE:
I lately went a bit too far
And told my husband I'd see
If I could get some other fixed star
To do what he does for me.
BALLAD SINGER:
No, no, no, no, no, no! Stop, Galileo, stop.
Once take a mad dog's muzzle off it spreads diseases
People must keep their place, some down and some on
    top.
(Although it's nice for once to do just as one pleases).

BOTH:

> Good people who have trouble here below
> In serving cruel lords and gentle Jesus
> Who bid you turn the other cheek just so
> They're better placed to strike the second blow:
> Obedience isn't going to cure your woe
> So each of you wake up, and do just as he pleases!

THE BALLAD SINGER: Honoured inhabitants, you will now see Galileo Galilei's amazing discovery: the earth circling round the sun!

He belabours the drum violently. The woman and child step forward. The woman holds a crude image of the sun while the child, with a pumpkin over its head to represent the earth, circles round her. The singer points elatedly at the child as if it were performing a dangerous leap as it takes jerky steps to single beats on the drum. Then comes drumming from the rear.

A DEEP VOICE *calls*: The procession!

Enter two men in rags pulling a little cart. On an absurd throne sits the 'Grand-Duke of Florence', a figure with a cardboard crown dressed in sacking and looking through a telescope. Above his throne a sign saying 'Looking for trouble'. Then four masked men march in carrying a big tarpaulin. They stop and toss a puppet representing a cardinal into the air. A dwarf has taken up position to one side with a sign saying 'The new age'. In the crowd a beggar gets up on his crutches and dances, stamping the ground till he crashes to earth. Enter an over-lifesize puppet, Galileo Galilei, bowing to the audience. Before it goes a boy carrying a gigantic bible, open, with crossed-out pages.

THE BALLAD-SINGER: Galileo Galilei, the bible-buster!

Huge laughter among the crowd.

11

1633: The Inquisition summons the world-famous scientist to Rome

> The depths are hot, the heights are chill
> The streets are loud, the court is still.

Antechamber and staircase in the Medici palace in Florence. Galileo and his daughter are waiting to be admitted by the Grand Duke.

VIRGINIA: This is taking a long time.

GALILEO: Yes.

VIRGINIA: There's that fellow again who followed us here. *She points out an individual who walks past without looking at them.*

GALILEO *whose eyes have suffered*: I don't know him.

VIRGINIA: I've seen him several times in the past few days, though. He gives me the creeps.

GALILEO: Rubbish. We're in Florence, not among Corsican bandits.

VIRGINIA: Here's Rector Gaffone.

GALILEO: He makes me want to run. That idiot will involve me in another of his interminable talks. *Down the stairs comes Mr Gaffone, rector of the university. He is visibly alarmed on seeing Galileo and walks stiffly past them barely nodding, his head awkwardly averted.*

GALILEO: What's got into the man? My eyes are bad again. Did he even greet us?

VIRGINIA: Barely. What's in your book? Could it be thought heretical maybe?

GALILEO: You're wasting too much time in church. You'll spoil what's left of your complexion with all this early rising and scurrying off to mass. You're praying for me, is that it?

VIRGINIA: Here's Mr Vanni the ironfounder you designed the furnace for. Don't forget to thank him for those quails. *A man has come down the stairs.*

VANNI: Were those good quails I sent you, Mr Galilei?

GALILEO: The quails were first-rate, Messer Vanni, many thanks again.

VANNI: Your name was mentioned upstairs. They're blaming you for those pamphlets against the bible that have been selling all over the place lately.

GALILEO: I know nothing about pamphlets. The Bible and Homer are my preferred reading.

VANNI: Even if that weren't so I'd like to take this chance to say that we manufacturers are behind you. I'm not the sort of fellow that knows much about the stars, but to me you're the man who's battling for freedom to teach what's new. Take that mechanical cultivator from Germany you were describing to me. In the past year alone five books on agriculture have been published in London. We'd be glad enough to have a book on the Dutch canals. The same sort of people as are trying to block you are stopping the Bologna doctors from dissecting bodies for medical research.

GALILEO: Your voice can be heard, Vanni.

VANNI: I should hope so. Do you realise that they've now got money markets in Amsterdam and London? Commercial schools too. Regularly printed papers with news in them. In this place we haven't even the freedom to make money. They're against ironfoundries because they imagine putting too many workers in one place leads to immorality. I sink or swim with people like you, Mr Galilei. If anybody ever tries launching anything against you, please remember you've friends in every branch of business. You've got the north Italian cities behind you, sir.

GALILEO: As far as I know nobody's thinking of launching anything against me.

VANNI: No?

GALILEO: No.

VANNI: I think you'd be better off in Venice. Fewer clerics. You could take up the cudgels from there. I've a travelling coach and horses, Mr Galilei.

GALILEO: I don't see myself as a refugee. I like my comforts.

VANNI: Surely. But from what I heard upstairs I'd say there was a hurry. It's my impression they'd be glad to know you weren't in Florence just now.

GALILEO: Nonsense. The Grand Duke is my pupil, and what's more the pope himself would never stand for any kind of attempt to trap me.

VANNI: I'm not sure you're good at distinguishing your friends from your enemies, Mr Galilei.

GALILEO: I can distinguish power from impotence. *He goes off brusquely.*

VANNI: Right. I wish you luck. *Exit.*

GALILEO *returning to Virginia*: Every local Tom, Dick and Harry with an axe to grind wants me to be his spokesman, particularly in places where it's not exactly helpful to me. I've written a book about the mechanics of the universe, that's all. What people make of it or don't make of it isn't my business.

VIRGINIA *loudly*: If they only knew how you condemned all those incidents at last carnival-time!

GALILEO: Yes. Give a bear honey and if the brute's hungry you risk losing your arm.

VIRGINIA *quietly*: Did the Grand Duke actually send for you today?

GALILEO: No, but I had myself announced. He wants to have the book, he has paid for it. Ask that official and tell him we don't like being kept waiting.

VIRGINIA *followed by the same individual, goes and addresses an official*: Mr Mincio, has his Highness been told my father wishes to speak with him?

THE OFFICIAL: How am I to know?

VIRGINIA: I don't call that an answer.

THE OFFICIAL: Don't you?

VIRGINIA: You're supposed to be polite.

The official half turns his back on her and yawns as he looks at the individual.

VIRGINIA *returning*: He says the Grand Duke is still busy.

GALILEO: I heard you say something about 'polite'. What was it?

VIRGINIA: I was thanking him for his polite answer, that's all. Can't you just leave the book here? You could use the time.

GALILEO: I'm beginning to wonder how much my time is worth. Perhaps I'll accept Sagredo's invitation to spend a few weeks in Padua after all. My health's not what it was.

VIRGINIA: You couldn't live without your books.

GALILEO: We could take a crate or two of that Sicilian wine in the coach with us.

VIRGINIA: You've always said it doesn't travel. And the court owes you three months' salary. They'll never forward it.

GALILEO: That's true.

The Cardinal Inquisitor comes down the stairs.

VIRGINIA: The Cardinal Inquisitor.

As he walks past he makes a deep bow to Galileo.

VIRGINIA: What's the Cardinal Inquisitor doing in Florence, Father?

GALILEO: I don't know. He behaved quite respectfully. I knew what I was doing when I came to Florence and kept quiet for all those years. They've paid me such tributes that now they're forced to accept me as I am.

THE OFFICIAL *calls out*: His Highness the Grand Duke!

Cosmo di Medici comes down the staircase. Galileo goes to meet him. Cosmo stops somewhat embarrassedly.

GALILEO: I wanted to bring my Dialogues on Two World Systems to your . . .

COSMO: Ah, yes. How are your eyes?

GALILEO: Not too good, your Highness. If your Highness permits, I have the book . . .

COSMO: The state of your eyes worries me. It worries me, truly. It shows me that you've been a little too eager to use that admirable tube of yours, haven't you?

He walks on without accepting the book.

GALILEO: He didn't take the book, did he?

VIRGINIA: Father, I'm scared.

GALILEO *firmly, in a low voice*: Control your feelings. We're not going home after this, we're going to Volpi the glazier's. I've fixed with him to have a cart full of empty barrels standing permanently in the yard of the winehouse next door, ready to take me out of the city.

VIRGINIA: So you knew . . .

GALILEO: Don't look round.

They start to go.

A HIGH OFFICIAL *comes down the stairs*: Mr Galilei, I have been charged to tell you that the court of Florence is no longer in a position to oppose the Holy Inquisition's wish to interrogate you in Rome. The coach of the Holy Inquisition awaits you, Mr Galilei.

12

The Pope

Room in the Vatican. Pope Urban VIII (formerly Cardinal Barberini) has received the Cardinal Inquisitor. In the course of the audience he is robed. Outside is heard the shuffling of many feet.

THE POPE *very loudly*: No! No! No!

THE INQUISITOR: So it is your Holiness's intention to go

before this gathering of doctors from every faculty, repre-
sentatives of every order and the entire clergy, all with their
naive faith in the word of God as set down in the scriptures,
who are now assembling here to have that trust confirmed
by your Holiness, and tell them that those scriptures can no
longer be regarded as true?

THE POPE: I am not going to have the multiplication table
broken. No!

THE INQUISITOR: Ah, it's the multiplication table, not the
spirit of insubordination and doubt: that's what these
people will tell you. But it isn't the multiplication table. No,
a terrible restlessness has descended on the world. It is the
restlessness of their own brain which these people have
transferred to the unmoving earth. They shout 'But look at
the figures'. But where do their figures come from? Everybody knows they originate in doubt. These people doubt
everything. Are we to base human society on doubt and no
longer on faith? 'You are my lord, but I doubt if that's a
good thing'. 'This is your house and your wife, but I doubt
if they shouldn't be mine.' Against that we have your
Holiness's love of art, to which we owe our fine collections,
being subjected to such disgraceful interpretations as we
see scrawled on the walls of Roman houses: 'The Barberinis
take what the Barbarians left.' And abroad? Your Holiness's
Spanish policy has been misinterpreted by short-sighted
critics, its antagonising of the Emperor regretted. For the last
fifteen years Germany has been running with blood, and
men have quoted the Bible as they hacked each other to
pieces. And at this moment, just when Christianity is being
shrivelled into little enclaves by plague, war and the
Reformation, a rumour is going through Europe that you
have made a secret pact with Protestant Sweden in order
to weaken the Catholic emperor. So what do these wretched
mathematicians do but go and point their tubes at the sky
and inform the whole world that your Holiness is hopelessly

at sea in the one area nobody has yet denied you? There's every reason to be surprised at this sudden interest in an obscure subject like astronomy. Who really cares how these spheres rotate? But thanks to the example of this wretched Florentine all Italy, down to the last stable boy, is now gossiping about the phases of Venus, nor can they fail at the same time to think about a lot of other irksome things that schools and others hold to be incontrovertible. Given the weakness of their flesh and their liability to excesses of all kinds, what would the effect be if they were to believe in nothing but their own reason, which this maniac has set up as the sole tribunal? They would start by wondering if the sun stood still over Gibeon, then extend their filthy scepticism to the offertory box. Ever since they began voyaging across the seas – and I've nothing against that – they have placed their faith in a brass ball they call a compass, not in God. This fellow Galileo was writing about machines even when he was young. With machines they hope to work miracles. What sort? God anyhow is no longer necessary to them, but what kind of miracle is it to be? The abolition of top and bottom, for one. They're not needed any longer. Aristotle, whom they otherwise regard as a dead duck, has said – and they quote this – that once the shuttle weaves by itself and the plectrum plays the zither of its own accord, then masters would need no apprentice and lords no servants. And they think they are already there. This evil man knows what he is up to when he writes his astronomical works not in Latin but in the idiom of fishwives and wool merchants.

THE POPE: That's very bad taste; I shall tell him.

THE INQUISITOR: He agitates some of them and bribes others. The north Italian ports are insisting more and more that they must have Mr Galilei's star charts for their ships. We'll have to give in to them, material interests are at stake.

THE POPE: But those star charts are based on his heretical theories. They presuppose certain motions on the part of the heavenly bodies which are impossible if you reject his doctrine. You can't condemn the doctrine and accept the charts.

THE INQUISITOR: Why not? It's the only way.

THE POPE: This shuffling is getting on my nerves. I cannot help listening to it.

THE INQUISITOR: It may speak to you more persuasively than I can, your Holiness. Are all these people to leave here with doubt in their hearts.

THE POPE: After all the man is the greatest physicist of our time, the light of Italy, and not just any old crank. He has friends. There is Versailles. There's the Viennese Court. They'll call Holy Church a cesspool of decomposing prejudices. Hands off him!

THE INQUISITOR: Practically speaking one wouldn't have to push it very far with him. He is a man of the flesh. He would give in immediately.

THE POPE: He enjoys himself in more ways than any man I have ever met. His thinking springs from sensuality. Give him an old wine or a new idea, and he cannot say no. But I won't have any condemnation of the physical facts, no war cries of 'Up the Church' 'Up Reason'. I let him write his book on condition that he finished it by saying that the last word lay with faith, not science. He met that condition.

THE INQUISITOR: But how? His book shows a stupid man, representing the view of Aristotle of course, arguing with a clever one who of course represents Mr Galilei's own; and which do you think, your Holiness, delivers the final remark?

THE POPE: What did you say? Well, which of them expresses our view?

THE INQUISITOR: Not the clever one.

THE POPE: Yes, that is an impertinence. All this stamping in the corridors is really unbearable. Is the whole world coming here?

THE INQUISITOR: Not the whole of it but its best part. *Pause. The Pope is now in his full robes.*

THE POPE: At the very most he can be shown the instruments.

THE INQUISITOR: That will be enough your Holiness. Instruments are Mr Galilei's speciality.

13

Before the Inquisition, on June 22nd 1633, Galileo recants his doctrine of the motion of the earth

> June twenty-second, sixteen thirty-three
> A momentous day for you and me.
> Of all the days that was the one
> An age of reason could have begun.

In the Florentine ambassador's palace in Rome. Galileo's pupils are waiting for news. Federzoni and the little monk are playing new-style chess with its sweeping moves. In one corner Virginia kneels saying the Ave Maria.

THE LITTLE MONK: The Pope wouldn't receive him. No more discussions about science.

FEDERZONI: That was his last hope. It's true what he told him years back in Rome when he was still Cardinal Barberini: We need you. Now they've got him.

ANDREA: They'll kill him. The Discorsi will never get finished.

FEDERZONI *gives him a covert look*: You think so?

ANDREA: Because he'll never recant.

Pause

THE LITTLE MONK: You keep getting quite irrelevant thoughts when you can't sleep. Last night for instance I kept on thinking, he ought never to have left the Venetian Republic.

ANDREA: He couldn't write his book there.

FEDERZONI: And in Florence he couldn't publish it.

Pause

THE LITTLE MONK: I also wondered if they'd let him keep his little stone he always carries in his pocket. His proving stone.

FEDERZONI: You don't wear pockets where they'll be taking him.

ANDREA *shouting*: They daren't do that! And even if they do he'll not recant. 'Someone who doesn't know the truth is just thick-headed. But someone who does know it and calls it a lie is a crook.'

FEDERZONI: I don't believe it either and I wouldn't want to go on living if he did it. But they do have the power.

ANDREA: Power can't achieve everything.

FEDERZONI: Perhaps not.

THE LITTLE MONK *softly*: This is his twenty-fourth day in prison. Yesterday was the chief hearing. And today they're sitting on it. *Aloud, as Andrea is listening*: That time I came to see him here two days after the decree we sat over there and he showed me the little Priapus by the sundial in the garden – you can see it from here – and he compared his own work with a poem by Horace which cannot be altered either. He talked about his sense of beauty, saying that was what forced him to look for the truth. And he quoted the motto 'Hieme et aestate, et prope et procul, usque dum vivam et ultra'. And he was referring to truth.

ANDREA *to the little monk*: Have you told him the way he stood in the Collegium Romanum when they were testing

his tube? Tell him! *The little monk shakes his head.* He behaved just as usual. He had his hands on his hams, thrust
out his tummy and said 'I would like a bit of reason, please,
gentlemen.'
Laughing, he imitates Galileo.
Pause

ANDREA *referring to Virginia*: She is praying that he'll
recant.

FEDERZONI: Leave her alone. She's been all confused ever
since they spoke to her. They brought her father confessor
down from Florence.

The individual from the Grand-Ducal palace in Florence enters.

INDIVIDUAL: Mr Galilei will be here shortly. He may need a
bed.

FEDERZONI: Have they released him?

INDIVIDUAL: It is expected that Mr Galilei will recant
around five o'clock at a full sitting of the Inquisition. The
great bell of St Mark's will be rung and the text of his
recantation will be proclaimed in public.

ANDREA: I don't believe it.

INDIVIDUAL: In view of the crowds in the streets Mr Galilei
will be brought to the garden gate here at the back of the
palace.
Exit

ANDREA *suddenly in a loud voice*: The moon is an earth and has
no light of its own. Likewise Venus has no light of its own
and is like the earth and travels round the sun. And four
moons revolve round the planet Jupiter which is on a level
with the fixed stars and is unattached to any crystal sphere.
And the sun is the centre of the cosmos and motionless, and
the earth is not the centre and not motionless. And he is the
one who showed us this.

THE LITTLE MONK: And no force will help them to make
what has been seen unseen.
Silence

FEDERZONI *looks at the sundial in the garden.* Five o'clock. *Virginia prays louder.*

ANDREA: I can't wait any more. They're beheading the truth. *He puts his hands over his ears, as does the little monk. But the bell is not rung. After a pause filled only by Virginia's murmured prayers, Federzoni shakes his head negatively. The others let their hands drop.*

FEDERZONI *hoarsely*: Nothing. It's three minutes past the hour.

ANDREA: He's holding out.

THE LITTLE MONK: He's not recanting.

FEDERZONI: No. Oh, how marvellous for us! *They embrace. They are ecstatically happy.*

ANDREA: So force won't do the trick. There are some things it can't do. So stupidity has been defeated, it's not invulnerable. So man is not afraid of death.

FEDERZONI: This truly is the start of the age of knowledge. This is the hour of its birth. Imagine if he had recanted.

THE LITTLE MONK: I didn't say, but I was worried silly. O ye of little faith!

ANDREA: But I knew.

FEDERZONI: Like nightfall in the morning, it would have been.

ANDREA: As if the mountain had said 'I'm a lake'.

THE LITTLE MONK *kneels down weeping*: Lord, I thank thee.

ANDREA: But today everything is altered. Man, so tormented, is lifting his head and saying 'I can live'. Such a lot is won when even a single man gets to his feet and says No. *At this moment the bell of Saint Mark's begins to toll. All stand rigid.*

VIRGINIA *gets up*: The bell of Saint Mark's. He is not damned!

From the street outside we hear the crier reading Galileo's recantation:

CRIER'S VOICE: 'I, Galileo Galilei, teacher of mathematics and physics in Florence, abjure what I have taught, namely that the sun is the centre of the cosmos and motionless and the earth is not the centre and not motionless. I foreswear, detest and curse, with sincere heart and unfeigned faith, all these errors and heresies as also any error and any further opinion repugnant to Holy Church.'

It grows dark.

When the light returns the bell is still tolling, but then stops.

Virginia has left. Galileo's pupils are still there.

FEDERZONI: You know, he never paid you for your work. You could never publish your own stuff or buy yourself new breeches. You stood for it because it was 'working for the sake of science'.

ANDREA *loudly*: Unhappy the land that has no heroes!

Galileo has entered, so completely changed by his trial as to be almost unrecognisable. He has heard Andrea's remark. For a few moments he stands at the gate waiting to be greeted. When he is not, and his pupils back away from him, he goes slowly and, on account of his bad eyes, uncertainly forward till he finds a stool and sits down.

ANDREA: I can't look at him. Get him away.

FEDERZONI: Calm down.

ANDREA *yells at Galileo*: Wine-pump! Snail-eater! Did you save your precious skin? *Sits down*: I feel ill.

GALILEO *quietly*: Give him a glass of water.

The little monk fetches Andrea a glass of water from outside. The others do nothing about Galileo, who sits on his stool and listens. Outside the crier's voice can again be heard in the distance.

ANDREA: I think I can walk with a bit of help.

They escort him to the door. At this juncture Galileo starts to speak.

GALILEO: No. Unhappy the land where heroes are needed.

A reading before the curtain:

Is it not obvious that a horse falling from a height of three or four ells will break its legs, whereas a dog would not suffer any damage, nor would a cat from a height of eight or nine ells, nor a cricket from a tower nor an ant even if it were to fall from the moon? And just as smaller animals are comparatively stronger than larger ones, so small plants too stand up better: an oak tree two hundred ells high cannot sustain its branches in the same proportion as a small oak tree, nor can nature let a horse grow as large as twenty horses or produce a giant ten times the size of man unless it changes all the proportions of the limbs and especially of the bones, which would have to be strengthened far beyond the size demanded by mere proportion. – The common assumption that large and small machines are equally durable is apparently erroneus.

Galileo. Discorsi.

14

1633–1642. Galileo Galilei lives in a house in the country near Florence, a prisoner of the Inquisition till he dies. The 'Discorsi'

A large room with table, leather chair and globe. Galileo, old now and half blind, is carefully experimenting with a bent wooden rail and a small ball of wood. In the antechamber sits a monk on guard. There is a knock at the door. The monk opens it and a peasant comes in carrying two plucked geese. Virginia emerges from the kitchen. She is now about forty years old.

THE PEASANT: They told me to deliver these.

VIRGINIA: Who? I didn't order any geese.

THE PEASANT: They told me to say it was someone passing through. *Exit. Virginia looks at the geese in amazement. The monk takes them from her and examines them dubiously. Then he gives them back to her, satisfied, and she carries them by their necks to Galileo in the large room.*

VIRGINIA: Somebody passing through has sent us a present.

GALILEO: What is it?

VIRGINIA: Can't you see?

GALILEO: No. *He walks over.* Geese. Any name on them?

VIRGINIA: No.

GALILEO *takes one of the geese from her*: Heavy. I could eat some of that.

VIRGINIA: Don't tell me you're hungry again; you've just had your supper. And what's wrong with your eyes this time? You should have been able to see them from where you are.

GALILEO: You're in the shadow.

VIRGINIA: I'm not in the shadow. *She takes the geese out.*

GALILEO: Put thyme with them, and apples.

VIRGINIA *to the monk*: We'll have to get the eye doctor in. Father couldn't see the geese from his table.

THE MONK: Not till I've cleared it with Monsignor Carpula. Has he been writing again?

VIRGINIA: No. He dictated his book to me, as you know. You've had pages 131 and 132, and those were the last.

THE MONK: He's an old fox.

VIRGINIA: He's doing nothing contrary to instructions. His repentance is genuine. I'll keep an eye on him. *She gives him the geese.* Tell them in the kitchen they're to fry the liver with an apple and an onion. *She goes back into the large room.* And now let's consider our eyes and leave that ball alone and dictate just a bit more of our weekly letter to the archbishop.

GALILEO: I'm not well enough. Read me some Horace.

VIRGINIA: Only last week Monsignor Carpula was telling me – and we owe him so much, you know; another lot of vegetables only the other day – that the archbishop keeps asking him what you think of those questions and quotations he sends you.

She has sat down to take dictation.

GALILEO: Where had I got to?

VIRGINIA: Section four: with respect to Holy Church's policy concerning the unrest in the Arsenal in Venice I agree with the attitude adopted by Cardinal Spoletti towards the disaffected rope-makers . . .

GALILEO: Yes. *He dictates*: I agree with the atittude adopted by Cardinal Spoletti towards the disaffected rope-makers, namely that it is better to hand out soup to them in the name of Christian brotherly love than to pay them more for their hawsers and bell ropes. Especially as it seems wiser to encourage their faith rather than their acquisitiveness. The apostle Paul says 'Charity never faileth'. – How's that?

VIRGINIA: That's wonderful, father.

GALILEO: You don't think a suspicion of irony might be read into it?

VIRGINIA: No, the archbishop will be delighted. He is so practical.

GALILEO: I trust your judgement. What's next?

VIRGINIA: A most beautiful saying: 'When I am weak then I am strong'.

GALILEO: No comment.

VIRGINIA: Why not?

GALILEO: What's next?

VIRGINIA: 'And to know the love of Christ, which passeth knowledge'. Saint Paul's Epistle to the Ephesians, iii, 19.

GALILEO: I am particularly grateful to your Eminence for the splendid quotation from the Epistle to the Ephesians. Stimulated by it I looked in our incomparable *Imitation* and found the following. *He quotes by heart*: 'He to whom speaketh the eternal word is free from much questioning.' May I take this opportunity to refer to my own affairs? I am still blamed for once having written an astronomical work in the language of the market-place. It was not my intention thereby to propose or approve the writing of books on infinitely more important matters, such as theology, in the jargon of pasta merchants. The argument for holding services in Latin – that it is a universal language and allows every nationality to hear holy mass in exactly the same way – seems to me a shade unfortunate in that our ever-present cynics might say this prevents any nationality from understanding the text. The cheap vulgarisation of sacred matters is something I can gladly do without. The church's Latin, which protects its eternal verities from the curiousity of the ignorant, inspires confidence when spoken by the priestly sons of the lower classes in the accents of the appropriate local dialect. – No, strike that out.

VIRGINIA: All of it?

GALILEO: Everything after the pasta merchants.
There is a knock at the door. Virginia goes into the antechamber. The monk opens. It is Andrea Sarti. He is now a man in his middle years.

ANDREA: Good evening. I am leaving Italy to do research in Holland and they asked me to look him up on the way through so I can say how he is.

VIRGINIA: I don't know that he'll want to see you. You never came.

ANDREA: Ask him. *Galileo has recognised his voice. He sits motionless. Virginia goes in to him.*

GALILEO: Is that Andrea?

VIRGINIA: Yes. Shall I send him away?

GALILEO *after a moment*: Show him in.
Virginia brings Andrea in.

VIRGINIA *to the monk*: He's harmless. Used to be his pupil. So now he's his enemy.

GALILEO: Leave us, Virginia.

VIRGINIA: I want to hear what he's got to say. *She sits down.*

ANDREA *coolly*: How are you?

GALILEO: Come closer. What are you doing now? Tell us about your work. I'm told you're on hydraulics.

ANDREA: Fabricius in Amsterdam has commissioned me to inquire about your health.

Pause

GALILEO: My health is good. They pay me every attention.

ANDREA: I am glad I can report that your health is good.

GALILEO: Fabricius will be glad to hear it. And you can tell him that I live in corresponding comfort. The depth of my repentance has earned me enough credit with my superiors to be permitted to conduct scientific studies on a modest scale under clerical supervision.

ANDREA: That's right. We too heard that the church is more than pleased with you. Your utter capitulation has been effective. We understand the authorities are happy to note that not a single paper expounding new theories has been published in Italy since you toed the line.

GALILEO *listening*: Unhappily there are still countries not under the wing of the church. I'm afraid the condemned doctrines are being pursued there.

ANDREA: There too your recantation caused a setback most gratifying to the church.

GALILEO: Really? *Pause.* Nothing from Descartes? No news from Paris?

ANDREA: On the contrary. When he heard about your recantation he shoved his treatise on the nature of light away in a drawer.

Long pause.

GALILEO: I feel concern for certain scientific friends whom I led into error. Did they learn anything from my recantation?

ANDREA: The only way I can do research is by going to Holland. They won't permit the ox anything that Jove won't permit himself.

GALILEO: I see.

ANDREA: Federzoni is back to grinding lenses in some shop in Milan.

GALILEO *laughs*: He doesn't know Latin.

ANDREA: Fulganzio, our little monk, has given up science and gone back to the bosom of the church.

GALILEO: Yes. *Pause.*

GALILEO: My superiors hope to achieve a spiritual cure in my case too. I am progressing better than anyone expected.

ANDREA: Indeed.

VIRGINIA: The Lord be praised.

GALILEO *roughly*: See to the geese, Virginia.

Virginia goes out angrily. The monk speaks to her as she passes.

THE MONK: I don't like that man.

VIRGINIA: He's harmless. You heard them. *Walking away*: There's some fresh goats-milk cheese arrived.

The monk follows her out.

ANDREA: I have to travel all night if I'm to cross the frontier early tomorrow. May I go?

GALILEO: I don't know why you came, Sarti. Was it to unsettle me? I've been living prudently and thinking prudently since coming here. Even so I get relapses.

ANDREA: I have no wish to arouse you, Mr Galilei.

GALILEO: Barberini called it the itch. He wasn't entirely free of it himself. I've been writing again.

ANDREA: Indeed.

GALILEO: I finished the 'Discorsi'.

ANDREA: What? The 'Discourses Concerning Two New Sciences: Mechanics and Local Motion'? Here?

GALILEO: Oh, they let me have pens and paper. My masters aren't stupid. They realise that deeply engrained vices can't be snapped off just like that. They shield me from any undesirable consequences by locking the pages away as I write them.

ANDREA: O God!

GALILEO: Did you say something?

ANDREA: They're making you plough water. They allow you pens and paper to keep you quiet. How can you possibly write when you know that's the purpose?

GALILEO: Oh, I'm a creature of habit.

ANDREA: The 'Discorsi' in the hands of the monks! With Amsterdam and London and Prague all slavering for it!

GALILEO: I can hear Fabricius grumbling away, insisting on his pound of flesh, meanwhile sitting safe and sound himself in Amsterdam.

ANDREA: Two new branches of science as good as lost!

GALILEO: It will no doubt relieve him and one or two others to hear that I've been risking the last pathetic remnants of my own comfort by making a transcript, more or less behind my back, by squeezing the very last ounce of light out of each reasonably clear night for the past six months.

ANDREA: You've got a transcript?

GALILEO: So far my vanity has stopped me destroying it.

ANDREA: Where is it?

GALILEO: 'If thine eye offend thee, pluck it out'. Whoever wrote that knew more about comfort than me. I suppose it's the height of folly to part with it. However, as I haven't managed to keep clear of scientific work you people might as well have it. The transcript is inside that globe. Should you think of taking it to Holland you would of course have to bear the entire responsibility. In that case you would have bought it from someone who had access to the original in the Holy Office.

Andrea has gone to the globe. He takes out the transcript.

ANDREA: The 'Discorsi'! *He leafs through the manuscript. Reads*: 'It is my purpose to establish an entirely new science in regard to a very old problem, namely, motion. By means of experiments I have discovered some of its properties, which are worth knowing.'

GALILEO: I had to do something with my time.

ANDREA: This will found a new physics.

GALILEO: Stuff it under your coat.

ANDREA: And we thought you had deserted! No voice against you was louder than mine!

GALILEO: Very proper. I taught you science and I denied the truth.

ANDREA: This alters everything. Everything.

GALILEO: Really?

ANDREA: You were hiding the truth. From the enemy. Even in matters of ethics you were centuries ahead of us.

GALILEO: Elaborate that, will you Andrea?

ANDREA: Like the man in the street we said 'He'll die, but he'll never recant.' You came back: 'I've recanted, but I'm going to live.' – 'Your hands are stained', we said. You're saying: 'Better stained than empty'.

GALILEO: Better stained than empty. Sounds realistic. Sounds like me. New science, new ethics.

ANDREA: I of all people should have known. I was eleven when you sold another man's telescope to the Venetian Senate. And I saw you put that instrument to immortal use. Your friends shook their heads when you bowed to that boy in Florence: science gained an audience. Even then you used to laugh at heroes. 'People who suffer are boring' you said. 'Misfortune comes from miscalculation'. And 'When there are obstacles the shortest line between two points may be a crooked one.'

GALILEO: I remember.

ANDREA: So in '33 when you chose to recant a popular point in your doctrine I ought to have known that you were simply backing out of a hopeless political wrangle in order to get on with the real business of science.

GALILEO: Which is . . .

ANDREA: Studying the properties of motion, mother of those machines which alone are going to make the earth so good to live on that heaven can be cleared away.

GALILEO: Aha.

ANDREA: You gained the leisure to write a scientific work which could be written by nobody else. If you had ended up at the stake in a halo of flames the other side would have won.

GALILEO: They did win. And there is no scientific work that can only be written by one particular man.

ANDREA: Why did you recant, then?

GALILEO: I recanted because I was afraid of physical pain.

ANDREA: No!

GALILEO: They showed me the instruments.

ANDREA: So it wasn't planned?

GALILEO: It was not.

Pause.

ANDREA *loudly*: Science makes only one demand: contribution to science.

GALILEO: And I met it. Welcome to the gutter, brother in science and cousin in betrayal! Do you eat fish? I have fish. What stinks is not my fish but me. I sell out, you are a buyer. O irresistible glimpse of the book, the sacred commodity! The mouth waters and the curses drown. The great whore of Babylon, the murderous beast, the scarlet woman, opens her thighs and everything is altered. Blessed be our horse-trading, whitewashing, death-fearing community!

ANDREA: Fearing death is human. Human weaknesses don't matter to science.

GALILEO: Don't they? – My dear Sarti, even as I now am I think I can still give you a tip or two as to what matters to that science you have dedicated yourself to.

A short pause

GALILEO *professorially, folding his hands over his stomach*:
In my spare time, of which I have plenty, I have gone over my case and considered how it is going to be judged by that world of science of which I no longer count myself a member. Even a wool merchant has not only to buy cheap and sell dear but also to ensure that the wool trade continues unimpeded. The pursuit of science seems to me to demand particular courage in this respect. It deals in knowledge procured through doubt. Creating knowledge

for all about all, it aims to turn all of us into doubters. Now the bulk of the population is kept by its princes, landlords and priests in a pearly haze of superstition and old saws which cloak what these people are up to. The poverty of the many is as old as the hills, and from pulpit and lecture platform we hear that it is as hard as the hills to get rid of. Our new art of doubting delighted the mass audience. They tore the telescope out of our hands and trained it on their tormentors, the princes, landlords and priests. These selfish and domineering men, having greedily exploited the fruits of science, found that the cold eye of science had been turned on a primaeval but contrived poverty that could clearly be swept away if they were swept away themselves. They showered us with threats and bribes, irresistible to feeble souls. But can we deny ourselves to the crowd and still remain scientists? The movements of the heavenly bodies have become more comprehensible, but the peoples are as far as ever from calculating the moves of their rulers. The battle for a measurable heaven has been won thanks to doubt; but thanks to credulity the Rome housewife's battle for milk will be lost time and time again. Science, Sarti, is involved in both these battles. A human race which shambles around in a pearly haze of superstition and old saws, too ignorant to develop its own powers, will never be able to develop those powers of nature which you people are revealing to it. To what end are you working? Presumably for the principle that science's sole aim must be to lighten the burden of human existence. If the scientists, brought to heel by self-interested rulers, limit themselves to piling up knowledge for knowledge's sake, then science can be crippled and your new machines will lead to nothing but new impositions. You may in due course discover all that there is to discover, and your progress will nonetheless be nothing but a progress away from mankind. The gap between you and it may one day become so wide that your cry of triumph at some new achievement will be echoed by a universal cry of horror. – As a scientist I had a unique opportunity. In my day astronomy emerged into the market place. Given this unique situation, if one man had put up a fight it might have had tremendous repercussions. Had I stood firm the scientists could have developed something like the doctors' Hippocratic oath, a vow to use their knowledge exclusively for mankind's benefit. As things are, the best that can be hoped for is a race of inventive dwarfs who can be hired for any purpose. What's more, Sarti, I have come to the conclusion that I was never in any real danger. For a few years I was as strong as the authorities. And I handed my knowledge to those in power for them to use, fail to use, misuse – whatever best suited their objectives.

Virginia has entered with a dish and come to a standstill.

GALILEO: I betrayed my profession. A man who does what I did cannot be tolerated in the ranks of science.

VIRGINIA: You are accepted in the ranks of the faithful.

She moves on and puts the dish on the table.

GALILEO: Correct. – Now I must eat.

Andrea holds out his hand. Galileo sees the hand but does not take it.

GALILEO: You're a teacher yourself now. Can you afford to take a hand like mine? *He goes to the table.* Somebody passing through sent me some geese. I still enjoy eating.

ANDREA: So you no longer believe a new age has started?

GALILEO: On the contrary – Look out for yourself when you pass through Germany, with the truth under your coat.

ANDREA *unable to tear himself away*: About your opinion of the author we were talking about. I don't know how to answer. But I cannot think your devastating analysis will be the last word.

GALILEO: Thank you very much, sir. *He begins eating.*

VIRGINIA *escorting Andrea out*: We don't like visitors from the past. They excite him.

Andrea leaves. Virginia comes back.

GALILEO: Got any idea who might have sent the geese?
VIRGINIA: Not Andrea.
GALILEO: Perhaps not. What's the night like?
VIRGINIA *at the window*: Clear.

15

1637. Galileo's book, the 'Discorsi' crosses the Italian frontier

> The great book o'er the border went
> And, good folk, that was the end.
> But we hope you'll keep in mind
> He and I were left behind.
> May you now guard science's light
> Kindle it and use it right
> Lest it be a flame to fall
> Downward to consume us all.
> Yes, us all.

Little Italian frontier town in the early morning. Children are playing by the barrier. Andrea, standing beside a coachman, is waiting to have his papers checked by the frontier guards. He is sitting on a small box reading Galileo's manuscript. On the other side of the barrier stands the coach.

THE CHILDREN *sing*:

> Mary, Mary sat her down
> Had a little old pink gown
> Gown was shabby and bespattered.
> But when chilly winter came
> Gown went round her just the same.
> Bespattered don't mean tattered.

THE FRONTIER GUARD: Why are you leaving Italy?

ANDREA: I'm a scholar.

THE FRONTIER GUARD *to his clerk*: Put under 'reason for leaving': scholar.

I must examine your luggage.

He does so

THE FIRST BOY *to Andrea*: Better not sit there. *He points to the hut outside which Andrea is sitting.* There's a witch lives inside.

THE SECOND BOY: Old Marina's no witch.

THE FIRST BOY: Want me to twist your wrist?

THE THIRD BOY: Course she's one. She flies through the air at night.

THE FIRST BOY: And why won't anyone in the town let her have a jug of milk even, if she's not a witch?

THE SECOND BOY: Who says she flies through the air? It can't be done. *To Andrea*: Can it?

THE FIRST BOY *referring to the second*: That's Giuseppe. He doesn't know a thing because he doesn't go to school because his trousers need patching.

THE FRONTIER GUARD: What's that book you've got?

ANDREA *without looking up*: It's by Aristotle, the great philosopher.

THE FRONTIER GUARD *suspiciously*: Who's he when he's at home?

ANDREA: He's been dead for years.

The boys mock Andrea's reading by walking round as if they were meanwhile reading books.

THE FRONTIER GUARD *to the clerk*: Have a look if there's anything about religion in it.

THE CLERK *turning the pages*: I can't see nothing.

THE FRONTIER GUARD: All this searching's a bit of a waste of time anyway. Nobody who wanted to hide something would put it under our noses like that. *To Andrea*: You're to sign that we've examined it all.

Andrea gets up reluctantly and accompanies the frontier guard into the house, still reading.

THE THIRD BOY *to the clerk, pointing at the box*: There's that too, see?

THE CLERK: Wasn't it there before?

THE THIRD BOY: The devil put it there. It's a box.

THE SECOND BOY: No, it belongs to that foreigner.

THE THIRD BOY: I wouldn't touch it. She put the evil eye on old Passi's horses. I looked through the hole in the roof made by the blizzard and heard them coughing.

THE CLERK *who was almost at the box, hesitates and turns back*: Devil's tricks, what? Well, we can't check everything. We'd never get done.

Andrea comes back with a jug of milk. He sits down on the box once more and goes on reading.

THE FRONTIER GUARD *following him with papers*: Shut the boxes. Is that everything?

THE CLERK: Yes.

THE SECOND BOY *to Andrea*: So you're a scholar. Tell us, can people fly through the air?

ANDREA: Wait a moment.

THE FRONTIER GUARD: You can go through.

The coachman has taken the luggage. Andrea picks up the box and is about to go.

THE FRONTIER GUARD: Halt! What's in that box?

ANDREA *taking up his book again*: Books.

THE FIRST BOY: It's the witch's.

THE FRONTIER GUARD: Nonsense. How could she bewitch a box?

THE THIRD BOY: She could if the devil helped.

THE FRONTIER GUARD *laughs*: That wouldn't work here. *To the clerk*: Open it.

The box is opened.

THE FRONTIER GUARD *unenthusiastically*: How many are there?

ANDREA: Thirty-four.

THE FRONTIER GUARD *to the clerk*: How long will they take to go through?

THE CLERK *who has begun superficially rummaging through the box*: Nothing but printed stuff. It'll mean you miss your breakfast, and when am I going to get over to Passi's stables to collect the road tax due on the sale of his house if I'm to go through this lot?

THE FRONTIER GUARD: Right, we need that money. *He kicks at the books*: After all, what can there be in those? *To the coachman*: Off with you!

Andrea crosses the frontier with the coachman carrying the box. Once across, he puts Galileo's manuscript in his travelling bag.

THE THIRD BOY *points at the jug which Andrea has left behind*: Look!

THE FIRST BOY: The box has gone too! Didn't I tell you it was the devil?

ANDREA *turning round*: No, it was me. You should learn to use your eyes. The milk's paid for, the jug too. The old woman can keep it. Oh, and I didn't answer your question, Giuseppe. People can't fly through the air on a stick. It'd have to have a machine on it, to say the least. But there's no machine like that so far. Maybe there never will be, as a human being's too heavy. But of course one never knows. There are a lot of things we don't know yet, Giuseppe. We're really just at the beginning.

The Resistible Rise of Arturo Ui

A parable play

Collaborator: M. STEFFIN

Translator: RALPH MANHEIM

Characters
THE ANNOUNCER
FLAKE
CARUTHER
BUTCHER } *Businessmen, directors of the*
MULBERRY *Cauliflower Trust*
CLARK
SHEET, *shipyard owner*
OLD DOGSBOROUGH
YOUNG DOGSBOROUGH
ARTURO UI, *gang leader*
ERNESTO ROMA, *his lieutenant*
EMANUELE GIRI, *gangster*
The florist GIUSEPPE GIVOLA, *gangster*
TED RAGG, *reporter on* The Star
DOCKDAISY

BOWL, *Sheet's chief accountant*
GOODWILL *and* GAFFLES, *members of the city council*
O'CASEY, *investigator*
AN ACTOR
HOOK, *wholesale vegetable dealer*
DEFENDANT FISH
THE DEFENCE COUNSEL
THE JUDGE
THE DOCTOR
THE PROSECUTOR
A WOMAN
YOUNG INNA, *Roma's familiar*
A LITTLE MAN
IGNATIUS DULLFEET
BETTY DULLFEET, *his wife*
Dogsborough's BUTLER

Bodyguards
Gunmen
Vegetable dealers of Chicago and Cicero
Reporters

Prologue

The Announcer steps before the curtain. Large notices are attached to the curtain: 'New developments in dock subsidy scandal' . . . 'The true facts about Dogsborough's will and confession' . . . 'Sensation at warehouse fire trial' . . . 'Friends murder gangster Ernesto Roma' . . . 'Ignatius Dullfeet blackmailed and murdered' . . . 'Cicero taken over by gangsters'. Behind the curtain popular dance music.

THE ANNOUNCER:
Friends, tonight we're going to show –
Pipe down, you boys in the back row!
And, lady, your hat is in the way! –
Our great historical gangster play
Containing, for the first time, as you'll see
The truth about the scandalous dock subsidy.
Further we give you, for your betterment
Dogsborough's confession and testament.
Arturo Ui's rise while the stock market fell.
The notorious warehouse fire trial. What a sell!
The Dullfeet murder! Justice in a coma!
Gang warfare: the killing of Ernesto Roma!
All culminating in our stunning last tableau:
Gangsters take over the town of Cicero!
Brilliant performers will portray
The most eminent gangsters of our day.
You'll see some dead and some alive
Some by-gone and others that survive
Some born, some made – for instance, here we show

The good old honest Dogsborough!
Old Dogsborough steps before the curtain.
His hair is white, his heart is black.
Corrupt old man, you may step back.
Dogsborough bows and steps back.
The next exhibit on our list
Is Givola –
Givola has stepped before the curtain.
                    – the horticulturist.
His tongue's so slippery he'd know how
To sell you a billy-goat for a cow!
Short, says the proverb, are the legs of lies.
Look at his legs, just use your eyes.
Givola steps back limping.
Now to Emanuele Giri, the super-clown.
Come out, let's look you up and down!
Giri steps before the curtain and waves his hand at the audience.
One of the greatest killers ever known!
Okay, beat it!
Giri steps back with an angry look.
And lastly Public Enemy Number One
Arturo Ui. Now you'll see
The biggest gangster of all times
Whom heaven sent us for our crimes
Our weakness and stupidity!
Arturo Ui steps before the curtain and walks out along the footlights.
Doesn't he make you think of Richard the Third?
Has anybody ever heard
Of blood so ghoulishly and lavishly shed
Since wars were fought for roses white and red?
In view of this the management
Has spared no cost in its intent
To picture his spectacularly vile
Manoeuvres in the grandest style.
But everything you'll see tonight is true.

Nothing's invented, nothing's new
Or made to order just for you.
The gangster play that we present
Is known to our whole continent.

*While the music swells and the sound of a machine-gun mingles
with it, the Announcer retires with an air of bustling self-
importance.*

I

a

Financial district. Enter five businessmen, the directors of the Cauliflower Trust.

FLAKE: The times are bad.
CLARK: It looks as if Chicago
   The dear old girl, while on her way to market
   Had found her pocket torn and now she's starting
   To scrabble in the gutter for her pennies.
CARUTHER: Last Thursday Jones invited me and eighty
   More to a partridge dinner to be held
   This Monday. If we really went, we'd find
   No one to greet us but the auctioneer.
   This awful change from glut to destitution
   Has come more quickly than a maiden's blush.
   Vegetable fleets with produce for this city
   Still ply the lakes, but nowhere will you find
   A buyer.
BUTCHER: It's like darkness at high noon.
MULBERRY: Robber and Clive are being auctioned off.
CLARK: Wheeler – importing fruit since Noah's ark –
   Is bankrupt.
FLAKE: And Dick Havelock's garages
   Are liquidiating.
CARUTHER: Where is Sheet?
FLAKE: Too busy
   To come. He's dashing round from bank to bank.
CLARK: What? Sheet?
   Pause.

In other words, the cauliflower
Trade in this town is through.

BUTCHER: Come, gentlemen
Chin up! We're not dead yet.

MULBERRY: Call this a life?

BUTCHER: Why all the gloom? The produce business in
This town is basically sound. Good times
And bad, a city of four million needs
Fresh vegetables. Don't worry. We'll pull through.

CARUTHER: How are the stores and markets doing?

MULBERRY: Badly.
The customers buy half a head of cabbage
And that on credit.

CLARK: Our cauliflower's rotting.

FLAKE: Say, there's a fellow waiting in the lobby –
I only mention it because it's odd –
The name is Ui . . .

CLARK: The gangster?

FLAKE: Yes, in person.
He's smelled the stink and thinks he sees an opening.
Ernesto Roma, his lieutenant, says
They can convince shopkeepers it's not healthy
To handle other people's cauliflower.
He promises our turnover will double
Because, he says, the shopkeepers would rather
Buy cauliflower than coffins.
They laugh dejectedly.

CARUTHER: It's an outrage.

MULBERRY, *laughing uproariously*:
Bombs and machine guns! New conceptions of
Salesmanship! That's the ticket. Fresh young
Blood in the Cauliflower Trust. They heard
We had insomnia, so Mr Ui
Hastens to offer us his services.
Well, fellows, we'll just have to choose. It's him

Or the Salvation Army. Which one's soup
Do you prefer?
CLARK: I tend to think that Ui's
Is hotter.
CARUTHER: Throw him out!
MULBERRY: Politely though.
How do we know what straits we'll come to yet?
They laugh.
FLAKE, *to Butcher*:
What about Dogsborough and a city loan?
To the others.
Butcher and I cooked up a little scheme
To help us through our pesent money troubles.
I'll give it to you in a nutshell. Why
Shouldn't the city that takes in our taxes
Give us a loan, let's say, for docks that we
Would undertake to build, so vegetables
Can be brought in more cheaply? Dogsborough
Is influential. He could put it through.
Have you seen Dogsborough?
BUTCHER: Yes. He refuses
To touch it.
FLAKE: He refuses? Damn it, he's
The ward boss on the waterfront, and he
Won't help us!
CARUTHER: I've contributed for years
To his campaign fund.
MULBERRY: Hell, he used to run
Sheet's lunchroom. Before he took up politics
He got his bread and butter from the Trust.
That's rank ingratitude. It's just like I've been
Telling you, Flake. All loyalty is gone!
Money is short, but loyalty is shorter.
Cursing, they scurry from the sinking ship
Friend turns to foe, employee snubs his boss
And our old lunchroom operator

Who used to be all smiles is one cold shoulder.
Morals go overboard in times of crisis.
CARUTHER: I'd never have expected that of Dogsborough.
FLAKE: What's his excuse?
BUTCHER: He says our proposition
Is fishy.
FLAKE: What's fishy about building docks?
Think of the men we'd put to work.
BUTCHER: He says
He has his doubts about our building docks.
FLAKE: Outrageous!
BUTCHER: What? Not building?
FLAKE: No. His doubts.
CLARK: Then find somebody else to push the loan.
MULBERRY: Sure, there are other people.
BUTCHER: True enough.
But none like Dogsborough. No, take it easy.
The man is good.
CLARK: For what?
BUTCHER: He's honest. And
What's more, reputed to be honest.
FLAKE: Rot!
BUTCHER: He's got to think about his reputation.
That's obvious.
FLAKE: Who gives a damn? We need
A loan from City Hall. His reputation
Is his affair.
BUTCHER: You think so? I should say
It's ours. It takes an honest man to swing
A loan like this, a man they'd be ashamed
To ask for proofs and guarantees. And such
A man is Dogsborough. Old Dogsborough's
Our loan. All right, I'll tell you why. Because they
Believe in him. They may have stopped believing
In God, but not in Dogsborough. A hard-boiled
Broker, who takes a lawyer with him to

His lawyer's, wouldn't hesitate to put his
Last cent in Dogsborough's apron for safe keeping
If he should see it lying on the bar.
Two hundred pounds of honesty. In eighty
Winters he's shown no weakness. Such a man
Is worth his weight in gold – especially
To people with a scheme for building docks
And building kind of slowly.
FLAKE: Okay, Butcher
He's worth his weight in gold. The deal he vouches
For is tied up. The only trouble is:
He doesn't vouch for ours.
CLARK: Oh no, not he!
'The city treasury is not a grab bag!'
MULBERRY: And 'All for the city, the city for itself!'
CARUTHER: Disgusting. Not an ounce of humour.
MULBERRY: Once
His mind's made up, an earthquake wouldn't change it.
To him the city's not a place of wood
And stone, where people live with people
Struggling to feed themselves and pay the rent
But words on paper, something from the Bible.
The man has always gotten on my nerves.
CLARK: His heart was never with us. What does he care
For cauliflower and the trucking business?
Let every vegetable in the city rot
You think he'd lift a finger? No, for nineteen years
Or is it twenty, we've contributed
To his campaign fund. Well, in all that time
The only cauliflower he's ever seen
Was on his plate. What's more, he's never once
Set foot in a garage.
BUTCHER: That's right.
CLARK: The devil
Take him!
BUTCHER: Oh no! We'll take him.

FLAKE: But Clark says
  It can't be done. The man has turned us down.
BUTCHER: That's so. But Clark has also told us why.
CLARK: The bastard doesn't know which way is up.
BUTCHER: Exactly. What's his trouble? Ignorance.
  He hasn't got the faintest notion what
  It's like to be in such a fix. The question
  Is therefore how to put him in our skin.
  In short, we've got to educate the man.
  I've thought it over. Listen, here's my plan.
  *A sign appears, recalling certain incidents in the recent past.**

b

Outside the produce exchange. Flake and Sheet in conversation.

SHEET: I've run from pillar to post. Pillar was out
  Of town, and Post was sitting in the bathtub.
  Old friends show nothing but their backs. A brother
  Buys wilted shoes before he meets his brother
  For fear his brother will touch him for a loan.
  Old partners dread each other so they use
  False names when meeting in a public place.
  Our citizens are sewing up their pockets.
FLAKE: So what about my proposition?
SHEET: No. I
  Won't sell. You want a five-course dinner for the
  Price of the tip. And to be thanked for the tip
  At that. You wouldn't like it if
  I told you what I think of you.
FLAKE: Nobody
  Will pay you any more.

* See the Chronological Table at the end of the play.

SHEET: And friends won't be
   More generous than anybody else.
FLAKE: Money is tight these days.
SHEET: Especially
   For those in need. And who can diagnose
   A friend's need better than a friend?
FLAKE: You'll lose
   Your shipyard either way.
SHEET: And that's not all
   I'll lose. I've got a wife who's likely to
   Walk out on me.
FLAKE: But if you sell . . .
SHEET: . . . she'll last another year. But what I'm curious
   About is why you want my shipyard.
FLAKE: Hasn't
   It crossed your mind that we – I mean the Trust –
   Might want to help you?
SHEET: No, it never crossed
   My mind. How stupid of me to suspect you
   Of trying to grab my property, when you
   Were only trying to help.
FLAKE: Such bitterness
   Dear Sheet, won't save you from the hammer.
SHEET: At least, dear Flake, it doesn't help the hammer.
   *Three men saunter past: Arturo Ui, the gangster, his lieutenant
   Ernesto Roma, and a bodyguard. In passing, Ui stares at Flake
   as though expecting to be spoken to, while, in leaving, Roma turns
   his head and gives Flake an angry look.*
SHEET: Who's that?
FLAKE: Arturo Ui, the gangster . . . How
   About it? Are you selling?
SHEET: He seemed eager
   To speak to you.
FLAKE, *laughing angrily*: And so he is. He's been
   Pursuing us with offers, wants to sell
   Our cauliflower with his tommy guns.

The town is full of types like that right now
Corroding it like leprosy, devouring
A finger, then an arm and shoulder. No one
Knows where it comes from, but we all suspect
From deepest hell. Kidnapping, murder, threats
Extortion, blackmail, massacre:
'Hands up!' 'Your money or your life!' Outrageous!
It's got to be wiped out.

SHEET, *looking at him sharply*: And quickly. It's contagious.

FLAKE: Well, how about it? Are you selling?

SHEET, *stepping back and looking at him*:
No doubt about it: a resemblance to
Those three who just passed by. Not too pronounced
But somehow there, one senses more than sees it.
Under the water of a pond sometimes
You see a branch, all green and slimy. It
Could be a snake. But no, it's definitely
A branch. Or is it? That's how you resemble
Roma. Don't take offence. But when I looked
At him just now and then at you, it seemed
To me I'd noticed it before, in you
And others, without understanding. Say it
Again, Flake: 'How about it? Are you selling?'
Even your voice, I think . . . No, better say
'Hands up!' because that's what you really mean.
He puts up his hands.
All right, Flake, Take the shipyard!
Give me a kick or two in payment. Hold it!
I'll take the higher offer. Make it two.

FLAKE: You're crazy!

SHEET: I only wish that that were true.

2

Back room in Dogsborough's restaurant. Dogsborough and his son are washing glasses. Enter Butcher and Flake.

DOGSBOROUGH: You didn't need to come. The answer is
    No. Your proposition stinks of rotten fish.
YOUNG DOGSBOROUGH: My father turns it down.
BUTCHER: Forget it, then.
    We ask you. You say no. So no it is.
DOGSBOROUGH: It's fishy. I know your kind of docks.
    I wouldn't touch it.
YOUNG DOGSBOROUGH: My father wouldn't touch it.
BUTCHER: Good.
    Forget it.
DOGSBOROUGH: You're on the wrong road, fellows.
    The city treasury is not a grab bag
    For everyone to dip his fingers into.
    Anyway, damn it all, your business is
    Perfectly sound.
BUTCHER: What did I tell you, Flake?
    You fellows are too pessimistic.
DOGSBOROUGH: Pessimism
    Is treason. You're only making trouble for
    Yourselves. I see it this way: What do you
    Fellows sell? Cauliflower. That's as good
    As meat and bread. Man doesn't live by bread
    And meat alone, he needs his green goods.
    Suppose I served up sirloin without onions
    Or mutton without beans. I'd never see
    My customers again. Some people are
    A little short right now. They hesitate
    To buy a suit. But people have to eat.

They'll always have a dime for vegetables.
Chin up! If I were you, I wouldn't worry.
FLAKE: It does me good to hear you, Dogsborough.
   It gives a fellow courage to go on.
BUTCHER: Dogsborough, it almost makes me laugh to find
   You so staunchly confident about the future
   Of cauliflower, because quite frankly we
   Have come here for a purpose. No, don't worry.
   Not what you think, that's dead and buried. Something
   Pleasant, or so at least we hope. Old man
   It's come to our attention that it's been
   Exactly-twenty three years this June, since you –
   Well known to us for having operated
   The lunchroom in one of our establishments for
   More than three decades – left us to devote
   Your talents to the welfare of this city.
   Yes, without you our town would not be what
   It is today. Nor, like the city, would
   The Trust have prospered as it has. I'm glad
   To hear you call it sound, for yesterday
   Moved by this festive occasion, we resolved
   In token of our high esteem, as proof
   That in our hearts we somehow still regard you
   As one of us, to offer you the major share
   Of stock in Sheet's shipyard for twenty thousand
   Dollars, or less than half its value.
   He lays the packet of stocks on the bar.
DOGSBOROUGH: I
   Don't understand.
BUTCHER: Quite frankly, Dogsborough
   The Cauliflower Trust is not reputed
   For tenderness of heart, but yesterday
   After we'd made our . . . well, our
   Stupid request about the loan, and heard
   Your answer, honest, incorruptible
   Old Dogsborough to a hair, a few of us –

It's not an easy thing to say – were close
To tears. Yes, one man said – don't interrupt
Me, Flake, I won't say who – 'Good God'
He said, 'the man has saved us from ourselves.'
For some time none of us could speak. Then this
Suggestion popped up of its own accord.

DOGSBOROUGH:
I've heard you, friends. But what is there behind it?

BUTCHER: What should there be behind it? It's an offer.

FLAKE: And one that we are really pleased to make.
For here you stand behind your bar, a tower
Of strength, a sterling name, the model of
An upright citizen. We find you washing
Glasses, but you have cleansed our souls as well.
And yet you're poorer than your poorest guest.
It wrings our hearts.

DOGSBOROUGH: I don't know what to say.

BUTCHER: Don't say a word. Just take this little package.
An honest man can use it, don't you think?
By golly, it's not often that the gravy train
Travels the straight and narrow. Take your boy here:
I know a good name's better than a bank
Account, and yet I'm sure he won't despise it.
Just take the stuff and let us hope you won't
Read us the riot act for *this*!

DOGSBOROUGH: Sheet's shipyard!

FLAKE: Look, you can see it from right here.

DOGSBOROUGH, *at the window*:   I've seen it
For twenty years.

FLAKE: We thought of that.

DOGSBOROUGH: And what is
Sheet going to do?

FLAKE: He's moving into beer.

BUTCHER: Okay?

DOGSBOROUGH: I certainly appreciate

Your oldtime sentiments, but no one gives
Away a shipyard for a song.

FLAKE: There's something
In that. But now the loan has fallen through
Maybe the twenty thousand will come in handy.

BUTCHER: And possibly right now we're not too eager
To throw our stock upon the open market . . .

DOGSBOROUGH: That sounds more like it. Not a bad deal if
It's got no strings attached.

FLAKE: None whatsoever.

DOGSBOROUGH: The price you say is twenty thousand?

FLAKE: Is it
Too much?

DOGSBOROUGH: No. And imagine, it's the selfsame
Shipyard where years ago I opened my first lunchroom.
As long as there's no nigger in the woodpile . . .
You've really given up the loan?

FLAKE: Completely.

DOGSBOROUGH: I might consider it. Hey, look here, son
It's just the thing for you. I thought you fellows
Were down on me and here you make this offer.
You see, my boy, that honesty sometimes
Pays off. It's like you say: When I pass on
The youngster won't inherit much more than
My name, and these old eyes have seen what evil
Can spring from penury.

BUTCHER: We'll feel much better
If you accept. The ugly aftertaste
Left by our foolish proposition would be
Dispelled. In future we could benefit
By your advice. You'd show us how to ride
The slump by honest means, because our business
Would be your business, Dogsborough, because
You too would be a cauliflower man
And want the Cauliflower Trust to win.

Dogsborough takes his hand.

DOGSBOROUGH: Butcher and Flake, I'm in.
YOUNG DOGSBOROUGH: My father's in.
  A sign appears.

3

Bookmaker's office on 122nd Street. Arturo Ui and his lieutenant Ernesto Roma, accompanied by bodyguards, are listening to the racing news on the radio. Next to Roma is Dockdaisy.

ROMA: I wish, Arturo, you could cure yourself
  Of this black melancholy, this inactive
  Dreaming. The whole town's talking.
  UI, *bitterly*:   Talking? Who's talking?
  Nobody talks about me any more.
  This city's got no memory. Short-lived
  Is fame in such a place. Two months without
  A murder, and a man's forgotten.
  He whisks through the newspapers.
                    When
  The rod falls silent, silence strikes the press.
  Even when I deliver murders by the
  Dozen, I'm never sure they'll print them.
  It's not accomplishment that counts; it's
  Influence, which in turn depends on my
  Bank balance. Things have come to such a pass
  I sometimes think of chucking the whole business.
  ROMA: The boys are chafing too from lack of cash.
  Morale is low. This inactivity's
  No good for them. A man with nothing but
  The ace of spades to shoot at goes to seed.
  I feel so sorry for those boys, Arturo
  I hate to show my face at headquarters. When
  They look at me, my 'Tomorrow we'll see action'

Sticks in my throat. Your vegetables idea was
So promising. Why don't we start right in?
UI: Not now. Not from the bottom. It's too soon.
ROMA: 'Too soon' is good. For four months now—
Remember? – since the Cauliflower Trust
Gave you the brush-off, you've been idly brooding.
Plans! Plans! Half-hearted feelers! That rebuff
Frizzled your spine. And then that little mishap –
Those cops at Harper's Bank – you've never gotten
Over it.
UI: But they fired!
ROMA: Only in
The air. That was illegal.
UI: Still too close
For me. I'd be in stir if they had plugged
My only witness. And that judge! Not two
Cent's worth of sympathy.
ROMA: The cops won't shoot
For grocery stores. They shoot for banks. Look here
Arturo, we'll start on Eleventh Street
Smash a few windows, wreck the furniture
Pour kerosene on the veg. And then we work
Our way to Seventh. Two or three days later
Giri, a posy in his buttonhole
Drops in and offers our protection for
A suitable percentage on their sales.
UI: No. First I need protection for myself
From cops and judges. Then I'll start to think
About protecting other people. We've
Got to start from the top.
Gloomily:

                    Until I've put the
Judge in my pocket by slipping something
Of mine in his, the law's against me. I
Can't even rob a bank without some two-bit cop
Shooting me dead.

ROMA: You're right. Our only hope is
  Givola's plan. He's got a nose for smells
  And if he says the Cauliflower Trust
  Smells promisingly rotten, I believe
  There's something in it. And there *was* some talk
  When, as they say, on Dogsborough's commendation
  The city made that loan. Since then I've heard
  Rumours about some docks that aren't being built
  But ought to be. Yet on the other hand
  Dogsborough recommended it. Why should
  That do-good peg for fishy business? Here comes
  Ragg of the 'Star'. If anybody knows
  About such things, it's him. Hi Ted.
RAGG, *slightly drunk*:   Hi, boys!
  Hi, Roma! Hi, Arturo! How are things in
  Capua?
UI: What's he saying?
RAGG: Oh, nothing much.
  That was a one-horse town where long ago
  An army went to pot from idleness
  And easy living.
UI: Go to hell!
ROMA, *to Ragg*:   No fighting.
  Tell us about that loan the Cauliflower
  Trust wangled.
RAGG: What do you care? Say! Could you
  Be going into vegetables? I've got it!
  You're angling for a loan yourselves. See Dogsborough.
  He'll put it through.
  Imitating the old man:
                    'Can we allow a business
  Basically sound but momentarily
  Threatened with blight, to perish?' Not an eye
  At City Hall but fills with tears. Deep feeling
  For cauliflower shakes the council members
  As though it were a portion of themselves.

Too bad, Arturo, guns call forth no tears.
The other customers laugh.
ROMA: Don't bug him, Ted. He's out of sorts.
RAGG: I shouldn't
Wonder. I hear that Givola has been
To see Capone for a job.
DOCKDAISY: You liar!
You leave Giuseppe out of this!
RAGG: Hi, Dockdaisy!
Still got your place in Shorty Givola's harem?
Introducing her:
Fourth super in the harem of the third
Lieutenant of a –
Points to Ui.

                       – fast declining star
Of second magnitude! Oh, bitter fate!
DOCKDAISY: Somebody shut the rotten bastard up!
RAGG: Posterity plaits no laurels for the gangster!
New heroes captivate the fickle crowd.
Yesterday's hero has been long forgotten
His mug-shot gathers dust in ancient files.
'Don't you remember, folks, the wounds I gave you?' –
'When?' – 'Once upon a time.' – 'Those wounds have
Turned to scars long since.' Alas, the finest scars
Get lost with those who bear them. 'Can it be
That in a world where good deeds go unnoticed
No monument remains to evil ones?' –
'Yes, so it is.' – 'Oh, lousy world!'
UI, *bellows:*   Shut
Him up!
The bodyguards approach Ragg.
RAGG, *turning pale:* Be careful, Ui. Don't insult
The press.
The other customers have risen to their feet in alarm.
ROMA: You'd better beat it, Ted. You've said
Too much already.

RAGG, *backing out, now very much afraid*:
> See you later, boys.

The room empties quickly.

ROMA: Your nerves are shot, Arturo.

UI: Those bastards
Treat me like dirt.

ROMA: Because of your long silence.
No other reason.

UI, *gloomily*:   Say, what's keeping Giri
And that accountant from the Cauliflower
Trust?

ROMA: They were due at three.

UI: And Givola?
What's this I hear about him seeing Capone?

ROMA: Nothing at all. He's in his flower shop
Minding his business, and Capone comes in
To buy some wreaths.

UI: Some wreaths? For who?

ROMA: Not us.

UI: I'm not so sure.

ROMA: You're seeing things too black.
Nobody's interested in us.

UI: Exactly.
They've more respect for dirt. Take Givola.
One setback and he blows. By God
I'll settle his account when things look up.

ROMA: Giri!

Enter Emanuele Giri with a rundown individual, Bowl.

GIRI: I've got him, boss.

ROMA, *to Bowl*:   They tell me you
Are Sheet's accountant at the Cauliflower
Trust.

BOWL: Was. Until last week that bastard . . .

GIRI: He hates the very smell of cauliflower.

BOWL: Dogsborough . . .

UI, *quickly*:   Dogsborough! What about him?

ROMA: What have you got to do with Dogsborough?

GIRI: That's why I brought him.

BOWL: Dogsborough
   Fired me.

ROMA: He fired you? From Sheet's shipyard?

BOWL: No, from his own. He took it over on
   September first.

ROMA: What's that?

GIRI: Sheet's shipyard
   Belongs to Dogsborough. Bowl here was present
   When Butcher of the Cauliflower Trust
   Handed him fifty-one percent of the stock.

UI: So what?

BOWL: So what? It's scandalous . . .

GIRI   Don't you
   Get it, boss?

BOWL: . . . Dogsborough sponsoring that
   Loan to the Cauliflower Trust . . .

GIRI: . . . when he
   Himself was secretly a member of
   The Cauliflower Trust.

UI, *who is beginning to see the light*:
                  Say, that's corrupt.
   By God the old man hasn't kept his nose
   Too clean.

BOWL: The loan was to the Cauliflower
   Trust, but they did it through the shipyard. Through
   Me. And I signed for Dogsborough. Not for Sheet
   As people thought.

GIRI: By golly, it's a killer.
   Old Dogsborough. The trusty and reliable
   Signboard. So honest. So responsible!
   Whose handshake was an honour and a pledge!
   The staunch and incorruptible old man!

BOWL: I'll make the bastard pay. Can you imagine?
   Firing me for embezzlement when he himself . . .

ROMA: Cool it! You're not the only one whose blood
   Boils at such abject villainy. What do
   You say, Arturo?
UI, *referring to Bowl*:
                    Will he testify?
GIRI: He'll testify.
UI, *grandly getting ready to leave*:
                    Keep an eye on him, boys. Let's go
   Roma. I smell an opening.
   *He goes out quickly, followed by Ernesto Roma and the body-
   guards.*
GIRI, *slaps Bowl on the back*: Bowl, I
   Believe you've set a wheel in motion, which . . .
BOWL: I hope you'll pay me back for any loss . . .
GIRI: Don't worry about that. I know the boss.
   A sign appears.

4

Dogsborough's country house. Dogsborough and his son.

DOGSBOROUGH: I should never have accepted this estate.
   Taking that package as a kind of gift was
   Beyond reproach.
YOUNG DOGSBOROUGH: Of course it was.
DOGSBOROUGH: And sponsoring
   That loan, when I discovered to my own
   Detriment that a thriving line of business
   Was languishing for lack of funds, was hardly
   Dishonest. But when, confident the shipyard
   Would yield a handsome profit, I accepted
   This house before I moved the loan, so secretly
   Acting in my own interest – that was wrong.
YOUNG DOGSBOROUGH: Yes, father.

DOGSBOROUGH: That was faulty judgment
   Or might be so regarded. Yes, my boy
   I should never have accepted this estate.
YOUNG DOGSBOROUGH: No.
DOGSBOROUGH: We've stepped into a trap.
YOUNG DOGSBOROUGH: Yes, father.
DOGSBOROUGH: That
   Package of stocks was like the salty titbit
   They serve free gratis at the bar to make
   The customer, appeasing his cheap hunger
   Work up a raging thirst.
   Pause.
                That inquiry
   At City Hall about the docks, has got
   Me down. The loan's used up. Clark helped
   Himself; so did Caruther, Flake and Butcher
   And so, I'm sad to say, did I. And no
   Cement's been bought yet, not a pound! The one
   Good thing is this: at Sheet's request I kept
   The deal a secret; no one knows of my
   Connection with the shipyard.
A BUTLER *enters*:   Telephone
   Sir, Mr Butcher of the Cauliflower
   Trust.
DOGSBOROUGH: Take it, son.
   Young Dogsborough goes out with the Butler. Church bells are
   heard in the distance.
DOGSBOROUGH   Now what can Butcher want?
   Looking out of the window.
   Those poplars are what tempted me to take
   The place. The poplars and the lake down there, like
   Silver before it's minted into dollars.
   And air that's free of beer fumes. The fir trees
   Are good to look at too, especially
   The tops. Grey-green and dusty. And the trunks –

Their colour calls to mind the leathers we used to wrap
   around
The taps when drawing beer. It was the poplars, though
That turned the trick. Ah yes, the poplars.
It's Sunday. Hm. The bells would sound so peaceful
If the world were not so full of wickedness.
But what can Butcher want on Sunday?
I never should have . . .

YOUNG DOGSBOROUGH, *returning*: Father, Butcher says ·
   Last night the City Council voted to
   Investigate the Cauliflower Trust's
   Projected docks. Father, what's wrong?

DOGSBOROUGH: My smelling salts!

YOUNG DOGSBOROUGH, *gives them to him*:
   Here.

DOGSBOROUGH: What does Butcher want?

YOUNG DOGSBOROUGH: He wants to come here.

DOGSBOROUGH: Here? I refuse to see him. I'm not well.
   My heart.
   He stands up. Grandly:
   I haven't anything to do
   With this affair. For sixty years I've trodden
   The narrow path, as everybody knows.
   They can't involve me in their schemes.

YOUNG DOGSBOROUGH: No, father.
   Do you feel better now?

THE BUTLER *enters*:   A Mr Ui
   Desires to see you, sir.

DOGSBOROUGH: The gangster!

THE BUTLER: Yes
   I've seen his picture in the papers. Says he
   Was sent by Mr Clark of the Cauliflower
   Trust.

DOGSBOROUGH:
   Throw him out! Who sent him? Clark? Good God!
   Is he threatening me with gangsters now? I'll . . . .

Enter Arturo Ui and Ernesto Roma.

UI: Mr
  Dogsborough.
DOGSBOROUGH: Get out!
ROMA: I wouldn't be in such
  A hurry, friend. It's Sunday. Take it easy.
DOGSBOROUGH: Get out, I said!
YOUNG DOGSBOROUGH: My father says: Get out!
ROMA: Saying it twice won't make it any smarter.
UI, *unruffled*:
  Mr Dogsborough.
DOGSBOROUGH: Where are the servants? Call the
  Police.
ROMA: I wouldn't leave the room if I
  Were you, son. In the hallway you might run
  Into some boys who wouldn't understand.
DOGSBOROUGH: Ho! Violence!
ROMA: I wouldn't call it that.
  Only a little emphasis perhaps.
UI: Mr Dogsborough. I am well aware that you
  Don't know me, or even worse, you know me but
  Only from hearsay. Mr Dogsborough
  I have been very much maligned, my image
  Blackened by envy, my intentions disfigured
  By baseness. When some fourteen years ago
  Yours truly, then a modest, unemployed
  Son of the Bronx, appeared within the gates
  Of this your city to launch a new career
  Which, I may say, has not been utterly
  Inglorious, my only followers
  Were seven youngsters, penniless like myself
  But brave and like myself determined
  To cut their chunk of meat from every cow
  The Lord created. I've got thirty now
  And will have more. But now you're wondering: What
  Does Arturo Ui want of me? Not much. Just this.

What irks me is to be misunderstood
To be regarded as a fly-by-night
Adventurer and heaven knows what else.
Clears his throat.
Especially by the police, for I
Esteem them and I'd welcome their esteem.
And so I've come to ask you – and believe me
Asking's not easy for my kind of man –
To put a word in for me with the precinct
When necessary.
DOGSBOROUGH, *incredulously*:
                Vouch for you, you mean?
UI: If necessary. That depends on whether
  We strike a friendly understanding with
  The vegetable dealers.
DOGSBOROUGH: What is your
  Connection with the vegetable trade?
UI: That's what I'm coming to. The vegetable
  Trade needs protection. By force if necessary.
  And I'm determined to supply it.
DOGSBOROUGH: No
  One's theatening it as far as I can see.
UI: Maybe not. Not yet. But I see further. And
  I ask you: How long with our corrupt police
  Force will the vegetable dealer be allowed
  To sell his vegetables in peace? A ruthless
  Hand may destroy his little shop tomorrow
  And make off with his cash-box. Would he not
  Prefer at little cost to arm himself
  Before the trouble starts, with powerful protection?
DOGSBOROUGH: I doubt it.
UI: That would mean he doesn't know
  What's good for him. Quite possible. The small
  Vegetable dealer, honest but short-sighted
  Hard-working but too often unaware
  Of his best interest, needs strong leadership.

Moreover, toward the Cauliflower Trust
That gave him everything he has, he feels
No sense of responsibility. That's where I
Come in again. The Cauliflower Trust
Must likewise be protected. Down with the welshers!
Pay up, say I, or close your shop! The weak
Will perish. Let them, that's the law of nature.
In short, the Trust requires my services.

DOGSBOROUGH: But what's the Cauliflower Trust to me?
Why come to me with this amazing plan?

UI: We'll get to that. I'll tell you what you need.
The Cauliflower Trust needs muscle, thirty
Determined men under my leadership.

DOGSBOROUGH:
Whether the Trust would want to change its typewriters
For tommy-guns I have no way of knowing.
You see, I'm not connected with the Trust.

UI: We'll get to that. You say: With thirty men
Armed to the teeth, at home on our premises
How do we know that we ourselves are safe?
The answer's very simple. He who holds
The purse strings holds the power. And it's you
Who hand out the pay envelopes. How could
I turn against you even if I wanted
Even without the high esteem I bear you?
For what do I amount to? What
Following have I got? A handful. And some
Are dropping out. Right now it's twenty. Or less.
Without your help I'm finished. It's your duty
Your human duty to protect me from
My enemies, and (I may as well be frank)
My followers too! The work of fourteen years
Hangs in the balance! I appeal to you
As man to man.

DOGSBOROUGH: As man to man I'll tell
You what I'll do. I'm calling the police.

UI: What? The police?

DOGSBOROUGH: Exactly, the police!

UI: Am I to understand that you refuse
  To help me as a man?
  Bellows.

                    Then I demand
  It of you as a criminal. Because
  That's what you are. I'm going to expose you.
  I've got the proofs. There's going to be a scandal
  About some docks. And you're mixed up in it. Sheet's
  Shipyard – that's you. I'm warning you! Don't
  Push me too far! They've voted to investigate.

DOGSBOROUGH, *very pale*:
  They never will. They can't. My friends . . .

UI: You haven't got any. You had some yesterday.
  Today you haven't got a single friend
  Tomorrow you'll have nothing but enemies.
  If anybody can rescue you, it's me
  Arturo Ui! Me! Me!

DOGSBOROUGH: Nobody's going to
  Investigate. My hair is white.

UI: But nothing else
  Is white about you, Dogsborough.
  Tries to seize his hand.
  Think, man! It's now or never. Let me save you!
  One word from you and any bastard who
  Touches a hair of yon white head, I'll drill him.
  Dogsborough, help me now. I beg you. Once.
  Just once! Oh, say the word, or I shall never
  Be able to face my boys again.
  He weeps.

DOGSBOROUGH: Never!
  I'd sooner die than get mixed up with you.

UI: I'm washed up and I know it. Forty
  And still a nobody. You've got to help me.

DOGSBOROUGH: Never.

UI: I'm warning you. I'll crush you.

DOGSBOROUGH: Never
  Never while I draw breath will you get away with
  Your green goods racket.

UI, *with dignity*:   Mr Dogsborough
  I'm only forty. You are eighty. With God's
  Help I'll outlast you. And one thing I know:
  I'll break into the green goods business yet.

DOGSBOROUGH: Never!

UI: Come, Roma. Let's get out of here.
  He makes a formal bow and leaves the room with Ernesto Roma.

DOGSBOROUGH: Air! Give me air. Oh, what a mug!
  Oh, what a mug! I should never have accepted
  This estate. But they won't dare. I'm sunk
  If they investigate, but they won't dare.

THE BUTLER *enters*: Goodwill and Gaffles of the city
  council.
  Enter Goodwill and Gaffles.

GOODWILL: Hello, Dogsborough.

DOGSBOROUGH: Hello, Goodwill and Gaffles.
  Anything new?

GOODWILL: Plenty, and not so good, I fear.
  But wasn't that Arturo Ui who
  Just passed us in the hall?

DOGSBOROUGH, *with a forced laugh*: Himself in person.
  Hardly an ornament to a country home.

GOODWILL: No.
  Hardly an ornament. It's no good wind
  That brings us. It's that loan we made the Trust
  To build their docks with.

DOGSBOROUGH, *stiffly*:   What about the loan?

GAFFLES: Well, certain council members said – don't get
  Upset – the thing looked kind of fishy.

DOGSBOROUGH: Fishy.

GOODWILL: Don't worry The majority flew off
  The handle. Fishy! We almost came to blows.

GAFFLES: Dogsborough's contracts fishy! they shouted.
   What
   About the Bible? Is that fishy too?
   It almost turned to an ovation for you
   Dogsborough. When your friends demanded an
   Investigation, some, infected with
   Our confidence, withdrew their motion and
   Wanted to shelve the whole affair. But the
   Majority, resolved to clear your name
   Of every vestige of suspicion, shouted:
   Dogsborough's more than a name. It stands for more
      than
   A man. It's an institution! In an uproar
   They voted the investigation.

DOGSBOROUGH: The
   Investigation.

GOODWILL: O'Casey is in charge.
   The cauliflower people merely say
   The loan was made directly to Sheet's shipyard.
   The contracts with the builders were to be
   Negotiated by Sheet's shipyard.

DOGSBOROUGH: By Sheet's shipyard.

GOODWILL: The best would be for you to send a man
   Of flawless reputation and impartiality
   Someone you trust, to throw some light on this
   Unholy rat's nest.

DOGSBOROUGH: So I will.

GAFFLES: All right
   That settles it. And now suppose you show us
   This famous country house of yours. We'll want
   To tell our friends about it.

DOGSBOROUGH: Very well.

GOODWILL:
   What blessed peace! And church bells! All one can
   Wish for.

GAFFLES, *laughing*:
>   No docks in sight.
DOGSBOROUGH: I'll send a man.
>   *They go out slowly.*
>   *A sign appears.*

5

City Hall. Butcher, Flake, Clark, Mulberry, Caruther. Across from them Dogsborough, who is as white as a sheet, O'Casey, Gaffles and Goodwill. Reporters.

BUTCHER, *in an undertone*:
>   He's late.
MULBERRY: He's bringing Sheet. Quite possibly
>   They haven't come to an agreement. I
>   Believe they've been discussing it all night.
>   Sheet *has* to say the shipyard still belongs
>   To him.
CARUTHER: It's asking quite a lot of Sheet
>   To come here just to tell us *he's* the scoundrel.
FLAKE: He'll never come.
CLARK: He's got to.
FLAKE: Why should he
>   Ask to be sent to prison for five years?
CLARK: It's quite a pile of dough. And Mabel Sheet
>   Needs luxury. He's still head over heels
>   In love with Mabel. He'll play ball all right.
>   And anyway he'll never serve his term.
>   Old Dogsborough will see to that.
>   *The shouts of newsboys are heard. A reporter brings in a paper.*
GAFFLES: Sheet's been found dead. In his hotel. A ticket
>   To San Francisco in his pocket.

BUTCHER: Sheet
  Dead?
O'CASEY, *reading*:
      Murdered.
MULBERRY: My God!
FLAKE, *in an undertone*:   He didn't come.
GAFFLES: What is it, Dogsborough?
DOGSBOROUGH, *speaking with difficulty*:
                          Nothing. It'll pass.
O'CASEY: Sheet's death . . .
CLARK: Poor Sheet. His unexpected death
  Would seem to puncture your investigation . . .
O'CASEY: Of course the unexpected often looks
  As if it were expected. Some indeed
  Expect the unexpected. Such is life.
  This leaves me in a pretty pickle and
  I hope you won't refer me and my questions
  To Sheet; for Sheet, according to this paper
  Has been most silent since last night.
MULBERRY: Your questions?
  You know the loan was given to the shipyard
  Don't you?
O'CASEY: Correct. But there remains a question:
  Who is the shipyard?
FLAKE, *under his breath*: Funny question! He's
  Got something up his sleeve.
CLARK, *likewise*:   I wonder what.
O'CASEY:
  Something wrong, Dogsborough? Could it be the air?
  To the others.
  I only mean: some people may be thinking
  That several shovelsful of earth are not
  Enough to load on Sheet, and certain muck
  Might just as well be added. I suspect . . .
CLARK: Maybe you'd better not suspect too much

O'Casey. Ever hear of slander? We've
Got laws agaist it.

MULBERRY: What's the point of these
Insinuations? Dogsborough, they tell me
Has picked a man to clear this business up.
Let's wait until he comes.

O'CASEY: He's late. And when
He comes, I hope Sheet's not the only thing
He'll talk about.

FLAKE: We hope he'll tell the truth
No more no less.

O'CASEY: You mean the man is honest?
That suits me fine. Since Sheet was still alive
Last night, the whole thing should be clear. I only –
To Dogsborough.
– Hope that you've chosen a good man.

CLARK, *cuttingly*:   You'll have
To take him as he is. Ah, here he comes.
Enter Arturo Ui and Ernesto Roma with bodyguards.

UI: Hi, Clark! Hi, Dogsborough! Hi, everybody!

CLARK: Hi, Ui.

UI: Well, it seems you've got some questions.

O'CASEY, *to Dogsborough*:
Is this your man?

CLARK: That's right, Not good enough?

GOODWILL: Dogsborough, can you be . . . ?
Commotion among the reporters.

O'CASEY: Quiet over there!

A REPORTER: It's Ui!
*Laughter. O'Casey bangs his gavel for order. Then he musters
the bodyguards.*

O'CASEY: Who are these men?

UI: Friends.

O'CASEY, *to Roma*:   And who
Are you?

UI: Ernesto Roma, my accountant.

GAFFLES: Hold it! Can you be serious, Dogsborough?
Dogsborough is silent.
O'CASEY: Mr
  Ui, we gather from Mr Dogsborough's
  Eloquent silence that you have his confidence
  And desire ours. Well then. Where are the contracts?
UI: What contracts?
CLARK, *seeing that O'Casey is looking at Goodwill*:
                    The contracts that the shipyard no doubt
  Signed with the builders with a view to enlarging
  Its dock facilities.
UI: I never heard
  Of any contracts.
O'CASEY: Really?
CLARK: Do you mean
  There are no contracts?
O'CASEY, *quickly*:   Did you talk with Sheet?
UI, *shaking his head*:
  No.
CLARK: Oh. You didn't talk with Sheet?
UI, *angrily*:   If any-
  One says I talked with Sheet, that man's a liar.
O'CASEY: Ui, I thought that Mr Dogsborough
  Had asked you to look into this affair?
UI: I have looked into it.
O'CASEY: And have your studies
  Borne fruit?
UI: They have. It wasn't easy to
  Lay bare the truth. And it's not a pleasant truth.
  When Mr Dogsborough, in the interest of
  This city, asked me to investigate
  Where certain city funds, the hard-earned savings
  Of taxpayers like you and me, entrusted
  To a certain shipyard in this city, had gone to
  I soon discovered to my consternation
  That they had been embezzled. That's Point One.

Point Two is who embezzled them. All right
I'll answer that one too. The guilty party
Much as it pains me is . . .

O'CASEY: Well, who is it?

UI: Sheet.

O'CASEY: Oh, Sheet! The silent Sheet you didn't talk to!

UI: Why look at me like that? The guilty party
Is Sheet.

CLARK: Sheet's dead. Didn't you know?

UI: What, dead?
I was in Cicero last night. That's why
I haven't heard. And Roma here was with me.
Pause.

ROMA: That's mighty funny. Do you think it's mere
Coincidence that . . .

UI: Gentlemen, it's not
An accident. Sheet's suicide was plainly
The consequence of Sheet's embezzlement.
It's monstrous!

O'CASEY: Except it wasn't suicide.

UI: What then? Of course Ernesto here and I
Were in Cicero last night. We wouldn't know.
But this we know beyond a doubt: that Sheet
Apparently an honest businessman
Was just a gangster.

O'CASEY: Ui, I get your drift.
You can't find words too damaging for Sheet
After the damage he incurred last night.
Well, Dogsborough, let's get to you.

DOGSBOROUGH: To me?

BUTCHER, *cuttingly*:
What about Dogsborough?

O'CASEY: As I understand Mr
Ui – and I believe I understand
Him very well – there was a shipyard which
Borrowed some money which has disappeared.

But now the question rises: Who is this
Shipyard? It's Sheet, you say. But what's a name?
What interests us right now is not its name
But whom it actually belonged to. Did it
Belong to Sheet? Unquestionably Sheet
Could tell us. But Sheet has buttoned up
About his property since Ui spent
The night in Cicero. But could it be
That when this swindle was put over someone
Else was the owner? What is your opinion
Dogsborough?

DOGSBOROUGH: Me?

O'CASEY: Yes, could it be that you
Were sitting in Sheet's office when a contract
Was ... well, suppose we say, not being drawn up?

GOODWILL: O'Casey!

GAFFLES, *to O'Casey*:
                      Dogsborough? You're crazy!

DOGSBOROUGH: I ...

O'CASEY: And earlier, at City Hall, when you
Told us how hard a time the cauliflower
People were having and how badly they
Needed a loan – could that have been the voice
Of personal involvement?

BUTCHER: Have you no shame?
The man's unwell.

CARUTHER: Consider his great age!

FLAKE:
His snow-white hair confounds your low suspicions.

ROMA: Where are your proofs?

O'CASEY: The proofs are ...

UI   Quiet, please!
Let's have a little quiet, friends.
Say something, Dogsborough!

A BODYGUARD, *suddenly roars*: The chief wants quiet!
Quiet!

Sudden silence.

UI: If I may say what moves me in
This hour and at this shameful sight – a white-
Haired man insulted while his friends look on
In silence – it is this. I trust you, Mr
Dogsborough. And I ask: Is this the face
Of guilt? Is this the eye of one who follows
Devious ways? Can you no longer
Distinguish white from black? A pretty pass
If things have come to such a pass!

CLARK: A man of
Untarnished reputation is accused
Of bribery.

O'CASEY: And more: of fraud. For I
Contend that this unholy shipyard, so
Maligned when Sheet was thought to be the owner
Belonged to Dogsborough at the time the loan
Went through.

MULBERRY: A filthy lie!

CARUTHER: I'll stake my head
For Dogsborough. Summon the population!
I challenge you to find one man to doubt him.

A REPORTER, *to another who has come in*:
Dogsborough's under suspicion.

THE OTHER REPORTER: Dogsborough?
Why not Abe Lincoln?

MULBERRY *and* FLAKE: Witnesses!

O'CASEY: Oh
It's witnesses you want? Hey, Smith, where *is*
Our witness? Is he here? I see he is.
*One of his men has stepped into the doorway and made a sign.
All look toward the door. Short pause. Then a burst of shots
and noise are heard. Tumult. The reporters run out.*

THE REPORTERS: It's outside. A machine-gun. – What's
your witness's name, O'Casey? – Bad business. – Hi, Ui!

O'CASEY, *going to the door*: Bowl! *Shouts out the door.* Come
on in!

THE MEN OF THE CAULIFLOWER TRUST: What's going
on? – Somebody's been shot – On the stairs – God damn it!

BUTCHER, *to Ui*:
More monkey business? Ui, it's all over
Between us if . . .

UI: Yes?

O'CASEY: Bring him in!
Policemen carry in a corpse.

O'CASEY: It's Bowl. My witness, gentlemen, I fear
Is not in a fit state for questioning.
*He goes out quickly. The policemen have set down Bowl's body
in a corner.*

DOGSBOROUGH:
For God's sake, Gaffles, get me out of here!
Without answering Gaffles goes out past him.

UI, *going toward Dogsborough with outstretched hand*:
Congratulations, Dogsborough. Don't doubt
One way or another, I'll get things straightened out.
A sign appears.

6

*Hotel Mammoth. Ui's suite. Two bodyguards lead a ragged actor
to Ui. In the background Givola.*

FIRST BODYGUARD: It's an actor, boss. Unarmed.

SECOND BODYGUARD: He can't afford a rod. He was able to
get tight because they pay him to declaim in the saloons
when they're tight. But I'm told that he's good. He's one
of them classical guys.

UI: Okay. Here's the problem. I've been given to understand
that my pronunciation leaves something to be desired. It

looks like I'm going to have to say a word or two on certain occasions, especially when I get into politics, so I've decided to take lessons. The gestures too.

THE ACTOR: Very well.

UI: Get the mirror.

A bodyguard comes front stage with a large standing mirror.

UI: First the walk. How do you guys walk in the theatre or the opera?

THE ACTOR: I see what you mean. The grand style. Julius Caesar, Hamlet, Romeo – that's Shakespeare. Mr Ui, you've come to the right man. Old Mahonney can teach you the classical manner in ten minutes. Gentlemen, you see before you a tragic figure. Ruined by Shakespeare. An English poet. If it weren't for Shakespeare, I could be on Broadway right now. The tragedy of a character. 'Don't play Shakespeare when you're playing Ibsen, Mahonney! Look at the calendar! This is 1912, sir!' – 'Art knows no calendar, sir!' say I. 'And art is my life.' Alas.

GIVOLA: I think you've got the wrong guy, boss. He's out of date.

UI: We'll see about that. Walk around like they do in this Shakespeare.

The actor walks around.

UI: Good!

GIVOLA: You can't walk like that in front of cauliflower men. It ain't natural.

UI: What do you mean it ain't natural? Nobody's natural in this day and age. When I walk I want people to know I'm walking.

He copies the actor's gait.

THE ACTOR: Head back. *Ui throws his head back.* The foot touches the ground toe first. *Ui's foot touches the ground toe first.* Good. Excellent. You have a natural gift. Only the arms. They're not quite right. Stiff. Perhaps if you joined your arms in front of your private parts. *Ui joins his arms in front of his private parts.* Not bad. Relaxed but firm. But

head back. Good. Just the right gait for your purposes, I
believe, Mr Ui. What else do you wish to learn?

UI: How to stand. In front of people.

GIVOLA: Have two big bruisers right behind you and you'll
be standing pretty.

UI: That's bunk. When I stand I don't want people looking
at the two bozos behind me. I want them looking at me.
Correct me!

He takes a stance, his arms crossed over his chest.

THE ACTOR: A possible solution. But common. You don't
want to look like a barber, Mr Ui. Fold your arms like this.
*He folds his arms in such a way that the backs of his hands
remain visible. His palms are resting on his arms not far from
the shoulder.* A trifling change, but the difference is in-
calculable. Draw the comparison in the mirror, Mr Ui.
Ui tries out the new position before the mirror.

UI: Not bad.

GIVOLA: What's all this for, boss? Just for those
Fancy-pants in the Trust?

UI: Hell, no! It's for
The little people. Why, for instance, do
You think this Clark makes such a show of grandeur?
Not for his peers. His bank account
Takes care of them, the same as my big bruisers
Lend me prestige in certain situations.
Clark makes a show of grandeur to impress
The little man. I mean to do the same.

GIVOLA: But some will say it doesn't look inborn.
Some people stick at that.

UI: I know they do.
But I'm not trying to convince professors
And smart-alecks. My object is the little
Man's image of his master.

GIVOLA: Don't overdo
The master, boss. Better the democrat
The friendly, reassuring type in shirtsleeves.

UI: I've got old Dogsborough for that.

GIVOLA: His image
  Is kind of tarnished, I should say. He's still
  An asset on the books, a venerable
  Antique. But people aren't as eager as they
  Were to exhibit him. They're not so sure
  He's genuine. It's like the family Bible
  Nobody opens any more since, piously
  Turning the yellowed pages with a group
  Of friends, they found a dried-out bedbug. But
  Maybe he's good enough for Cauliflower.

UI: I decide who's respectable.

GIVOLA: Sure thing, boss.
  There's nothing wrong with Dogsborough. We can
  Still use him. They haven't even dropped him
  At City Hall. The crash would be too loud.

UI: Sitting.

THE ACTOR: Sitting. Sitting is almost the hardest, Mr Ui.
  There are men who can walk; there are men who can
  stand; but find me a man who can sit. Take a chair with a
  back-rest, Mr Ui. But don't lean against it. Hands on thighs,
  level with the abdomen, elbows away from body. How
  long can you sit like that, Mr Ui?

UI: As long as I please.

THE ACTOR: Then everything's perfect, Mr Ui.

GIVOLA: You know, boss, when old Dogsborough passes
  on
  Giri could take his place. He's got the
  Popular touch. He plays the funny man
  And laughs so loud in season that the plaster
  Comes tumbling from the ceiling. Sometimes, though
  He does it out of season, as for instance
  When you step forward as the modest son of
  The Bronx you really were and talk about
  Those seven determined youngsters.

UI: Then he laughs?

GIVOLA: The plaster tumbles from the ceiling. Don't
Tell him I said so or he'll think I've got
It in for him. But maybe you could make
Him stop collecting hats.
UI: What kind of hats?
GIVOLA: The hats of people he's rubbed out. And running
Around with them in public. It's disgusting.
UI: Forget it. I would never think of muzzling
The ox that treads my corn. I overlook
The petty foibles of my underlings.
To the actor.
And now to speaking! Speak a speech for me!
THE ACTOR: Shakespeare. Nothing else. Julius Caesar. The
Roman hero. *He draws a little book from his pocket.* What
do you say to Mark Antony's speech? Over Caesar's body.
Against Brutus. The ringleader of Caesar's assassins. A
model of demagogy. Very famous. I played Antony in
Zenith in 1908. Just what you need, Mr Ui. *He takes a
stance and recites Mark Antony's speech line for line.*
Friends, Romans, countrymen, lend me your ears!
*Reading from the little book, Ui speaks the lines after him. Now
and then the actor corrects him, but in the main Ui keeps his
rough staccato delivery.*
THE ACTOR: I come to bury Caesar, not to praise him.
The evil that men do lives after them;
The good is oft interred with their bones;
So let it be with Caesar. The noble Brutus
Hath told you Caesar was ambitious.
If it were so, it was a grievous fault,
And grievously hath Caesar answer'd it.
UI, *continues by himself*:
Here, under leave of Brutus and the rest –
For Brutus is an honourable man;
So are they all, all honourable men –
Come I to speak in Caesar's funeral.
He was my friend, faithful and just to me;

But Brutus says he was ambitious;
And Brutus is an honourable man.
He hath brought many captives home to Rome,
Whose ransoms did the general coffers fill;
Did this in Caesar seem ambitious?
When that the poor have cried, Caesar hath wept;
Ambition should be made of sterner stuff.
Yet Brutus says he was ambitious;
And Brutus is an honourable man.
You all did see that on the Lupercal
I thrice presented him a kingly crown,
Which he did thrice refuse. Was this ambition?
Yet Brutus says he was ambitious;
And sure he is an honourable man.
I speak not to disprove what Brutus spoke,
But here I am to speak what I do know.
You all did love him once, not without cause?
What cause withholds you then, to mourn for him?
During the last lines the curtain slowly falls.
A sign appears.

7

Offices of the Cauliflower Trust. Arturo Ui, Ernesto Roma, Giuseppe Givola, Emanuele Giri and bodyguards. A group of small vegetable dealers is listening to Ui. Old Dogsborough, who is ill, is sitting on the platform beside Ui. In the background Clark.

UI, *bellowing*: Murder! Extortion! Highway robbery!
   Machine-guns sputtering on our city streets!
   People going about their business, law-abiding
   Citizens on their way to City Hall
   To make a statement, murdered in broad daylight!
   And what, I ask you, do our town fathers do?

Nothing! These honourable men are much
Too busy planning their shady little deals
And slandering respectable citizens
To think of law enforcement.

GIVOLA: Hear!

UI: In short
Chaos is rampant. Because if everybody
Can do exactly what he pleases, if
Dog can eat dog without a second thought
I call it chaos. Look. Suppose I'm sitting
Peacefully in my vegetable store
For instance, or driving my cauliflower truck
And someone comes barging not so peacefully
Into my store: 'Hands up!' Or with his gun
Punctures my tyres. Under such conditions
Peace is unthinkable. But once I know
The score, once I recognise that men are not
Innocent lambs, then I've got to find a way
To stop these men from smashing up my shop and
Making me, when it suits them put 'em up
And keep 'em up, when I could use my hands
For better things, for instance, counting pickles.
For such is man. He'll never put aside
His hardware of his own free will, say
For love of virtue, or to earn the praises
Of certain silver tongues at City Hall.
If I don't shoot, the other fellow will.
That's logic. Okay. And maybe now you'll ask:
What's to be done? I'll tell you. But first get
This straight: What you've been doing so far is
Disastrous: Sitting idly at your counters
Hoping that everything will be all right
And meanwhile disunited, bickering
Among yourselves, instead of mustering
A strong defence force that would shield you from
The gangsters' depredations. No, I say

This can't go on. The first thing that's needed
Is unity. The second is sacrifices.
What sacrifices? you may ask. Are we
To part with thirty cents on every dollar
For mere protection? No, nothing doing.
Our money is too precious. If protection
Were free of charge, then yes, we'd be all for it.
Well, my dear vegetable dealers, things
Are not so simple. Only death is free:
Everything else costs money. And that includes
Protection, peace and quiet. Life is like
That, and because it never will be any different
These gentlemen and I (there are more outside)
Have resolved to offer you protection.
Givola and Roma applaud.

                                              But

To show you that we mean to operate
On solid business principles, we've asked
Our partner, Mr Clark here, the wholesaler
Whom you all know, to come here and address you.
*Roma pulls Clark forward. A few of the vegetable dealers
applaud.*

GIVOLA: Mr Clark, I bid you welcome in the name
Of this assembly. Mr Ui is honoured
To see the Cauliflower Trust supporting his
Initiative. I thank you, Mr Clark.

CLARK: We of the Cauliflower Trust observe
Ladies and gentlemen, with consternation
How hard it's getting for you vegetable
Dealers to sell your wares. 'Because,' I hear
You say, 'they're too expensive.' Yes, but why
Are they expensive? It's because our packers
And teamsters, pushed by outside agitators
Want more and more. And that's what Mr Ui
And Mr Ui's friends will put an end to.

FIRST DEALER: But if the little man gets less and less
  How is he going to buy our vegetables?
UI: Your question is a good one. Here's my answer:
  Like it or not, this modern world of ours
  Is inconceivable without the working man
  If only as a customer. I've always
  Insisted that honest work is no disgrace.
  Far from it. It's constructive and conducive
  To profits. As an individual
  The working man has all my sympathy.
  It's only when he bands together, when he
  Presumes to meddle in affairs beyond
  His understanding, such as profits, wages
  Etcetera, that I say: Watch your step
  Brother, a worker is somebody who works.
  But when you strike, when you stop working, then
  You're not a worker any more. Then you're
  A menace to society. And that's
  Where I step in.
  Clark applauds.
                            However, to convince you
  That everything is open and above
  Board, let me call your attention to the presence
  Here of a man well-known, I trust, to
  Everybody here for his sterling honesty
  And incorruptible morality.
  His name is Dogsborough.
  The vegetable dealers applaud a little louder.
                            Mr Dogsborough
  I owe you an incomparable debt
  Of gratitude. Our meeting was the work
  Of Providence. I never will forget –
  Not if I live to be a hundred – how
  You took me to your arms, an unassuming
  Son of the Bronx and chose me for your friend
  Nay more, your son.

He seizes Dogsborough's limply dangling hand and shakes it.

GIVOLA, *in an undertone*: How touching! Father and Son!

GIRI, *steps forward*:
Well, folks, the boss has spoken for us all.
I see some questions written on your faces.
Ask them! Don't worry. We won't eat you. You
Play square with us and we'll play square with you.
But get this straight: we haven't got much patience
With idle talk, especially the kind
That carps and cavils and finds fault
With everything. You'll find us open, though
To any healthy, positive suggestion
On ways and means of doing what must be done.
So fire away!
The vegetable dealers don't breathe a word.

GIVOLA, *unctuously*: And no holds barred. I think
You know me and my little flower shop.

A BODYGUARD: Hurrah for Givola!

GIVOLA: Okay, then. Do
You want protection? Or would you rather have
Murder, extortion and highway robbery?

FIRST DEALER: Things have been pretty quiet lately. I
Haven't had any trouble in my store.

SECOND DEALER: Nothing's wrong in my place.

THIRD DEALER: Nor in mine.

GIVOLA: That's odd.

SECOND DEALER: We've heard that recently in bars
Things have been happening just like Mr Ui
Was telling us, that glasses have been smashed
And gin poured down the drain in places that
Refused to cough up for protection. But
Things have been peaceful in the greengoods business.
So far at least, thank God.

ROMA: And what about
Sheet's murder? And Bowl's death? Is that
What you call peaceful?

SECOND DEALER: But is that connected
With cauliflower, Mr Roma?
ROMA: No. Just a minute.
*Roma goes over to Ui, who after his big speech has been sitting
there exhausted and listless. After a few words he motions to
Giri to join them. Givola also takes part in a hurried whispered
conversation. Then Giri motions to one of the bodyguards and
goes out quickly with him.*
GIVOLA: Friends, I've been asked to tell you that a poor
Unhappy woman wishes to express
Her thanks to Mr Ui in your presence.
*He goes to the rear and leads in a heavily made-up and flashily
dressed woman – Dockdaisy – who is holding a little girl by the
hand. The three stop in front of Ui, who has stood up.*
GIVOLA: Speak, Mrs Bowl.
To the vegetable dealers.
                        It's Mrs Bowl, the young
Widow of Mr Bowl, the late accountant
Of the Cauliflower Trust, who yesterday
While on his way to City Hall to do
His duty, was struck down by hand unknown.
Mrs Bowl!
DOCKDAISY: Mr Ui, in my profound bereavement over my
husband who was foully murdered while on his way to
City Hall in the exercise of his civic duty, I wish to express
my heartfelt thanks for the flowers you sent me and my
little girl, aged six, who has been robbed of her father.
To the vegetable dealers. Gentlemen I'm only a poor widow
and all I have to say is that without Mr Ui I'd be out in
the street as I shall gladly testify at any time. My little girl,
aged five, and I will never forget it, Mr Ui.
Ui gives Dockdaisy his hand and chucks the child under the chin.
GIVOLA: Bravo!
*Giri wearing Bowl's hat cuts through the crowd, followed by
several gangsters carrying large gasoline cans. They make their
way to the exit.*

UI: Mrs Bowl, my sympathies. This lawlessness
This crime wave's got to stop because . . .

GIVOLA, *as the dealers start leaving*:   Hold it!
The meeting isn't over. The next item
Will be a song in memory of poor Bowl
Sung by our friend James Greenwool, followed by
A collection for the widow. He's a baritone.

*One of the bodyguards steps forward and sings a sentimental song
in which the word 'home' occurs frequently. During the performance the gangsters sit rapt, their heads in their hands, or leaning
back with eyes closed, etc. The meagre applause at the end is
interrupted by the howling of police and fire sirens. A red glow
is seen in a large window in the background.*

ROMA: Fire on the waterfront!

A VOICE: Where?

A BODYGUARD *entering*:   Is there a vegetable
Dealer named Hook in the house?

SECOND DEALER: That's me. What's wrong?

THE BODYGUARD: Your warehouse is on fire.

*Hook, the dealer, rushes out. A few follow him. Others go to the
window.*

ROMA: Hold it!
Nobody leave the room!
To the bodyguard.
                    Is it arson?

THE BODYGUARD: It must be. They've found some gasoline
cans.

THIRD DEALER: Some gasoline cans were taken out of here!

ROMA, *in a rage*: What's that? Is somebody insinuating
We did it?

A BODYGUARD, *pokes his automatic into the man's ribs*:
                    What was being taken out
Of here? Did you see any gasoline cans?

OTHER BODYGUARDS, *to other dealers*:
Did you see any cans? – Did you?

THE DEALERS: Not I . . .
  Me neither.
ROMA: That's better.
GIVOLA, *quickly*:   Ha. The very man
  Who just a while ago was telling us
  That all was quiet on the green goods front
  Now sees his warehouse burning, turned to ashes
  By malefactors. Don't you see? Can you
  Be blind? You've got to get together. And quick!
UI, *bellowing*: Things in this town are looking very sick!
  First murder and now arson! This should show
  You men that no one's safe from the next blow!
  A sign appears.

8

The warehouse fire trial. Press. Judge. Prosecutor. Defence counsel.
Young Dogsborough. Giri. Givola. Dockdaisy. Bodyguards.
Vegetable dealers and Fish, the accused.

a

Emanuele Giri stands in front of the witness's chair, pointing at
Fish, the accused, who is sitting in utter apathy.

GIRI, *shouting*: There sits the criminal who lit the fire!
  When I challenged him he was slinking down the street
  Clutching a gasoline can to his chest.
  Stand up, you bastard, when I'm talking to you.
  Fish is pulled to his feet. He stands swaying.
THE JUDGE: Defendant, pull yourself together. This is a

court of law. You are on trial for arson. That is a very serious matter, and don't forget it!

FISH, *in a thick voice*: Arlarlarl.

THE JUDGE: Where did you get that gasoline can?

FISH: Arlarl.

At a sign from the judge an excessively well-dressed, sinister-looking doctor bends down over Fish and exchanges glances with Giri.

THE DOCTOR: Simulating.

DEFENCE COUNSEL: The defence moves that other doctors be consulted.

THE JUDGE, *smiling*: Denied.

DEFENCE COUNSEL: Mr Giri, how did you happen to be on the spot when this fire, which reduced twenty-two buildings to ashes, broke out in Mr Hook's warehouse?

GIRI: I was taking a walk for my digestion.

Some of the bodyguards laugh. Giri joins in the laughter.

DEFENCE COUNSEL: Are you aware, Mr Giri, that Mr Fish, the defendant, is an unemployed worker, that he had never been in Chicago before and arrived here on foot the day before the fire?

GIRI: What? When?

DEFENCE COUNSEL: Is the registration number of your car XXXXXX?

GIRI: Yes.

DEFENCE COUNSEL: Was this car parked outside Dogsborough's restaurant on 87th Street during the four hours preceding the fire, and was defendant Fish dragged out of that restaurant in a state of unconsciousness?

GIRI: How should I know? I spent the whole day on a little excursion to Cicero, where I met fifty-two persons who are all ready to testify that they saw me.

The bodyguards laugh.

DEFENCE COUNSEL: Your previous statement left me with the impression that you were taking a walk for your digestion in the Chicago waterfront area.

GIRI: Any objection to my eating in Cicero and digesting in Chicago?

Loud and prolonged laughter in which the judge joins. Darkness. An organ plays Chopin's Funeral March *in dance rhythm.*

b

When the lights go on, Hook, the vegetable dealer, is sitting in the witness's chair.

DEFENCE COUNSEL: Did you ever quarrel with the defendant, Mr Hook? Did you ever see him before?

HOOK: Never.

DEFENCE COUNSEL: Have you ever seen Mr Giri?

HOOK: Yes. In the office of the Cauliflower Trust on the day of the fire.

DEFENCE COUNSEL: Before the fire?

HOOK: Just before the fire. He passed through the room with four men carrying gasoline cans.

Commotion on the press bench and among the bodyguards.

THE JUDGE: Would the gentlemen of the press please be quiet.

DEFENCE COUNSEL: What premises does your warehouse adjoin, Mr Hook?

HOOK: The premises of the former Sheet shipyard. There's a passage connecting my warehouse with the shipyard.

DEFENCE COUNSEL: Are you aware, Mr Hook, that Mr Giri lives in the former Sheet shipyard and consequently has access to the premises?

HOOK: Yes. He's the stockroom superintendent.

Increased commotion on the press bench. The bodyguards boo and take a menacing attitude toward Hook, the defence and the press. Young Dogsborough rushes up to the judge and whispers something in his ear.

JUDGE: Order in the court! The defendant is unwell. The
court is adjourned.
Darkness. The organ starts again to play Chopin's Funeral
March *in dance rhythm.*

c

*When the lights go on, Hook is sitting in the witness's chair. He is
in a state of collapse, with a cane beside him and bandages over his
head and eyes.*

THE PROSECUTOR: Is your eyesight poor, Hook?
HOOK, *with difficulty*: Yes.
THE PROSECUTOR: Would you say you were capable of
recognising anyone clearly and definitely?
HOOK: No.
THE PROSECUTOR: Do you, for instance, recognise this
man?
He points at Giri.
HOOK: No.
THE PROSECUTOR: You're not prepared to say that you
ever saw him before?
HOOK: No.
THE PROSECUTOR: And now, Hook, a very important
question. Think well before you answer. Does your ware-
house adjoin the premises of the former Sheet shipyard?
HOOK, *after a pause*: No.
THE PROSECUTOR: That is all.
Darkness. The organ starts playing again.

d

When the lights go on, Dockdaisy is sitting in the witness's chair.

DOCKDAISY, *mechanically*: I recognise the defendant perfectly because of his guilty look and because he is five feet eight inches tall. My sister-in-law has informed me that he was seen outside City Hall on the afternoon my husband was shot while entering City Hall. He was carrying a Webster sub-machine gun and made a suspicious impression.
Darkness. The organ starts playing again.

e

When the lights go on, Giuseppe Givola is sitting in the witness's chair. Greenwool, the bodyguard, is standing near him.

THE PROSECUTOR: It has been alleged that certain men were seen carrying gasoline cans out of the offices of the Cauliflower Trust before the fire. What do you know about this?
GIVOLA: It couldn't be anybody but Mr Greenwool.
THE PROSECUTOR: Is Mr Greenwool in your employ?
GOVOLA: Yes.
THE PROSECUTOR: What is your profession, Mr Givola?
GIVOLA: Florist.
THE PROSECUTOR: Do florists use large quantities of gasoline?
GIVOLA, *seriously*: No, only for plant lice.

THE PROSECUTOR: What was Mr Greenwool doing in the offices of the Cauliflower Trust?

GIVOLA: Singing a song.

THE PROSECUTOR: Then he can't very well have carried any gasoline cans to Hook's warehouse at the same time.

GIVOLA: It's out of the question. It's not in his character to start fires. He's a baritone.

THE PROSECUTOR: If it please the court, I should like witness Greenwool to sing the fine song he was singing in the offices of the Cauliflower Trust while the warehouse was being set on fire.

THE JUDGE: The court does not consider it necessary.

GIVOLA: I protest.

He rises.

The bias in this courtroom is outrageous.
Cleancut young fellows who in broadest daylight
Fire a well-meant shot or two are treated
Like shady characters. It's scandalous.
Laughter. Darkness. The organ starts playing again.

f

When the lights go on, the courtroom shows every indication of utter exhaustion.

THE JUDGE: The press has dropped hints that this court might be subject to pressure from certain quarters. The court wishes to state that it has been subjected to no pressure of any kind and is conducting this trial in perfect freedom. I believe this will suffice.

THE PROSECUTOR: Your Honour! In view of the fact that defendant Fish persists in simulating dementia, the prosecution holds that he cannot be questioned any further. We therefore move . . .

DEFENCE COUNSEL: Your honour. The defendant is coming to!
Commotion.

FISH, *seems to be waking up*: Arlarlwaratarlawatrla.

DEFENCE COUNSEL: Water! Your Honour! I ask leave to question defendant Fish.
Uproar.

THE PROSECUTOR: I object. I see no indication that Fish is in his right mind. It's all a machination on the part of the defence, cheap sensationalism, demagogy!

FISH: Watr.

Supported by the defence counsel, he stands up.

DEFENCE COUNSEL: Fish. Can you answer me?

FISH: Yarl.

DEFENCE COUNSEL: Fish, tell the court: Did you, on the 28th of last month, set fire to a vegetable warehouse on the waterfront? Yes or no?

FISH: N-n-no.

DEFENCE COUNSEL: When did you arrive in Chicago, Fish?

FISH: Water.

DEFENCE COUNSEL: Water!

Commotion. Young Dogsborough has stepped up to the judge and is talking to him emphatically.

GIRI *stands up square-shouldered and bellows*: Frame-up! Lies! Lies!

DEFENCE COUNSEL: Did you ever see this man – *He indicates Giri.* – before?

FISH: Yes. Water.

DEFENCE COUNSEL: Where? Was it in Dogsborough's restaurant on the waterfront?

FISH, *faintly*: Yes.

Uproar. The bodyguards draw their guns and boo. The doctor comes running in with a glass. He pours the contents into Fish's mouth before the defence counsel can take the glass out of his hand.

DEFENCE COUNSEL: I object. I move that this glass be examined.

THE JUDGE, *exchanging glances with the prosecutor*: Motion denied.

DOCKDAISY *screams at Fish*: Murderer!

DEFENCE COUNSEL: Your Honour!
Because the mouth of truth cannot be stopped with earth
They're trying to stop it with a piece of paper
A sentence to be handed down as though
Your Honour – that's their hope – should properly
Be titled Your Disgrace. They cry to justice:
Hands up! Is this our city, which has aged
A hundred years in seven days beneath
The onslaught of a small but bloody brood
Of monsters, now to see its justice murdered
Nay, worse than murdered, desecrated by
Submission to brute force? Your Honour!
Suspend this trial!

THE PROSECUTOR: I object!

GIRI: You dog!
You lying, peculating dog! Yourself
A poisoner! Come on! Let's step outside!
I'll rip your guts out! Gangster!

DEFENCE COUNSEL: The whole
Town knows this man.

GIRI, *fuming*: Shut up!
When the judge tries to interrupt him:
You too!
Just keep your trap shut if you want to live!
He runs short of breath and the judge manages to speak.

THE JUDGE: Order in the court. Defence counsel will incur charges of contempt of court. Mr Giri's indignation is quite understandable. *To the defence counsel*: Continue.

DEFENCE COUNSEL: Fish! Did they give you anything to drink at Dogsborough's restaurant? Fish! Fish!

GIEI, *bellowing*: Go on and shout! Looks like his tyre's gone
   down.
   We'll see who's running things in this here town!
   Uproar. Darkness. The organ starts again to play Chopin's
   Funeral March *in dance rhythm.*

g

As the lights go on for the last time, the judge stands up and in a
toneless voice delivers the sentence. The defendant is deathly pale.

THE JUDGE: Charles Fish, I find you guilty of arson and
   sentence you to fifteen years at hard labour.
   A sign appears.

9

a

Cicero. A woman climbs out of a shot-up truck and staggers
forward.

THE WOMAN: Help! Help! Don't run away. Who'll testify?
   My husband is in that truck. They got him. Help!
   My arm is smashed . . . And so's the truck. I need
   A bandage for my arm. They gun us down
   Like rabbits. God! Won't anybody help?
   You murderers! My husband! I know who's
   Behind it. Ui! *Raging*: Fiend! Monster! Shit!
   You'd make an honest piece of shit cry out:
   Where can I wash myself? You lousy louse!
   And people stand for it. And we go under.

Hey you! It's Ui!
A burst of machine-gun fire nearby. She collapses.
Ui did this job!
Where's everybody? Help! who'll stop that mob?

b

Dogsborough's country house. Night toward morning.
Dogsborough is writing his will and confession.

DOGSBOROUGH:
    And so I, honest Dogsborough acquiesced
    In all the machinations of that bloody gang
    After full eighty years of uprightness.
    I'm told that those who've known me all along
    Are saying I don't know what's going on
    That if I knew I wouldn't stand for it.
    Alas, I know it all. I know who set
    Fire to Hook's warehouse. And I know who dragged
    Poor Fish into the restaurant and doped him.
    I know that when Sheet died a bloody death
    His steamship ticket in his pocket, Roma
    Was there. I know that Giri murdered Bowl
    That afternoon outside of City Hall
    Because he knew too much about myself
    Honest old Dogsborough. I know that he
    Shot Hook, and saw him with Hook's hat.
    I know that Givola committed five
    Murders, here itemised. I also know
    All about Ui, and I know he knew
    All this – the deaths of Sheet and Bowl, Givola's
    Murderers and all about the fire. All this
    Your honest Dogsborough knew. All this
    He tolerated out of sordid lust
    For gain, and fear of forfeiting your trust.

Hotel Mammoth. Ui's suite. Ui is sitting slumped in a deep chair,
staring into space. Givola is writing and two bodyguards are looking
over his shoulder, grinning.

GIVOLA: And so I, Dogsborough, bequeath my bar
    To good hard-working Givola. My country
    House to the brave, though somewhat hot-headed Giri.
    And I bequeath my son to honest Roma.
    I furthermore request that you appoint
    Roma police chief, Giri judge, and Givola
    Commissioner of welfare. For my own
    Position I would warmly recommend
    Arturo Ui, who, believe your honest
    Old Dogsborough, is worthy of it. – That's
    Enough, I think, let's hope he kicks in soon.
    This testament will do wonders. Now that the old
    Man's known to be dying and the hope arises
    Of laying him to rest with relative
    Dignity, in clean earth, it's well to tidy up
    His corpse. A pretty epitaph is needed.
    Ravens from olden time have battened on
    The reputation of the fabulous
    White raven that somebody saw sometime
    And somewhere. This old codger's their white raven.
    I guess they couldn't find a whiter one.
    And by the way, boss, Giri for my taste
    Is too much with him. I don't like it.
UI, *starting up*:   Giri?
    What about Giri?

GIVOLA: Only that he's spending
A little too much time with Dogsborough.
UI: I
Don't trust him.
Giri comes in wearing a new hat, Hook's.
GIVOLA: I don't either. Hi, Giri
How's Dogsborough's apoplexy?
GIRI: He refuses
To let the doctor in.
GIVOLA: Our brilliant doctor
Who took such loving care of Fish?
GIRI: No other
Will do. The old man talks too much.
UI: Maybe somebody's talked too much to him . . .
GIRI: What's that? *To Givola*: You skunk, have you been
    stinking up
The air around here again?
GIVOLA, *alarmed*:   Just read the will
Dear Giri.
GIRI, *snatches it from him*:
                      What! Police chief? Him? Roma?
You must be crazy.
GIVOLA: He demands it. I'm
Against it too. The bastard can't be trusted
Across the street.
Roma comes in followed by bodyguards.
                      Hi, Roma. Take a look at
This will.
ROMA, *grabbing it out of his hands*:
                      Okay, let's see it. What do you know!
Giri a judge! But where's the old man's scribble?
GIRI: Under his pillow. He's been trying to
Smuggle it out. Five times I've caught his son.
ROMA *holds out his hand*:
Let's have it, Giri.
GIRI: What? I haven't got it.

ROMA: Oh yes, you have!
They glare at each other furiously.
                              I know what's on your mind.
There's something about Sheet. That concerns me.
GIRI: Bowl figures in it too. That concerns *me*.
ROMA: Okay, but you're both jerks, and I'm a man.
I know you, Giri, and you too, Givola.
I'd even say your crippled leg was phony.
Why do I always find you bastards here?
What are you cooking up? What lies have they
Been telling you about me, Arturo? Watch
Your step, you pipsqueaks. If I catch you trying
To cross me up, I'll rub you out like blood spots.
GIRI: Roma, you'd better watch your tongue. I'm not
One of your two-bit gunmen.
ROMA, *to his bodyguards*:   That means you!
That's what they're calling you at headquarters.
They hobnob with the Cauliflower Trust –
Pointing to Giri.
That shirt was made to order by Clark's tailor –
You two-bit gunmen do the dirty work –
And you – *To Ui.* – put up with it.
UI, *as though waking up*:   Put up with what?
GIVOLA: His shooting up Caruther's trucks. Caruther's
A member of the Trust.
UI: Did you shoot up
Caruther's trucks?
ROMA: I gave no orders. Just
Some of the boys. Spontaneous combustion.
They don't see why it's always the small grocers
That have to sweat and bleed. Why not the big wheels?
Damn it, Arturo, I myself don't get it.
GIVOLA: The Trust is good and mad.
GIRI: Clark says they're only
Waiting for it to happen one more time.
He's put in a complaint with Dogsborough.

UI, *morosely*: Ernesto, these things mustn't happen.

GIRI: Crack down, boss!
These guys are getting too big for their breeches.

GIVOLA: The Trust is good and mad, boss.

ROMA *pulls his gun. To Giri and Givola*:
Okay. Hands up!
To their bodyguards:
                           You too!
Hands up the lot of you. No monkey business!
Now back up to the wall.
*Givola, his men, and Giri raise their hands and with an air of
resignation back up to the wall.*

UI, *indifferently*:   What is all this?
Ernesto, don't make them nervous. What are you guys
Squabbling about? So some palooka's wasted
Some bullets on a cauliflower truck.
Such misunderstandings can be straightened out.
Everything is running smooth as silk.
The fire was a big success. The stores
Are paying for protection. Thirty cents
On every dollar. Almost half the city
Has knuckled under in five days. Nobody
Raises a hand against us. And I've got
Bigger and better projects.

GIVOLA, *quickly*:   Projects? What
For instance?

GIRI: Fuck your projects. Get this fool
To let me put my hands down.

ROMA: Safety first, Arturo.
We'd better leave them up.

GIVOLA: Won't it look sweet
If Clark comes in and sees us here like this?

UI: Ernesto, put that rod away!

ROMA: No dice!
Wake up, Arturo. Don't you see their game?
They're selling you out to the Clarks and Dogsboroughs.

'If Clark comes in and sees us!' What, I ask you
Has happened to the shipyard's funds? We haven't
Seen a red cent. The boys shoot up the stores
Tote gasoline to warehouses and sigh:
We made Arturo what he is today
And he doesn't know us any more. He's playing
The shipyard owner and tycoon. Wake up
Arturo!

GIRI: Right. And speak up. Tell us where
You stand.

UI *jumps up*:   Are you boys trying to pressure me
At gunpoint? Better not, I'm warning you
You won't get anywhere with me like that.
You'll only have yourselves to blame for
The consequences. I'm a quiet man. But
I won't be threatened. Either trust me blindly
Or go your way. I owe you no accounting.
Just do your duty, and do it to the full.
The recompense is up to me, because
Duty comes first and then the recompense.
What I demand of you is trust. You lack
Faith, and where faith is lacking, all is lost.
How do you think I got this far? By faith!
Because of my fanatical, my unflinching
Faith in the cause. With faith and nothing else
I flung a challenge at this city and forced
It to its knees. With faith I made my way
To Dogsborough. With faith I climbed the steps
Of City Hall. With nothing in my naked
Hands but indomitable faith.

ROMA: And
A tommy gun.

UI: No, other men have them
But lack firm faith in their predestination
To leadership. And that is why you too
Need to have faith in me. Have faith! Believe that

I know what's best for you and that I'm
Resolved to put it through. That I will find
The road to victory. If Dogsborough
Passes away, then I decide who gets to
Be what. I say no more, but rest assured:
You'll all be satisfied.

GIVOLA *puts his hand on his heart*:
Arturo!

ROMA, *sullenly*:   Scram
You guys!
*Giri, Givola and Givola's bodyguard go out slowly with their
hands up.*

GIRI, *leaving, to Roma*: I like your hat.

GIVOLA, *leaving*:   Dear Roma . . .

ROMA: Scram!
Giri, you clown, don't leave your laugh behind.
And Givola, you crook, be sure to take
Your clubfoot, though I'm pretty sure you stole it.
When they are gone, Ui relapses into his brooding.

UI: I want to be alone.

ROMA, *standing still*:   Arturo, if I
Hadn't the kind of faith you've just described
I'd sometimes find it hard to look my
Men in the face. We've got to act. And quickly.
Giri is cooking up some dirty work.

UI: Don't worry about Giri. I am planning
Bigger and better things. And now, Ernesto
To you, my oldest friend and trusted lieutenant
I will divulge them.

ROMA, *beaming*:   Speak, Arturo. Giri
And what I had to say of him can wait.
He sits down with Ui. Roma's men stand waiting in the corner.

UI: We're finished with Chicago. I need more.

ROMA: More?

UI: Vegetables are sold in other cities.

ROMA: But how are you expecting to get in?

UI: Through
  The front door, through the back door, through the
    windows.
  Resisted, sent away, called back again.
  Booed and acclaimed. With threats and supplications
  Appeals and insults, gentle force and steel
  Embrace. In short, the same as here.
ROMA: Except
  Conditions aren't the same in other places.
UI: I have in mind a kind of dress rehearsal
  In a small town. That way we'll see
  Whether conditions are so different. I
  Doubt it.
ROMA: And where have you resolved to stage
  This dress rehearsal?
UI: In Cicero.
ROMA: But there
  They've got this Dullfeet with his Journal
  For Vegetables and Positive Thinking
  Which every Saturday accuses me
  Of murdering Sheet.
UI: That's got to stop.
ROMA: It will. These journalists have enemies.
  Their black and white makes certain people
  See red. Myself, for instance. Yes, Arturo
  I think these accusations can be silenced.
UI: I'm sure they can. The Trust is negotiating
  With Cicero right now. For the time being
  We'll just sell cauliflower peacefully.
ROMA: Who's doing this negotiating?
UI: Clark.
  But he's been having trouble. On our account.
ROMA: I see. So Clark is in it. I wouldn't trust
  That Clark around the corner.
UI: In Cicero
  They say we're following the Cauliflower

Trust like its shadow. They want cauliflower, but
They don't want us. The shopkeepers don't like us.
A feeling shared by others: Dullfeet's wife
For instance, who for years now has been running
A greengoods wholesale house. She'd like to join
The Trust, and would have joined except for us.
ROMA: You mean this plan of moving in on Cicero
Didn't start with you at all, but with the Trust?
Arturo, now I see it all. I see
Their rotten game.
UI: Whose game?
ROMA: The Trust's.
The goings-on at Dogsborough's! His will!
It's all a machination of the Trust.
They want the Cicero connection. You're in
The way. But how can they get rid of you?
You've got them by the balls, because they needed
You for their dirty business and connived at
Your methods. But now they've found a way:
Old Dogsborough confesses and repairs
In ash and sackcloth to his coffin.
The cauliflower boys with deep emotion
Retrieve this paper from his hands and sobbing
Read it to the assembled press: how he repents
And solemnly adjures them to wipe out
The plague which he – as he confesses – brought
In, and restore the cauliflower trade
To its time-honoured practices.
That's what they plan, Arturo. They're all in it:
Giri, who gets Dogsborough to scribble wills
And who is hand in glove with Clark, who's having
Trouble in Cicero because of us
And wants pure sunshine when he shovels shekels.
Givola, who smells carrion. – This Dogsborough
Honest old Dogsborough with his two-timing will
That splatters you with muck has got to be

Rubbed out, Arturo, or your best-laid plans
For Cicero are down the drain.

UI: You think
It's all a plot? It's true. They've kept me out
Of Cicero. I've noticed that.

ROMA: Arturo
I beg you: let me handle this affair.
I tell you what: my boys and I will beat
It out to Dogsborough's tonight
And take him with us. To the hospital
We'll tell him – and deliver him to the morgue.

UI: But Giri's with him at the villa.

ROMA: He
Can stay there.
They exchange glances.
                    Two birds one stone.

UI: And Givola?

ROMA: On the way back I'll drop in at the florist's
And order handsome wreaths for Dogsborough.
For Giri too, the clown. And I'll pay cash.
He pats his gun.

UI: Ernesto, this contemptible project of
The Dogsboroughs and Clarks and Dullfeets
To squeeze me out of Cicero's affairs
By coldly branding me a criminal
Must be frustrated with an iron hand.
I put my trust in you.

ROMA: And well you may.
But you must meet with us before we start
And give the boys a talk to make them see
The matter in its proper light. I'm not
So good at talking.

UI, *shaking his hand*: It's a deal.

ROMA: I knew it
Arturo. This was how it had to be
Decided. Say, the two of us! Say, you

And me! Like in the good old days.
To his men.

What did
I tell you, boys? He gives us the green light.

UI: I'll be there.

ROMA: At eleven.

UI: Where?

ROMA: At the garage.
I'm a new man. At last we'll see some fight!
*He goes out quickly with his men. Pacing the floor, Ui prepares
the speech he is going to make to Roma's men.*

UI: Friends, much as I regret to say it, word
Has reached me that behind my back perfidious
Treason is being planned. Men close to me
Men whom I trusted implicitly
Have turned against me. Goaded by ambition
And crazed by lust for gain, these despicable
Fiends have conspired with the cauliflower
Moguls – no, that won't do – with who? I've got it!
With the police, to coldly liquidate you
And even, so I hear, myself. My patience
Is at an end. I therefore order you
Under Ernesto Roma who enjoys
My fullest confidence, tonight . . .
Enter Clark, Giri and Betty Dullfeet.

GIRI, *noticing that Ui looks frightened*: It's only
Us, boss.

CLARK: Ui, let me introduce
Mrs Dullfeet of Cicero. The Trust
Asks you to give her your attention, and hopes
The two of you will come to terms.

UI, *scowling*:   I'm listening.

CLARK: A merger, as you know, is being considered
Between Chicago's Cauliflower Trust
And Cicero's purveyors. In the course
Of the negotiations, Cicero

Objected to your presence on the board.
The Trust was able, after some discussion
To overcome this opposition. Mrs Dullfeet
Is here . . .

MRS DULLFEET: To clear up the misunderstanding.
Moreover, I should like to point out that
My husband, Mr Dullfeet's newspaper
Campaign was not directed against you
Mr Ui.

UI: Against who was it directed?

CLARK: I may as well speak plainly, Ui. Sheet's
'Suicide' made a very bad impression
In Cicero. Whatever else Sheet may
Have been, he was a shipyard owner
A leading citizen, and not some Tom
Dick or Harry whose death arouses no
Comment. And something else. Caruther's
Garage complains of an attack on one of
Its trucks. And one of your men, Ui, is
Involved in both these cases.

MRS DULLFEET: Every child in
Cicero knows Chicago's cauliflower
Is stained with blood.

UI: Have you come here to insult me?

MRS DULLFEET:
No, no. Not you, since Mr Clark has vouched
For you. It's this man Roma.

CLARK, *quickly*:   Cool it, Ui!

GIRI: Cicero . . .

UI: You can't talk to me like this!
What do you take me for? I've heard enough!
Ernesto Roma is my man. I don't
Let anybody tell me who to pal with.
This is an outrage.

GIRI: Boss!

MRS DULLFEET: Ignatius Dullfeet

Will fight the Romas of this world to his
Last breath.
CLARK, *coldly*: And rightly so. In that the Trust
Is solidly behind him. Think it over.
Friendship and business are two separate things.
What do you say?
UI, *likewise coldly*:   You heard me, Mr Clark.
CLARK: Mrs Dullfeet, I regret profoundly
The outcome of this interview.
On his way out, to Ui:

                                    Most unwise, Ui.
Left alone, Ui and Giri do not look at each other.   .
GIRI: This and the business with Caruther's truck
Means war. That's plain.
UI: I'm not afraid of war.
GIRI: Okay, you're not afraid. You'll only have
The Trust, the papers, the whole city, plus
Dogsborough and his crowd against you.
Just between you and me, boss, I'd think twice . . .
UI: I know my duty and need no advice.
A sign appears.

11

*Garage. Night. The sound of rain. Ernesto Roma and young Inna.
In the background gunmen.*

INNA: It's one o'clock.
ROMA: He must have been delayed.
INNA: Could he be hesitating?
ROMA: He could be.
Arturo's so devoted to his henchmen
He'd rather sacrifice himself than them.
Even with rats like Givola and Giri

He can't make up his mind. And so he dawdles
And wrestles with himself. It might be two
Or even three before he gets a move on.
But never fear, he'll come. Of course he will.
I know him, Inna.
Pause.
                          When I see that Giri
Flat on the carpet, pouring out his guts
I'll feel as if I'd taken a good leak.
Oh well, it won't be long.

INNA: These rainy nights are
Hard on the nerves.

ROMA: That's what I like about them.
Of nights the blackest
Of cars the fastest
And of friends
The most resolute.

INNA: How many years have
You known him?

ROMA: Going on eighteen.

INNA: That's a long time.

A GUNMAN *comes forward*:
The boys want whisky.

ROMA: No. Tonight I need
Them sober.
A little man is brought in by the bodyguards.

THE LITTLE MAN, *out of breath*:
                          Dirty work at the crossroads!
Two armoured cars outside police H.Q.
Jam-packed with cops.

ROMA: Okay, boys, get the
Bullet-proof shutter down. Those cops have got
Nothing to do with us, but foresight's better
Than hindsight.
Slowly an iron shutter falls, blocking the garage door.
                    Is the passage clear?

INNA *nods*: It's a funny thing about tobacco. When a man
  Is smoking, he looks calm. And if you imitate
  A calm-looking man and light a cigarette, you
  Get to be calm yourself.
ROMA, *smiling*:   Hold out your hand.
INNA *does so*: It's trembling. That's no good.
ROMA: Don't worry. It's all
  Right. I don't go for bruisers. They're unfeeling.
  Nothing can hurt them and they won't hurt you.
  Not seriously. Tremble all you like.
  A compass needle is made of steel but trembles
  Before it settles on its course. Your hand
  Is looking for its pole. That's all.
A SHOUT, *from the side*:   Police car
  Coming down Church Street.
ROMA, *intently*:   Is it stopping?
THE VOICE: No.
A GUNMAN *comes in*:
  Two cars with blacked-out lights have turned the corner.
ROMA: They're waiting for Arturo. Givola and
  Giri are laying for him. He'll run straight
  Into their trap. We've got to head him off.
  Let's go!
A GUNMAN: It's suicide.
ROMA: If suicide it is
  Let it be suicide! Hell! Eighteen years
  Of friendship!
INNA, *loud and clear*: Raise the shutter!
  Machine-gun ready?
A GUNMAN: Ready.
INNA: Up she goes.
  The bullet-proof shutter rises slowly. Ui and Givola enter briskly,
  followed by bodyguards.
ROMA: Arturo!
INNA, *under his breath*: Yeah, and Givola.
ROMA: What's up?

Arturo, man, you had us worried. *Laughs loudly.* Hell!
But everything's okay.

UI, *hoarsely*:   Why wouldn't it be okay?

INNA: We thought
Something was wrong. If I were you I'd give him
The glad-hand, boss. He was going to lead
Us all through fire to save you. Weren't you, Roma?
*Ui goes up to Roma, holding out his hand. Roma grasps it,
laughing. At this moment, when Roma cannot reach for his gun,
Givola shoots him from the hip.*

UI: Into the corner with them!
*Roma's men stand bewildered. Inna in the lead, they are driven
into the corner. Givola bends down over Roma, who is lying on the
floor.*

GIVOLA: He's still breathing.

UI: Finish him off.
To the men lined up against the wall.
Your vicious plot against me is exposed.
So are your plans to rub out Dogsborough.
I caught you in the nick of time. Resistance
Is useless. I'll teach you to rebel against me!
You bastards!

GIVOLA: Not a single one unarmed!
Speaking of Roma:
He's coming to. He's going to wish he hadn't.

UI: I'll be at Dogsborough's country house tonight.
He goes out quickly.

INNA: You stinking rats! You traitors!

GIVOLA, *excitedly*:   Let 'em have it!
*The men standing against the wall are mowed down by machine-
gun fire.*

ROMA *comes to*:
Givola! Christ.
Turns over, his face chalky-white.
                      What happened over there?

GIVOLA: Nothing. Some traitors have been executed.

ROMA: You dog! My men! What have you done to them?
Givola does not answer.
And where's Arturo? You've murdered him. I knew it!
Looking for him on the floor.
Where is he?
GIVOLA: He's just left.
ROMA, *as he is being dragged to the wall*: You stinking dogs!
GIVOLA, *coolly*: You say my leg is short, I say your brain is
    small.
Now let your pretty legs convey you to the wall!
A sign appears.

12

*Givola's flower shop. Ignatius Dullfeet, a very small man, and
Betty Dullfeet come in.*

DULLFEET: I don't like this at all.
BETTY: Why not? They've gotten rid
    Of Roma.
DULLFEET: Yes, they've murdered him.
BETTY: That's how
    They do it. Anyway, he's gone. Clark says
    That Ui's years of storm and stress, which even
    The best of men go through, are over. Ui
    Has shown he wants to mend his uncouth ways.
    But if you persevere in your attacks
    You'll only stir his evil instincts up
    Again, and you, Ignatius, will be first
    To bear the brunt. But if you keep your mouth shut
    They'll leave you be.
DULLFEET: I'm not so sure my silence
    Will help.

BETTY: It's sure to. They're not beasts.
Giri comes in from one side, wearing Roma's hat.
GIRI: Hi. Here already? Mr Ui's inside.
   He'll be delighted. Sorry I can't stay.
   I've got to beat it quick before I'm seen.
   I've swiped a hat from Givola.
He laughs so hard that plaster falls from the ceiling, and goes out, waving.
DULLFEET:
   Bad when they growl. No better when they laugh.
BETTY: Don't say such things, Ignatius. Not here.
DULLFEET, *bitterly*:   Nor
   Anywhere else.
BETTY: What can you do? Already
   The rumour's going around in Cicero
   That Ui's stepping into Dogsborough's shoes.
   And worse, the greengoods men of Cicero
   Are flirting with the Cauliflower Trust.
DULLFEET:
   And now they've smashed two printing presses on me.
   Betty, I've got a dark foreboding.
Givola and Ui come in with outstretched hands.
BETTY: Hi, Ui!
UI: Welcome. Dullfeet!
DULLFEET: Mr Ui
   I tell you frankly that I hesitated
   To come, because . . .
UI: Why hesitate? A man
   Like you is welcome everywhere.
GIVOLA: So is a
   Beautiful woman.
DULLFEET: Mr Ui, I've felt
   It now and then to be my duty to
   Come out against . . .
UI: A mere misunderstanding!
   If you and I had known each other from

The start, it never would have happened. It
Has always been my fervent wish that what
Had to be done should be done peacefully.

DULLFEET: Violence . . .

UI: No one hates it more than I do.
If men were wise, there'd be no need of it.

DULLFEET: My aim . . .

UI: Is just the same as mine. We both
Want trade to thrive. The small shopkeeper whose
Life is no bed of roses nowadays
Must be permitted to sell his greens in peace.
And find protection when attacked.

DULLFEET, *firmly*:   And be
Free to determine whether he desires·
Protection. I regard that as essential.

UI: And so do I. He's *got* to be free to choose.
Why? Because when he chooses his protector
Freely, and puts his trust in somebody he himself
Has chosen, then the confidence, which is
As necessary in the greengoods trade
As anywhere else, will prevail. That's always been
My stand.

DULLFEET: I'm glad to hear it from your lips.
For, no offence intended, Cicero
Will never tolerate coercion.

UI: Of course not.
No one, unless he has to, tolerates
Coercion.

DULLFEET: Frankly, if this merger with the Trust
Should mean importing the ungodly bloodbath
That plagues Chicago to our peaceful town
I never could approve it.
Pause.

UI: Frankness calls
For frankness, Mr Dullfeet. Certain things
That might not meet the highest moral standards

May have occurred in the past. Such things
Occur in battle. Among friends, however
They cannot happen. Dullfeet, what I want
Of you is only that in the future you should
Trust me and look upon me as a friend
Who never till the seas run dry will forsake
A friend – and, to be more specific, that
Your paper should stop printing these horror stories
That only make bad blood. I don't believe
I'm asking very much.

DULLFEET: It's easy not
To write about what doesn't happen, sir.

UI: Exactly. And if now and then some trifling
Incident should occur, because the earth
Is inhabited by men and not by angels
You will abstain, I hope, from printing lurid
Stories about trigger-happy criminals.
I wouldn't go so far as to maintain that
One of our drivers might not on occasion
Utter an uncouth word. That too is human.
And if some vegetable dealer stands
One of our men to a beer for punctual
Delivery of his carrots, let's not rush
Into print with stories of corruption.

BETTY: Mr
Ui, my husband's human.

GIVOLA: We don't doubt it.
And now that everything has been so amiably
Discussed and settled among friends, perhaps
You'd like to see my flowers . . .

UI, *to Dullfeet*:   After you.

They inspect Givola's flower shop. Ui leads Betty, Givola leads Dullfeet. In the following they keep disappearing behind the flower displays. Givola and Dullfeet emerge.

GIVOLA: These, my dear Dullfeet, are Malayan fronds.

DULLFEET: Growing, I see, by little oval ponds.

GIVOLA: Stocked with blue carp that stay stock-still for hours.

DULLFEET: The wicked are insensitive to flowers.

They disappear. Ui and Betty emerge.

BETTY: A strong man needs no force to win his suit.

UI: Arguments carry better when they shoot.

BETTY: Sound reasoning is bound to take effect.

UI: Except when one is trying to collect.

BETTY: Intimidation, underhanded tricks . . .

UI: I prefer to speak of pragmatic politics.

They disappear. Givola and Dullfeet emerge.

DULLFEET: Flowers are free from lust and wickedness.

GIVOLA: Exactly why I love them, I confess.

DULLFEET: They live so quietly. They never hurry.

GIVOLA, *mischievously*:

No problems. No newspapers. No worry.

They disappear. Ui and Betty emerge.

BETTY: They tell me you're as abstinent as a vicar.

UI: I never smoke and have no use for liquor.

BETTY: A saint perhaps when all is said and done.

UI: Of carnal inclinations I have none.

They disappear. Givola and Dullfeet emerge.

DULLFEET: Your life with flowers must deeply satisfy.

GIVOLA: It would, had I not other fish to fry.

They disappear. Ui and Betty emerge.

BETTY: What, Mr Ui, does religion mean to you?

UI: I am a Christian. That will have to do.

BETTY: Yes. But the Ten Commandments, where do they Come in?

UI: In daily life they don't, I'd say.

BETTY: Forgive me if your patience I abuse
But what exactly are your social views?

UI: My social views are balanced, clear and healthy.
What proves it is: I don't neglect the wealthy.

They disappear. Givola and Dullfeet emerge.

DULLFEET: The flowers have their life, their social calls.

GIVOLA: I'll say they do. Especially funerals!

DULLFEET: Oh, I forgot that flowers were your bread.

GIVOLA: Exactly. My best clients are the dead.

DULLFEET: I hope that's not your only source of trade.

GIVOLA: Some people have the sense to be afraid.

DULLFEET: Violence, Givola, brings no lasting glory.

GIVOLA: It gets results, though.

DULLFEET: That's another story.

GIVOLA: You look so pale.

DULLFEET: The air is damp and close.

GIVOLA: The heavy scent affects you, I suppose.

They disappear. Ui and Betty emerge.

BETTY: I am so glad you two have worked things out.

UI: Once frankness showed what it was all about . . .

BETTY: Foul-weather friends will never disappoint . . .

UI, *putting his arm around her shoulder*:

    I like a woman who can get the point.

*Givola and Dullfeet, who is deathly pale, emerge. Dullfeet sees
the hand on his wife's shoulder.*

DULLFEET: Betty, we're leaving.

UI *comes up to him, holding out his hand*:

                                Mr Dullfeet, your

    Decision honours you. It will redound to

    Cicero's welfare. A meeting between such men

    As you and me can only be auspicious.

GIVOLA, *giving Betty flowers*:

    Beauty to beauty!

BETTY: Look, how nice, Ignatius!

    Oh, I'm so happy. 'Bye, 'bye.

GIVOLA: Now we can

    Start going places.

UI, *darkly*:   I don't like that man.

    A sign appears.

13

Bells. A coffin is being carried into the Cicero funeral chapel, followed by Betty Dullfeet in widow's weeds, and by Clark, Ui, Giri and Givola bearing enormous wreaths. After handing in their wreaths, Giri and Givola remain outside the chapel. The pastor's voice is heard from inside.

VOICE: And so Ignatius Dullfeet's mortal frame
  Is laid to rest. A life of meagrely
  Rewarded toil is ended, of toil devoted
  To others than the toiler who has left us.
  The angel at the gates of heaven will set
  His hand upon Ignatius Dullfeet's shoulder
  Feel that his cloak has been worn thin and say:
  This man has borne the burdens of his neighbours.
  And in the city council for some time
  To come, when everyone has finished speaking
  Silence will fall. For so accustomed are
  His fellow citizens to listen to
  Ignatius Dullfeet's voice that they will wait
  To hear him. 'Tis as though the city's conscience
  Had died. This man who met with so untimely
  An end could walk the narrow path unseeing.
  Justice was in his heart. This man of lowly
  Stature but lofty mind created in
  His newspaper a rostrum whence his voice
  Rang out beyond the confines of our city.
  Ignatius Dullfeet, rest in peace! Amen.
GIVOLA: A tactful man: no word of how he died.
GIRI, *wearing Dullfeet's hat*:
  A tactful man? A man with seven children.
  Clark and Mulberry come out of the chapel.

CLARK: God damn it! Are you mounting guard for fear
    The truth might be divulged beside his coffin?
GIVOLA: Why so uncivil, my dear Clark? I'd think
    This holy place would curb your temper. And
    Besides, the boss is out of sorts. He doesn't
    Like the surroundings here.
MULBERRY: You murderers!
    Ignatius Dullfeet kept his word – and silence.
GIVOLA: Silence is not enough. The kind of men
    We need must be prepared not only to
    Keep silent for us but to speak – and loudly.
MULBERRY: What could he say except to call you butchers?
GIVOLA: He had to go. That little Dullfeet was
    The pore through which the greengoods dealers oozed
    Cold sweat. He stank of it unbearably.
GIRI: And what about your cauliflower? Do
    You want it sold in Cicero or don't
    You?
MULBERRY: Not by slaughter.
GIRI: Hypocrite, how else?
    Who helps us eat the calf we slaughter, eh?
    You're funny bastards, clamouring for meat
    Then bawling out the cook because he uses
    A cleaver. We expect you guys to smack
    Your lips and all you do is gripe. And now
    Go home!
MULBERRY: A sorry day, Clark, when you brought
    These people in.
CLARK: You're telling me?
    The two go out, deep in gloom.
GIRI: Boss
    Don't let those stinkers keep you from enjoying
    The funeral!
GIVOLA: Pst! Betty's coming.
    Leaning on another woman, Betty comes out of the chapel.
    Ui steps up to her. Organ music from the chapel.

UI: Mrs
  Dullfeet, my sympathies.
  She passes him without a word.
GIRI, *bellowing*:   Hey, you!
  She stops still and turns around. Her face is white.
UI: I said, my
  Sympathies, Mrs Dullfeet. Dullfeet – God
  Have mercy on his soul – is dead. But cauliflower –
  Your cauliflower – is still with us. Maybe you
  Can't see it, because your eyes are still
  Blinded with tears. This tragic incident
  Should not, however, blind you to the fact
  That shots are being fired from craven ambush
  On law-abiding vegetable trucks.
  And kerosene dispensed by ruthless hands
  Is spoiling sorely needed vegetables.
  My men and I stand ready to provide
  Protection. What's your answer?
BETTY, *looking heavenward*:   This
  With Dullfeet hardly settled in his grave!
UI: Believe me, I deplore the incident:
  The man by ruthless hand extinguished was
  My friend.
BETTY: The hand that felled him was the hand
  That shook his hand in friendship. Yours!
UI: Am I
  Never to hear the last of these foul rumours
  This calumny which poisons at the root
  My noblest aspirations and endeavours
  To live in harmony with my fellow men?
  Oh, why must they refuse to understand me?
  Why will they not requite my trust? What malice
  To speak of threats when I appeal to reason!
  To spurn the hand that I hold out in friendship!
BETTY: You hold it out to murder.

UI: No!
  I plead with them and they revile me.
BETTY: You
  Plead like a serpent pleading with a bird.
UI: You've heard her. That's how people talk to me.
  It was the same with Dullfeet. He mistook
  My warm, my open-hearted offer of friendship
  For calculation and my generosity
  For weakness. How, alas, did he requite
  My friendly words? With stony silence. Silence
  Was his reply when what I hoped for
  Was joyful appreciation. Oh, how I longed to
  Hear him respond to my persistent, my
  Well-nigh humiliating pleas for friendship, or
  At least for a little understanding, with
  Some sign of human warmth. I longed in vain.
  My only reward was grim contempt. And even
  The promise to keep silent that he gave me
  So sullenly and God knows grudgingly
  Was broken on the first occasion. Where
  I ask you is this silence that he promised
  So fervently? New horror stories are being
  Broadcast in all directions. But I warn you:
  Don't go too far, for even my proverbial
  Patience has got its breaking point.
BETTY: Words fail me.
UI: Unprompted by the heart, they always fail.
BETTY: You call it heart that makes you speak so glibly?
UI: I speak the way I feel.
BETTY: Can anybody feel
  The way you speak? Perhaps he can. Your murders
  Come from the heart. Your blackest crimes are
  As deeply felt as other men's good deeds.
  As we believe in faith, so you believe in
  Betrayal. No good impulse can corrupt you.
  Unwavering in your inconstancy!

True to disloyalty, staunch in deception!
Kindled to sacred fire by bestial deeds!
The sight of blood delights you. Violence
Exalts your spirit. Sordid actions move you
To tears, and good ones leave you with deep-seated
Hatred and thirst for vengeance.

UI: Mrs Dullfeet
I always – it's a principle of mine –
Hear my opponent out, even when
His words are gall. I know that in your circle
I'm not exactly loved. My origins –
Never have I denied that I'm a humble
Son of the Bronx – are held against me.
'He doesn't even know,' they say, 'which fork
To eat his fish with. How then can he hope
To be accepted in big business? When
Tariffs are being discussed, or similar
Financial matters, he's perfectly capable
Of reaching for his knife instead of his pen.
Impossible! We can't use such a man!'
My uncouth tone, my manly way of calling
A spade a spade are used as marks against me.
These barriers of prejudice compel me
To bank exclusively on my own achievement.
You're in the cauliflower business. Mrs
Dullfeet, and so am I. There lies the bridge
Between us.

BETTY: And the chasm to be bridged
Is only foul murder.

UI: Bitter experience
Teaches me not to stress the human angle
But speak to you as a man of influence
Speaks to the owner of a greengoods business.
And so I ask you: How's the cauliflower
Business? For life goes on despite our sorrows.

BETTY: Yes, it goes on – and I shall use my life

To warn the people of this pestilence.
I swear to my dead husband that in future
I'll hate my voice if it should say 'Good morning'
Or 'Pass the bread' instead of one thing only:
'Extinguish Ui!'

GIRI, *in a threatening tone*: Don't overdo it, kid!

UI: Because amid the tombs I dare not hope
For milder feelings, I'd better stick to business
Which knows no dead.

BETTY: Oh Dullfeet, Dullfeet! Now
I truly know that you are dead.

UI: Exactly.
Bear well in mind that Dullfeet's dead. With him
Has died the only voice in Cicero
That would have spoken out in opposition
To crime and terror. You cannot deplore
His loss too deeply. Now you stand defenceless
In a cold world where, sad to say, the weak
Are always trampled. You've got only one
Protector left. That's me, Arturo Ui.

BETTY: And this to me, the widow of the man
You murdered! Monster! Oh, I knew you'd be here
Because you've always gone back to the scene of
Your crimes to throw the blame on others. 'No
It wasn't me, it was somebody else.'
'I know of nothing.' 'I've been injured'
Cries injury. And murder cries: 'A murder!
Murder must be avenged!'

UI: My plan stands fast.
Protection must be given to Cicero.

BETTY, *feebly*: You won't succeed.

UI: I will. That much I know.

BETTY: From this protector God protect us!

UI: Give
Me your answer.

He holds out his hand.

                              Is it friendship?
BETTY: Never while I live!
Cringing with horror, she runs out.
A sign appears.

14

Ui's bedroom at the Hotel Mammoth. Ui tossing in his bed,
plagued by a nightmare. His bodyguards are sitting in chairs, their
revolvers on their laps.

UI, *in his sleep*: Out, bloody shades! Have pity! Get you gone!
The wall behind him becomes transparent. The ghost of Ernesto
Roma appears, a bullet-hole in his forehead.
ROMA: It will avail you nothing. All this murder
   This butchery, these threats and slaverings
   Are all in vain, Arturo, for the root of
   Your crimes is rotten. They will never flower.
   Treason is made manure. Murder, lie
   Deceive the Clarks and slay the Dullfeets, but
   Stop at your own. Conspire against the world
   But spare your fellow conspirators.
   Trample the city with a hundred feet
   But trample not the feet, you treacherous dog!
   Cozen them all, but do not hope to cozen
   The man whose face you look at in the mirror!
   In striking me, you struck yourself, Arturo!
   I cast my lot with you when you were hardly
   More than a shadow on a bar-room floor.
   And now I languish in this drafty
   Eternity, while you sit down to table
   With sleek and proud directors. Treachery
   Made you, and treachery will unmake you.

Just as you betrayed Ernesto Roma, your
Friend and lieutenant, so you will betray
Everyone else, and all, Arturo, will
Betray you in the end. The green earth covers
Ernesto Roma, but not your faithless spirit
Which hovers over tombstones in the wind
Where all can see it, even the grave-diggers.
The day will come when all whom you struck down
And all you will strike down will rise, Arturo
And, bleeding but made strong by hate, take arms
Against you. You will look around for help
As I once looked. Then promise, threaten, plead.
No one will help. Who helped me in my need?

UI, *jumping up with a start*:
Shoot! Kill him! Traitor! Get back to the dead!
The bodyguards shoot at the spot on the wall indicated by Ui.

ROMA, *fading away*:
What's left of me is not afraid of lead.

15

*Financial District. Meeting of the Chicago vegetable dealers.
They are deathly pale.*

FIRST VEGETABLE DEALER:
Murder! Extortion! Highway robbery!

SECOND VEGETABLE DEALER:
And worse: Submissiveness and cowardice!

THIRD VEGETABLE DEALER:
What do you mean, submissiveness? In January
When the first two came barging into
My store and threatened me at gunpoint, I
Gave them, a steely look from top to toe
And answered firmly: I incline to force.

I made it plain that I could not approve
Their conduct or have anything to do
With them. My countenance was ice.
It said: So be it, take your cut. But only
Because you've got those guns.
FOURTH VEGETABLE DEALER: Exactly!
I wash my hands in innocence! That's what
I told my missus.
FIRST VEGETABLE DEALER, *vehemently*:
What do you mean, cowardice?
We used our heads. If we kept quiet, gritted
Our teeth and paid, we thought those bloody fiends
Would put their guns away. But did they? No! It's
Murder! Extortion! Highway robbery!
SECOND VEGETABLE DEALER:
Nobody else would swallow it. No backbone!
FIFTH VEGETABLE DEALER:
No tommy gun, you mean. I'm not a gangster.
My trade is selling greens.
THIRD VEGETABLE DEALER: My only hope
Is that the bastard some day runs across
Some guys who show their teeth. Just let him try his
Little game somewhere else!
FOURTH VEGETABLE DEALER: In Cicero
For instance.
The Cicero vegetable dealers come in. They are deathly pale.
THE CICERONIANS: Hi, Chicago!
THE CHICAGOANS: Hi, Cicero!
What brings *you* here?
THE CICERONIANS: We were told to come.
THE CHICAGOANS: By who?
THE CICERONIANS: By him.
FIRST CHICAGOAN: Who says so? How can he command
You? Throw his weight around in Cicero?
FIRST CICERONIAN: With
His gun.

SECOND CICERONIAN: Brute force. We're helpless.

FIRST CHICAGOAN: Stinking
    cowards!

Can't you be men? Is there no law in Cicero?

FIRST CICERONIAN: No.

SECOND CICERONIAN: No longer.

THIRD CHICAGOAN: Listen, friends. You've got
    To fight. This plague will sweep the country
    If you don't stop it.

FIRST CHICAGOAN: First one city, then another.
    Fight to the death! You owe it to your country.

SECOND CICERONIAN:
    Why us? We wash our hands in innocence.

FOURTH CHICAGOAN:
    We only hope with God's help that the bastard
    Some day comes across some guys that show
    Their teeth.

*Fanfares. Enter Arturo Ui and Betty Dullfeet – in mourning –
followed by Clark, Giri, Givola and bodyguards. Flanked by
the others, Ui passes through. The bodyguards line up in the
background.*

GIRI: Hi, friends! Is everybody here
    From Cicero?

FIRST CICERONIAN: All present.

GIRI: And Chicago?

FIRST CHICAGOAN: All present.

GIRI, *to Ui:*   Everybody's here.

GIVOLA: Greetings, my friends. The Cauliflower Trust
    Wishes you all a hearty welcome. Our
    First speaker will be Mr Clark. *To Clark:* Mr Clark.

CLARK: Gentlemen, I bring news. Negotiations
    Begun some weeks ago and patiently
    Though sometimes stormily pursued – I'm telling
    Tales out of school – have yielded fruit. The wholesale
    House of I. Dullfeet, Cicero, has joined
    The Cauliflower Trust. In consequence

The Cauliflower Trust will now supply
Your greens. The gain for you is obvious:
Secure delivery. The new prices, slightly
Increased, have already been set. It is
With pleasure, Mrs Dullfeet, that the Trust
Welcomes you as its newest member.
Clark and Betty Dullfeet shake hands.

GIVOLA: And now: Arturo Ui.

Ui steps up to the microphone.

UI: Friends, countrymen!
Chicagoans and Ciceronians! When
A year ago old Dogsborough, God rest
His honest soul, with tearful eyes
Appealed to me to protect Chicago's green-
Goods trade, though moved, I doubted whether
My powers would be able to justify
His smiling confidence. Now Dogsborough
Is dead. He left a will which you're all free
To read. In simple words therein he calls me
His son. And thanks me fervently for all
I've done since I responded to his appeal.
Today the trade in vegetables –
Be they kohlrabi, onions, carrots or what
Have you – is amply protected in Chicago.
Thanks, I make bold to say, to resolute
Action on my part. When another civic
Leader, Ignatius Dullfeet, to my surprise
Approached me with the same request, this time
Concerning Cicero, I consented
To take that city under my protection.
But one condition I stipulated, namely:
The dealers had to want me. I would come
Only pursuant to their free decision
Freely arrived at. Cicero, I told
My men, in no uncertain terms, must not be
Subjected to coercion or constraint.

The city has to elect me in full freedom.
I want no grudging 'Why not?', no teeth-gnashing
'We might as well'. Half-hearted acquiescence
Is poison in my books. What I demand
Is one unanimous and joyful 'Yes'
Succinct and, men of Cicero, expressive.
And since I want this and everything else I want
To be complete, I turn again to you
Men of Chicago, who, because you know
Me better, hold me, I have reason to believe
In true esteem, and ask you: Who is for me?
And just in passing let me add: If anyone's
Not for me he's against me and has only
Himself to blame for anything that happens.
Now you may vote.

GIVOLA: But first a word from Mrs
Dullfeet, the widow, known to all of you, of
A man beloved by all.

BETTY: Dear friends
Your faithful friend and my beloved husband
Ignatius Dullfeet is no longer with us to . . .

GIVOLA: God rest his soul!

BETTY: . . . sustain and help you. I
Advise you all to put your trust in Mr
Ui, as I do now that in these grievous days
I've come to know him better.

GIVOLA: Time to vote!

GIRI: All those in favour of Arturo Ui
Raise your right hands!
Some raise their hands.

A CICERONIAN: Is it permissible to leave?

GIVOLA: Each man
Is free to do exactly as he pleases.
*Hesitantly the Ciceronian goes out. Two bodyguards follow him.
A shot is heard.*

GIRI: All right, friends, Let's have your free decision!
All raise both hands.

GIVOLA: They've finished voting, boss. With deep
   emotion
Teeth chattering for joy, the greengoods dealers
Of Cicero and Chicago thank you
For your benevolent protection.

UI: With
Pride I accept your thanks. Some fifteen years
Ago, when I was only a humble, unemployed
Son of the Bronx; when following the call
Of destiny I sallied forth with only
Seven staunch men to brave the Windy City
I was inspired by an iron will
To create peace in the vegetable trade.
We were a handful then, who humbly but
Fanatically strove for this ideal
Of peace! Today we are a multitude.
Peace in Chicago's vegetable trade
Has ceased to be a dream. Today it is
Unvarnished reality. And to secure
This peace I have put in an order
For more machine-guns, rubber truncheons
Etcetera. For Chicago and Cicero
Are not alone in clamouring for protection.
There are other cities: Washington and Milwaukee!
Detroit! Toledo! Pittsburgh! Cincinnati!
And other towns where vegetables are traded!
Philadelphia! Columbus! Charleston! And New York!
They all demand protection! And no 'Phooey!'
No 'That's not nice!' will stop Arturo Ui!
Amid drums and fanfares the curtain falls.
A sign appears.

Epilogue

Therefore learn how to see and not to gape.
To act instead of talking all day long.
The world was almost won by such an ape!
The nations put him where his kind belong.
But don't rejoice too soon at your escape –
The womb he crawled from still is going strong.

Chronological Table

1. 1929–1932. Germany is hard hit by the world crisis. At the height of the crisis a number of Prussian Junkers try to obtain government loans, for a long time without success. The big industrialists in the Ruhr dream of expansion.

2. By way of winning President Hindenburg's sympathy for their cause, the Junkers make him a present of a landed estate.

3. In the autumn of 1932, Adolf Hitler's party and private army are threatened with bankruptcy and disintegration. To save the situation Hitler tries desperately to have himself appointed Chancellor, but for a long time Hindenburg refuses to see him.

4. In January 1933 Hindenburg appoints Hitler Chancellor in return for a promise to prevent the exposure of the *Osthilfe* (East Aid) scandal, in which Hindenburg himself is implicated.

5. After coming to power legally, Hitler surprises his high patrons by extremely violent measures, but keeps his promises.

6. The gang leader quickly transforms himself into a statesman. He is believed to have taken lessons in declamation and bearing from one, Basil, a provincial actor.

7. February 1933, the Reichstag fire. Hitler accuses his enemies of instigating the fire and gives the signal for the Night of the Long Knives.

8. The Supreme Court in Leipzig condemns an unemployed worker to death for causing the fire. The real incendiaries get off scot-free.

9. and 10. The impending death of the aged Hindenburg provokes bitter struggles in the Nazi camp. The Junkers

and industrialists demand Röhm's removal. The occupation of Austria is planned.

11. On the night of 30 June 1934 Hitler overpowers his friend Röhm at an inn where Röhm has been waiting for him. Up to the last moment Röhm thinks that Hitler is coming to arrange for a joint strike against Hindenburg and Göring.

12. Under compulsion the Austrian Chancellor Engelbert Dollfuss agrees to stop the attacks on Hitler that have been appearing in the Austrian press.

13. Dollfuss is murdered at Hitler's instigation, but Hitler goes on negotiating with Austrian rightist circles.

15. On 11 March 1938 Hitler marches into Austria. An election under the Nazi terror results in a 98% vote for Hitler.

The Caucasian Chalk Circle

Collaborator: R. BERLAU

Translators: JAMES AND TANIA STERN, *with* W. H. AUDEN

Characters

Delegates of the Galinsk goat-breeding kolchos: an old peasant, a peasant woman, a young peasant, a very young workman · Members of the Rosa Luxemburg fruit-growing kolchos: an old peasant, a peasant woman, the agronomist, the girl tractor driver; the wounded soldier and other peasants from the kolchos · The expert from the capital · The singer Arkadi Cheidze · His musicians · Georgi Abashvili, the Governor · His wife, Natella · Their son, Michael · Shalva, the adjutant · Arsen Kazbeki, the fat prince · The rider from the capital · Niko Mikadze and Mikha Loladze, doctors · Simon Chachava, a soldier · Grusha Vachnadze, a kitchen-maid · Three architects · Four chambermaids: Assia, Masha, Sulika and Fat Nina · A nurse · A man cook · A woman cook · A stableman · Servants in the governor's palace · The governor's and the fat prince's Ironshirts and soldiers · Beggars and petitioners · The old peasant with the milk · Two elegant ladies · The innkeeper · The servant · A corporal · 'Blockhead', a soldier · A peasant woman and her husband · Three merchants · Lavrenti Vachnadze, Grusha's brother · His wife, Aniko · Their stableman · The peasant woman, for a time Grusha's mother-in-law · Yussup, her son · Brother Anastasius, a monk · Wedding guests · Children · Azdak, the village clerk · Shauva, a policeman · A refugee, the Grand Duke · The doctor · The invalid · The limping man · The blackmailer · Ludovica, the innkeeper's daughter-in-law · A poor old peasant woman · Her brother-in-law Irakli, a bandit · Three farmers · Illo Shaboladze and Sandro Oboladze, lawyers · The very old married couple

THE STRUGGLE FOR THE VALLEY

Among the ruins of a badly shelled Caucasian village the members of two kolchos villages are sitting in a circle, smoking and drinking wine. They consist mainly of women and old men, but there are also a few soldiers among them. With them is an expert of the State Reconstruction Commission from the capital.

A PEASANT WOMAN *left, pointing:* In those hills over there we stopped three Nazi tanks. But the apple orchard had already been destroyed.

AN OLD PEASANT *right:* Our beautiful dairy farm. All in ruins.

A GIRL TRACTOR DRIVER *left:* I set fire to it, Comrade. *Pause.*

THE EXPERT: Now listen to the report: the delegates of the Galinsk goat-breeding kolchos arrived in Nukha. When the Hitler armies were approaching, the kolchos had been ordered by the authorities to move its goat-herds further to the east. The kolchos now considers resettling in this valley. Its delegates have investigated the village and the grounds and found a high degree of destruction. *The delegates on the right nod.* The neighbouring Rosa Luxemburg fruit-growing kolchos—*to the left*—moves that the former grazing land of the Galinsk kolchos, a valley with scanty growth of grass, should be used for the replanting of orchards and vineyards. As an expert of the Reconstruction Commission, I request the two kolchos villages to decide between themselves whether the Galinsk kolchos shall return here or not.

AN OLD MAN *right:* First of all, I want to protest against the restriction of time for discussion. We of the Galinsk kolchos have spent three days and three nights getting here. And now we are allowed a discussion of only half a day.

A WOUNDED SOLDIER *left:* Comrade, we no longer have as many villages and no longer as many working hands and no longer as much time.

THE GIRL TRACTOR DRIVER *left:* All pleasures have to be rationed. Tobacco is rationed, and wine and discussion, too.

THE OLD MAN *right, sighing:* Death to the Fascists! But I will come to the point and explain to you why we want to have our valley back. There are a great many reasons, but I want to begin with one of the simplest. Makinae Abakidze, unpack the goat cheese.

A peasant woman, right, takes from a basket an enormous cheese wrapped in a cloth. Applause and laughter.

Help yourselves, comrades. Start in.

AN OLD PEASANT *left, suspiciously:* Is this meant to influence us, perhaps?

THE OLD MAN *right, amidst laughter:* How could it be meant as an influence, Surab, you valley-thief? Everyone knows that you will take the cheese and the valley, too. *Laughter.* All I expect from you is an honest answer: Do you like the cheese?

THE OLD MAN *left:* The answer is yes.

THE OLD MAN *right:* Oh. *Bitterly.* I might have guessed you know nothing about cheese.

THE OLD MAN *left:* Why not? When I tell you I like it!

THE OLD MAN *right:* Because you can't like it. Because it's not what it was in the old days. And why isn't it? Because our goats don't like the new grass as they used to like the old. Cheese is not cheese because grass is not grass, that's it. Mind you put that in your report.

THE OLD MAN *left:* But your cheese is excellent.

THE OLD MAN *right:* It's not excellent. Barely decent. The new grazing land is no good, whatever the young people may say. I tell you, it's impossible to live there. It doesn't even smell of morning there in the morning.

Several people laugh.

THE EXPERT: Don't mind their laughter. They understand you all the same. Comrades, why does one love one's country? Because the bread tastes better there, the sky is higher, the air smells better, voices sound stronger, the ground is easier to walk on. Isn't that so?

THE OLD MAN *right:* The valley has belonged to us for centuries.

THE SOLDIER *left:* What does that mean—for centuries? Nothing belongs to anyone for centuries. When you were young you didn't even belong to yourself, but to Prince Kazbeki.

THE OLD MAN *right:* According to the law the valley belongs to us.

THE GIRL TRACTOR DRIVER: The laws will have to be re-examined in any case, to see whether they are still valid.

THE OLD MAN *right:* That's obvious. You mean to say it makes no difference what kind of tree stands beside the house where one was born? Or what kind of neighbour one has? Doesn't that make any difference? We want to go back just to have you next door to our kolchos, you valley-thieves. Now you can laugh that one off.

THE OLD MAN *left, laughing:* Then why don't you listen to what your 'neighbour', Kato Vachtang, our agronomist, has to say about the valley?

A PEASANT WOMAN *right:* We haven't said anywhere near all we have to say about our valley. Not all the houses are destroyed. At least the foundation wall of the dairy farm is still standing.

THE EXPERT: You can claim State support—both here and there. You know that.

A PEASANT WOMAN *right:* Comrade Expert, we're not trading now. I can't take your cap and hand you another, and say: 'This one's better.' The other one might be better, but you prefer yours.

THE GIRL TRACTOR DRIVER: A piece of land is not like a cap. Not in our country, comrade.

THE EXPERT: Don't get angry. It's true that we have to consider a piece of land as a tool with which one produces something useful. But it's also true that we must recognize the love for a particular piece of land. Before we continue the discussion I suggest that you explain to the comrades

222 The Caucasian Chalk Circle

of the Galinsk kolchos just what you intend to do with the disputed valley.

THE OLD MAN *right:* Agreed.

THE OLD MAN *left:* Yes, let Kato speak.

THE EXPERT: Comrade Agronomist!

THE AGRONOMIST *rising. She is in military uniform:* Last winter, comrades, while we were fighting here in these hills as partisans, we discussed how after the expulsion of the Germans we could increase our orchards to ten times their former size. I have prepared a plan for an irrigation project. With the help of a dam on our mountain lake, three hundred hectares of unfertile land can be irrigated. Our kolchos could then grow not only more fruit, but wine as well. The project, however, would pay only if the disputed valley of the Galinsk kolchos could also be included. Here are the calculations. *She hands the expert a briefcase.*

THE OLD MAN *right:* Write into the report that our kolchos plans to start a new stud farm.

THE GIRL TRACTOR DRIVER: Comrades, the project was conceived during the days and nights when we had to take cover in the mountains and often were without ammunition for our few rifles. Even to get a pencil was difficult.

Applause from both sides.

THE OLD MAN *right:* Our thanks to the comrades of the Rosa Luxemburg kolchos and to all those who defended our country.

They shake hands and embrace.

THE PEASANT WOMAN *left:* Our thoughts were that our soldiers—both your men and our men—should return to a still more fertile homeland.

THE GIRL TRACTOR DRIVER: As the poet Mayakovsky said: 'The home of the Soviet people shall also be the home of Reason!'

The delegates on the right (except the old man) have risen and, with the expert, study the agronomist's plans. Exclamations such as: 'Why is there a fall of 66 feet?'—'This rock here is to be dynamited!'—'Actually, all they need is cement and dynamite!'— 'They force the water to come down here, that's clever!'

A VERY YOUNG WORKMAN *right, to the old man, right:* They are going to irrigate all the fields between the hills—look at that, Alleko.

THE OLD MAN *right:* I am not going to look at it. I knew the project would be good. I won't have a revolver pointed at my chest.

THE SOLDIER: But they are only pointing a pencil at your chest.

Laughter.

THE OLD MAN *right. He gets up gloomily and walks over to look at the drawings:* These valley-thieves know only too well that we can't resist machines and projects in this country.

THE PEASANT WOMAN *right:* Alleko Bereshvili, you yourself are the worst one at new projects. That is well known.

THE EXPERT: What about my report? May I write that in your kolchos you will support the transfer of your old valley for the project?

THE PEASANT WOMAN *right:* I will support it. What about you, Alleko?

THE OLD MAN *right, bent over the drawings:* I move that you give us copies of the drawings to take along.

THE PEASANT WOMAN *right:* Then we can sit down to eat. Once he has the drawings and is ready to discuss them, the affair is settled. I know him. And it will be the same with the rest of us.

The delegates embrace again amidst laughter.

THE OLD MAN *left:* Long live the Galinsk kolchos and good luck to your new stud farm!

THE PEASANT WOMAN *left:* Comrades, in honour of the visit of the delegates from the Galinsk kolchos and of the expert we have arranged a play featuring the singer Arkadi Cheidze, which has some bearing on our problem.

Applause.

The girl tractor driver has gone off to fetch the singer.

THE PEASANT WOMAN *right:* Comrades, your play will have to be good. We're going to pay for it with a valley.

THE PEASANT WOMAN *left:* Arkadi Cheidze knows 21,000 verses by heart.

THE OLD MAN *left:* We rehearsed the play under his direction. It is very difficult to get him, by the way. You and the Planning Commission should see to it that he comes north more often, comrade.

THE EXPERT: We are more concerned with economy.

THE OLD MAN *left, smiling:* You arrange the new distribution of grapevines and tractors. Why not of songs, too?

Enter the singer Arkadi Cheidze, led by the girl tractor driver. He is a sturdy man of simple manners, accompanied by musicians with their instruments. The artistes are greeted with applause.

THE GIRL TRACTOR DRIVER: This is the comrade expert, Arkadi.

The singer greets those round him.

THE PEASANT WOMAN *right:* I am very honoured to make your acquaintance. I've heard about your songs ever since I was at school.

THE SINGER: This time it's a play with songs, and almost the whole kolchos takes part. We have brought along the old masks.

THE OLD MAN *right:* Is it going to be one of the old legends?

THE SINGER: A very old one. It is called 'The Chalk Circle' and is derived from the Chinese. But we will recite it in a changed version. Yura, show the masks. Comrades, we consider it an honour to entertain you after such a difficult debate. We hope you will find that the voice of the old poet also sounds well in the shadow of Soviet tractors. It may be mistaken to mix different wines, but old and new wisdom mix very well. Now I hope we will all be given something to eat before the recital begins. That usually helps.

VOICES: Of course.—Everyone into the club house.

All go cheerfully to the meal. While they begin to move off, the expert turns to the singer.

THE EXPERT: How long will the story take, Arkadi? I have to get back to Tiflis tonight.

THE SINGER *casually:* It is actually two stories. A few hours.

THE EXPERT *very confidentially:* Couldn't you make it shorter?

THE SINGER: No.

2

THE NOBLE CHILD

THE SINGER, *who is seen sitting on the floor in front of his musicians, a black sheepskin cloak round his shoulders, leafing through a small, well-thumbed script:*

> Once upon a time
> A time of bloodshed
> When this city was called
> The city of the damned
> It had a Governor.
> His name was Georgi Abashvili
> Once upon a time.
>
> He was very rich
> He had a beautiful wife
> He had a healthy child
> Once upon a time.
>
> No other governor in Grusinia
> Had as many horses in his stable
> As many beggars on his doorstep
> As many soldiers in his service
> As many petitioners in his courtyard
> Once upon a time.
>
> Georgi Abashvili, how shall I describe him?
> He enjoyed his life:
> On Easter Sunday morning
> The Governor and his family went to church
> Once upon a time.

Beggars and petitioners stream from a palace gateway, holding up thin children, crutches, and petitions. They are followed by two Ironshirts and then by the Governor's family, elaborately dressed.

THE BEGGARS AND PETITIONERS: Mercy, Your Grace, the taxes are beyond our means ... I lost my leg in the

Persian War, where can I get ... My brother is innocent, Your Grace, a misunderstanding ... My child is starving in my arms ... We plead for our son's discharge from the army, our one remaining son ... Please, Your Grace, the water inspector is corrupt.

A servant collects the petitions, another distributes coins from a purse. Soldiers push back the crowd, lashing at it with thick leather whips.

SOLDIER: Get back! Make way at the church door!

Behind the Governor, his wife and his Adjutant, the Governor's child is driven through the gateway in an ornate pram. The crowd surges forward to see it.

THE SINGER *while the crowd is driven back with whips:*

> For the first time on this Easter Sunday, the people see the heir.
> Two doctors never leave the child, the noble child
> Apple of the Governor's eye.

Cries from the crowd: 'The child!' ... 'I can't see it, stop pushing!' ... 'God bless the child, Your Grace!'

THE SINGER:

> Even the mighty Prince Kazbeki
> Bows before it at the church door.

A fat prince steps forward and bows before the family.

THE FAT PRINCE: Happy Easter, Natella Abashvili!

A command is heard. A rider arrives at the gallop and holds out to the Governor a roll of documents. At a nod from the Governor the Adjutant, a handsome young man, approaches the rider and stops him. There follows a brief pause during which the fat prince eyes the rider suspiciously.

THE FAT PRINCE: What a magnificent day! While it was raining in the night I thought to myself: gloomy holidays. But this morning: a gay sky. I love a bright sky, a simple heart, Natella Abashvili. And little Michael, a governor from head to foot, tititi! *He tickles the child.* Happy Easter, little Michael, tititi!

THE GOVERNOR'S WIFE: What do you think of this, Arsen? Georgi has finally decided to start building the new wing on the east side. All these miserable slum houses are to be torn down to make room for a garden.

THE FAT PRINCE: That's good news after so much bad. What's the latest about the war, Brother Georgi? *The Governor shows his lack of interest.* A strategic retreat, I hear? Well, minor reverses invariably occur. Sometimes things go well, sometimes not so well. Such are the fortunes of war. Doesn't mean much, eh?

THE GOVERNOR'S WIFE: He's coughing! Georgi, did you hear?

Sharply to the two doctors, dignified men, who stand close to the pram: He's coughing!

FIRST DOCTOR *to the second:* May I remind you, Niko Mikadze, that I was against the lukewarm bath? A minor oversight in warming the bath water, Your Grace.

SECOND DOCTOR *equally polite:* I can't possibly agree with you, Mikha Loladze. The temperature of the bath water was the one prescribed by our great and beloved Mishiko Oboladze. More likely a slight draught in the night, Your Grace.

THE GOVERNOR'S WIFE: But do take better care of him. He looks feverish, Georgi.

FIRST DOCTOR *bending over the child:* No cause for alarm, Your Grace. The bath water will be warmer. It won't happen again.

SECOND DOCTOR *with a poisonous glance at the first:* I won't forget it, dear Mikha Loladze. No cause for alarm, Your Grace.

THE FAT PRINCE: Well, well, well! I always say: one pain in my liver and the doctor gets fifty strokes on the soles of his feet. And that's only because we live in such a decadent age. In the old days it would have been: Off with his head!

THE GOVERNOR'S WIFE: Let's go into the church. Very likely it's the draught here.

The procession, consisting of the family and servants, turns into the church doorway. The fat prince follows. The Adjutant leaves the procession and points at the rider.

THE GOVERNOR: Not before divine service, Shalva.

ADJUTANT *to the rider*: The Governor doesn't want to be bothered with reports before the service—especially if they are, as I suspect, of a depressing nature. Go and get yourself something to eat in the kitchen, my friend.

The Adjutant joins the procession while the rider enters the palace gateway, cursing. A soldier appears from the palace and remains standing in the gateway.

THE SINGER

The city lies still.

On the church square the pigeons preen themselves.

A soldier of the palace guard

Is jesting with the kitchen maid

As she comes up from the river with a bundle.

A girl tries to pass through the gateway, a bundle of large green leaves under her arm.

THE SOLDIER: What! The young lady is not in church? Shirking service?

GRUSHA: I was already dressed to go. But they wanted one more goose for the Easter banquet. And they asked me to fetch it. I know something about geese.

THE SOLDIER: A goose? *Feigning suspicion.* I'd like to see that goose.

Grusha doesn't understand.

One has to be on one's guard with women. They say: 'I only went to fetch a goose', and then it turns out to be something quite different.

GRUSHA *walks resolutely towards him and shows him the goose*: There it is. And if it isn't a fifteen-pound goose, and they haven't stuffed it with corn, I'll eat the feathers.

THE SOLDIER: A queen of a goose. It will be eaten by the Governor himself. So the young lady has been down to the river again?

GRUSHA: Yes, at the poultry farm.

THE SOLDIER: I see! At the poultry farm, down by the river. Not higher up, near those—those willows?

GRUSHA: I go to the willows only to wash linen.

THE SOLDIER *insinuatingly:* Exactly.

GRUSHA: Exactly what?

THE SOLDIER *winking:* Exactly that.

GRUSHA: Why shouldn't I wash my linen near the willows?

THE SOLDIER *with exaggerated laughter:* 'Why shouldn't I wash my linen near the willows!' That's a good one, that is!

GRUSHA: I don't understand the soldier. What's so good about it?

THE SOLDIER *slyly:* If someone knew what someone's told, she'd grow hot, she'd grow cold.

GRUSHA: I don't know what I could know about those willows.

THE SOLDIER: Not even if there were a bush opposite? From which everything could be seen? Everything that happens there when a certain person is washing linen?

GRUSHA: What happens there? Won't the soldier say what he means and have done with it?

THE SOLDIER: Something happens. And perhaps something can be seen.

GRUSHA: Could the soldier mean that—once in a while on a hot day—I put my toes in the water? For otherwise there's nothing.

THE SOLDIER: And more—the toes and more.

GRUSHA: More what? At most the foot.

THE SOLDIER: The foot and a little more. *He laughs heartily.*

GRUSHA *angrily:* Simon Chachava, you ought to be ashamed of yourself! To sit in a bush on a hot day and wait till someone comes along and puts her leg in the river! And most likely with another soldier! *She runs off.*

THE SOLDIER *shouting after her:* Not with another soldier!

As the singer resumes his story the soldier runs after Grusha.

THE SINGER

> The city lies still, but why are there armed men?
> The Governor's palace lies at peace
> But why is it a fortress?

*From the doorway at the left the fat prince enters quickly. He
stands still and looks around. Before the gateway at the right two
Ironshirts are waiting. Noticing them, the prince walks slowly past
them, signs to them, then exits quickly. One Ironshirt exits through
the gateway, the other remains on guard. Muffled voices come from
different sides in the rear: 'To your posts!' The palace is surrounded. Distant church bells. Enter through the doorway the
procession and the Governor's family returning from church.*

THE SINGER

    Then the Governor returned to his palace
    Then the fortress was a trap
    Then the goose was plucked and roasted
    Then the goose was no longer eaten
    Then noon was no longer the hour to eat
    Then noon was the hour to die.

THE GOVERNOR'S WIFE *in passing:* It's quite impossible to
live in this slum. But Georgi, of course, builds only for his
little Michael. Never for me. Michael is everything, everything for Michael!

THE GOVERNOR: Did you hear Brother Kazbeki bid me a
'Happy Easter'? That's all very well, but so far as I know it
didn't rain in Nukha last night. It rained where Brother
Kazbeki was. Where was Brother Kazbeki?

THE ADJUTANT: That will have to be investigated.

THE GOVERNOR: Yes, at once. Tomorrow.

*The procession turns into the gateway. The rider, who has mean-
while returned from the palace, walks towards the Governor.*

THE ADJUTANT: Don't you want to listen to the rider from
the capital, Your Excellency? He arrived this morning with
confidential papers.

THE GOVERNOR *in passing:* Not before the banquet, Shalva!

THE ADJUTANT *to the rider, while the procession disappears into
the palace and only two Ironshirts remain at the gate as palace
guards:* The Governor doesn't wish to be disturbed by military reports before the banquet. The afternoon His Excellency will devote to conferences with prominent architects
who have also been invited to the banquet. Here they are

already. *Enter three men. As the rider goes off, the Adjutant greets the architects.* Gentlemen, His Excellency is awaiting you at the banquet. His entire time will be devoted to you. To the great new plans! Come, let us go!

ONE OF THE ARCHITECTS: We are impressed that his Excellency thinks of building in spite of the disquieting rumours that the war in Persia has taken a turn for the worse.

THE ADJUTANT: All the more reason for building! That's nothing. Persia is far away. The garrison here would let itself be chopped to pieces for its Governor.

Uproar from the palace. Shrill screams of a woman. Orders are shouted. Dumbfounded, the Adjutant moves towards the gateway. An Ironshirt steps out and holds him up at the point of a lance.

What's going on here? Put down that lance, you dog! *To the palace guard, furiously.* Disarm him! Can't you see an attempt is being made on the Governor's life?

The palace guard Ironshirts refuse to obey. Staring coldly, indifferently, at the Adjutant, they watch the proceedings without interest. The Adjutant fights his way into the palace.

ONE OF THE ARCHITECTS: The Princes! Don't you realize that the Princes met last night in the capital? And that they are against the Grand Duke and his governors? Gentlemen, we'd better make ourselves scarce.

They rush off.

THE SINGER

> Oh, blindness of the great! They walk like gods
> Great over bent backs, sure
> Of hired fists, trusting
> In their power which has already lasted so long.
> But long is not forever.
> Oh, Wheel of Fortune! Hope of the people!

From the gateway, enter the Governor with a grey face, manacled, between two soldiers armed to the teeth.

> Walk, Your Highness, walk even now with head up.
> From your Palace the eyes of many foes follow you!
> You no longer need an architect, a carpenter will do.

You will not move into a new palace, but into a little hole
in the ground.
Just look about you once more, you blind man!
The arrested Governor looks about him.
Does all you once possessed still please you? Between the
Easter Mass and the banquet
You are walking to that place from which no one returns.
*The Governor is led away. The palace guard follows. A horn
sounds. Noise behind the gateway.*
When the houses of the great collapse
Many little people are slain.
Those who had no share in the fortunes of the mighty
Often have a share in their misfortunes. The plunging
wain
Drags the sweating beasts with it into the abyss.
Servants come rushing through the gateway in panic.
THE SERVANTS *in confusion:* The hampers!—Take them all
into the third courtyard! Food for five days!—Her Ladyship has fainted! Someone must carry her down. She must
get away.—And what about us? We'll be slaughtered like
chickens, it's the old story.—Jesus and Mary, what's going
to happen? There's already bloodshed in the town, they
say.—Nonsense, the Governor has just been asked politely
to appear at a Princes' meeting. Everything'll be all right. I
have this on the best authority.
The two doctors rush into the courtyard.
FIRST DOCTOR *trying to restrain the other:* Niko Mikadze, it is
your duty as a doctor to attend Natella Abashvili.
SECOND DOCTOR: My duty? It's yours!
FIRST DOCTOR: Niko Mikadze, who is in charge of the child
today? You or me?
SECOND DOCTOR: Do you really think, Mikha Loladze, I'm
going to stay another minute in this cursed house for that
little brat?
*They start fighting. All one hears is: 'You neglect your duty!' and
'Duty be damned!' Then the second doctor knocks down the first.*
SECOND DOCTOR: Oh, go to hell! *Exit.*

THE SERVANTS: There's time enough before night. The soldiers won't be drunk till then.—Does anyone know if they've started a mutiny yet?—The Palace Guard has ridden away.—Doesn't anyone know what's happened?

GRUSHA: Meliva the fisherman says a comet with a red tail has been seen in the sky over the capital. That means bad luck.

THE SERVANTS: Yesterday they were saying in the capital that the Persian War is lost.—The Princes have started a great revolt. There's a rumour that the Grand Duke has already fled. All his Governors are to be hanged.—The likes of us will be left alone. I have a brother in the Iron-shirts.

Enter the soldier Simon Chachava, searching the crowd for Grusha.

THE ADJUTANT *appearing in the doorway:* Everyone into the third courtyard! All hands help with the packing!

He drives the servants out. Simon finally finds Grusha.

SIMON: There you are at last, Grusha! What are you going to do?

GRUSHA: Nothing. If the worst comes to the worst, I've a brother with a farm in the mountains. But what about you?

SIMON: Don't worry about me. *Polite again.* Grusha Vach-nadze, your desire to know my plans fills me with satis-faction. I've been ordered to accompany Madam Natella Abashvili as her guard.

GRUSHA: But hasn't the Palace Guard mutinied?

SIMON *serious:* That they have.

GRUSHA: But isn't it dangerous to accompany the woman?

SIMON: In Tiflis they say: how can stabbing harm the knife?

GRUSHA: You're not a knife. You're a man, Simon Chachava. What has this woman to do with you?

SIMON: The woman has nothing to do with me. But I have my orders, and so I go.

GRUSHA: The soldier is a pig-headed man; he gets himself into danger for nothing—nothing at all. *As she is called from the palace:* Now I must go into the third courtyard. I'm in a hurry.

SIMON: As there's a hurry we oughtn't to quarrel. For a good quarrel one needs time. May I ask if the young lady still has parents?

GRUSHA: No, only a brother.

SIMON: As time is short—the second question would be: Is the young lady as healthy as a fish in water?

GRUSHA: Perhaps once in a while a pain in the right shoulder; but otherwise strong enough for any work. So far no one has complained.

SIMON: Everyone knows that. Even if it's Easter Sunday and there's the question who shall fetch the goose, then it's she. The third question is this: Is the young lady impatient? Does she want cherries in winter?

GRUSHA: Impatient, no. But if a man goes to war without any reason, and no message comes, that's bad.

SIMON: A message will come. *Grusha is again called from the palace.* And finally the main question . . .

GRUSHA: Simon Chachava, because I've got to go to the third courtyard and I'm in a hurry, the answer is 'Yes'.

SIMON *very embarrassed:* Hurry, they say, is the wind that blows down the scaffolding. But they also say: The rich don't know what hurry is.—I come from . . .

GRUSHA: Kutsk.

SIMON: So the young lady has already made inquiries? Am healthy, have no dependents, earn ten piastres a month, as a paymaster twenty, and am asking honourably for your hand.

GRUSHA: Simon Chachava, that suits me.

SIMON *taking from his neck a thin chain from which hangs a little cross:* This cross belonged to my mother, Grusha Vachnadze. The chain is silver. Please wear it.

GRUSHA: I thank you, Simon. *He fastens it round her neck.*

SIMON: Now I must harness the horses. The young lady will understand that. It would be better for the young lady to go into the third courtyard. Otherwise there'll be trouble.

GRUSHA: Yes, Simon.

They stand together undecided.

SIMON: I'll just take the woman to the troops who've remained loyal. When the war's over, I'll come back. In two weeks. Or three. I hope my intended won't get tired waiting for my return.

GRUSHA: Simon Chachava, I shall wait for you.

> Go calmly into battle, soldier
> The bloody battle, the bitter battle
> From which not everyone returns.
> When you return I will be there.
> I will be waiting for you under the green elm
> I will be waiting for you under the bare elm
> I will wait until the last soldier has returned
> And even longer.
> When you return from the battle
> No boots will lie before the door
> The pillow beside mine will be empty
> My mouth will be unkissed.
> When you return, when you return
> You will be able to say: all is as it was.

SIMON: I thank you, Grusha Vachnadze, and farewell!
He bows low before her; she bows low before him. Then she runs off without looking round. Enter the Adjutant from the gateway.

THE ADJUTANT *harshly:* Harness the horses to the big carriage! Don't stand there doing nothing, idiot!
Simon Chachava leaps to attention and goes off. Two servants crawl in from the gateway, loaded down with heavy trunks. Behind them, supported by her women, stumbles Natella Abashvili. She is followed by another woman carrying Michael.

THE GOVERNOR'S WIFE: As usual, nobody's paying the slightest attention. I hardly know if I'm standing on my head or my feet. Where's Michael? Don't hold him so clumsily! Pile the trunks on to the carriage! Shalva, is there any word from the Governor?

THE ADJUTANT *shaking his head:* You must get away at once.

THE GOVERNOR'S WIFE: Is there any news from the town?

THE ADJUTANT: No. So far all is quiet. But there isn't a minute to lose. There's not enough room for the trunks on the carriage. Please pick out what you need.
Exit the Adjutant quickly.

THE GOVERNOR'S WIFE: Only essentials! Quick, open the trunks. I'll tell you what I've got to have.
The trunks are lowered and opened.

THE GOVERNOR'S WIFE *pointing at some brocade dresses:* That green one! And of course that one with the fur trimming. Where are the doctors? I'm getting this terrible migraine again. It always starts in the temples. This one with the little pearl buttons . . . *Enter Grusha.* You're taking your time, eh? Go and get the hot water bottles at once!
Grusha runs off, and returns with hot water bottles. The Governor's wife orders her about by signs.

THE GOVERNOR'S WIFE *watching a young woman attendant:* Don't tear the sleeve!

THE YOUNG WOMAN: I promise you, madam, no harm has come to the dress.

THE GOVERNOR'S WIFE: Because I caught you. I've been watching you for a long time. Nothing in your head but making eyes at the Adjutant. I'll kill you, you bitch! *She beats her.*

THE ADJUTANT *returning:* I must ask you to make haste, Natella Abashvili. They are fighting in the town. *Exit the Adjutant.*

THE GOVERNOR'S WIFE *letting go of the young woman:* My God, do you think they'll do something to me? Why should they? *All are silent. She herself begins to rummage in the trunks.* Where's my brocade jacket? Help me! What about Michael? Is he asleep?

THE NURSE: Yes, madam.

THE GOVERNOR'S WIFE: Then put him down a moment and go and fetch my little morocco slippers from the bedchamber. I need them to go with the green dress. *The nurse puts down the child and goes off. To the young woman:* Don't

stand around, you! *The young woman runs off.* Stay here, or
I'll have you flogged! Just look at the way these things
have been packed! No love! No understanding! If one
doesn't give every order oneself ... At such moments one
realizes what one's servants are like! Masha! *She gives her an
order with a wave of the hand.* You all gorge yourselves, but
never a sign of gratitude! I won't forget this.

THE ADJUTANT *very excited:* Natella, you must leave at once!
Orbeliani, Judge of the Supreme Court, has just been
hanged! The carpet weavers are in revolt!

THE GOVERNOR'S WIFE: Why? I must have the silver dress
—it cost 1000 piastres. And that one there, and all my furs.
And where's the wine-coloured dress?

THE ADJUTANT *trying to pull her away:* Riots have broken out
in the outer town! We've got to leave this minute! *A
servant runs off.* Where's the child?

THE GOVERNOR'S WIFE *to the nurse:* Maro, get the child
ready! Where are you?

THE ADJUTANT *leaving:* We'll probably have to do without
the carriage. And ride.
*The Governor's wife still rummages among her dresses, throws
some on to the heap to go with her, then takes them off again. Drums
are heard. The sky begins to redden.*

THE GOVERNOR'S WIFE *rummaging desperately:* I can't find
that wine-coloured dress. *Shrugging her shoulders, to the second
woman:* Take the whole heap and carry it to the carriage.
Why hasn't Maro come back? Have you all gone off your
heads? I told you it's right at the bottom.

THE ADJUTANT *returning:* Quick! Quick!

THE GOVERNOR'S WIFE *to the second woman:* Run! Just throw
them into the carriage!

THE ADJUTANT: We're not going by carriage. Come at once
or I'll ride off on my own!

THE GOVERNOR'S WIFE: Maro! Bring the child! *To the
second woman:* Go and look, Masha. No, first take the dresses
to the carriage. It's all nonsense, I wouldn't dream of
riding! *Turning round, she sees the fire-reddened sky and starts*

back in horror. Fire! *She rushes off, followed by the Adjutant. The second woman, shaking her head, follows with a heap of dresses. Servants enter from the gateway.*

THE COOK: That must be the East Gate that's burning.

THE CHEF: They've gone. And without the food wagon. How are we going to get away now?

A STABLEMAN: This is going to be an unhealthy place for some time. *To the third chambermaid:* Suleika, I'm going to fetch some blankets, we're clearing out.

THE NURSE *entering through the gateway with her mistress's slippers:* Madam!

A FAT WOMAN: She's gone.

THE NURSE: And the child. *She rushes to the child, and picks it up.* They left it behind, those brutes! *She hands the child to Grusha.* Hold it for a moment. *Deceitfully.* I'm going to look for the carriage.

She runs off, following the Governor's wife.

GRUSHA: What have they done to the Governor?

THE STABLEMAN *drawing his index finger across his throat:* Fft.

THE FAT WOMAN *seeing the gesture, becomes hysterical:* Oh God! Oh God! Oh God! Our master Georgi Abashvili! At morning Mass he was a picture of health! And now! Oh, take me away! We're all lost! We must die in sin! Like our master, Georgi Abashvili!

THE THIRD WOMAN *trying to calm her:* Calm down, Nina. You'll get away. You've done no one any harm.

THE FAT WOMAN *being led out:* Oh God! Oh God! Oh God! Let's all get out before they come! Before they come!

THE THIRD WOMAN: Nina takes it to heart more than the mistress. People like that get others even to do their weeping for them! *Seeing the child in Grusha's arms.* The child! What are you doing with it?

GRUSHA: It's been left behind.

THE THIRD WOMAN: She just left it? Michael, who was never allowed to be in a draught!

The servants gather round the child.

GRUSHA: He's waking up.

THE STABLEMAN: Better put him down, I tell you. I'd rather not think what'd happen to the person seen with that child. I'll get our things. You wait here. *Exit into the palace.*

THE COOK: He's right. Once they start they slaughter whole families. I'll go and fetch my belongings.

All go except the cook, the third woman and Grusha with the child in her arms.

THE THIRD WOMAN: Didn't you hear? Better put him down!

GRUSHA: The nurse asked me to hold him for a moment.

THE COOK: That one won't come back, you silly!

THE THIRD WOMAN: Keep your hands off him.

THE COOK: They'll be more after him than after his mother. He's the heir. Grusha, you're a good soul. But you know you're not too bright. I tell you, if he had the plague it couldn't be worse. Better see to it that you get away.

The stableman has come back carrying bundles which he distributes among the women. All except Grusha prepare to leave.

GRUSHA *stubbornly:* He hasn't got the plague. He looks at you like a human being.

THE COOK: Then don't you look back. You're just the kind of fool who always gets put upon. If someone says to you: Run and get the lettuce, you have the longest legs!—you run. We're taking the ox-cart, you can have a lift if you hurry. Jesus, by now the whole neighbourhood must be in flames!

THE THIRD WOMAN: Haven't you packed anything yet? There isn't much time, you know. The Ironshirts will soon be here from the barracks.

Exit both women and the stableman.

GRUSHA: I'm coming.

Grusha lays the child down, looks at it for a moment, then takes clothes from the trunks lying about and covers the sleeping child. Then she runs into the palace to get her things. Sounds of horses' hoofs and of women screaming. Enter the fat prince with drunken Ironshirts. One of them carries the head of the Governor on a lance.

THE FAT PRINCE: Put it here. Right in the middle! *One Ironshirt climbs on to the back of another, takes the head and holds it over the gateway.* That's not the middle. Further to the right. Good. What I do, my friends, I do well. *While an Ironshirt with hammer and nail fastens the head by its hair:* This morning at the church door I said to Georgi Abashvili: 'I love a clear sky'. Actually, what I prefer is lightning from a clear sky. Oh, yes. But it's a pity they took the brat away. I need him. Badly. Search the whole of Grusinia for him! 1000 piastres reward!

As Grusha enters cautiously through the doorway, the fat prince and the Ironshirts leave. Trampling of horses' hoofs again. Carrying a bundle, Grusha walks towards the gateway. At the last moment, she turns to see if the child is still there. Promptly the singer begins to sing. She stands rooted to the spot.

THE SINGER

As she was standing between courtyard and gate, she heard
Or thought she heard, a low voice. The child
Called to her, not whining but calling quite sensibly
At least so it seemed to her: 'Woman', it said, 'Help me'.
Went on calling not whining but calling quite sensibly:
'Don't you know, woman, that she who does not listen to a cry for help
But passes by shutting her ears, will never hear
The gentle call of a lover
Nor the blackbird at dawn, nor the happy
Sigh of the exhausted grape-picker at the sound of the Angelus.'
Hearing this

Grusha walks a few steps towards the child and bends over it.

she went back to the child
Just for one more look, just to sit with it
For a moment or two till someone should come
Its mother, perhaps, or someone else—

She sits down opposite the child, and leans against a trunk.

Just for a moment before she left, for now the danger was too great
The city full of flame and grief.

The light grows dimmer as though evening and night were falling, Grusha has gone into the palace and fetched a lamp and some milk, which she gives the child to drink.

THE SINGER *loudly:*

Terrible is the temptation to do good!

Grusha now settles down to keep watch over the child through the night. Once, she lights a small lamp to look at it. Once, she tucks it in with a brocade coat. Now and again she listens and looks up to see if someone is coming.

For a long time she sat with the child.
Evening came, night came, dawn came.
Too long she sat, too long she watched
The soft breathing, the little fists
Till towards morning the temptation grew too strong.
She rose, she leaned over, she sighed, she lifted the child
She carried it off.

She does what the singer says as he describes it.

Like booty she took it for herself
Like a thief she sneaked away.

3

THE FLIGHT INTO THE NORTHERN MOUNTAINS

THE SINGER

As Grusha Vachnadze left the city
On the Grusinian highway
Towards the northern mountains
She sang a song, she bought some milk.

THE MUSICIANS

How will the merciful escape the merciless
The bloodhounds, the trappers?
Into the deserted mountains she wandered
Along the Grusinian highway she wandered
She sang a song, she bought some milk.

Grusha Vachnadze continues on her way. On her back she carries the child in a sack, in one hand a bundle, in the other a big stick.

GRUSHA *singing:*

Four generals set off for Iran
Four generals but not one man.
The first did not strike a blow
The second did not beat the foe
For the third the weather was not right
For the fourth the soldiers would not fight.
Four generals went forth to attack
Four generals turned back.

Sosso Robakidse marched to Iran
Sosso Robakidse was a man.
He struck a sturdy blow
He certainly beat the foe
For him the weather was good enough
For him the soldiers fought with love
Sosso Robakidse marched to Iran
Sosso Robakidse is our man.

A peasant's cottage appears.

GRUSHA *to the child:* Noontime, eating time. Now we'll sit here quietly in the grass, while the good Grusha goes and buys a little jug of milk. *She lays the child down and knocks at the cottage door. An old peasant opens it.* Grandpa, could I have a little mug of milk? And perhaps a corn cake?

THE OLD MAN: Milk? We haven't any milk. The soldiers from the city took our goats. If you want milk, go to the soldiers.

GRUSHA: But Grandpa, you surely have a jug of milk for a child?

THE OLD MAN: And for a 'God Bless You', eh?

GRUSHA: Who said anything about a 'God Bless You'? *She pulls out her purse.* We're going to pay like princes. Head in the clouds, bottom in the water! *The peasant goes off grumbling to fetch milk.* And how much is this jug?

THE OLD MAN: Three piastres. Milk has gone up.

GRUSHA: Three piastres for that drop? *Without a word the old man slams the door in her face.* Michael, did you hear that?

Three piastres! We can't afford that. *She goes back, sits down again and gives the child her breast.* Well, we must try again like this. Suck. Think of the three piastres. There's nothing there, but you think you're drinking, and that's something. *Shaking her head, she realizes the child has stopped sucking. She gets up, walks back to the door, and knocks again.* Open, Grandpa, we'll pay. *Under her breath:* May God strike you! *When the old man appears again:* I thought it would be half a piastre. But the child must have something. What about one piastre?

THE OLD MAN: Two.

GRUSHA: Don't slam the door again. *She rummages a long time in her purse.* Here are two piastres. But this milk has got to last. We still have a long journey ahead of us. These are cut-throat prices. It's a sin.

THE OLD MAN: If you want milk, kill the soldiers.

GRUSHA *letting the child drink:* That's an expensive joke. Drink, Michael. This is half a week's pay. The people here think we've earned our money sitting on our bottom. Michael, Michael, I certainly took on a nice burden with you! *Looking at the brocade coat in which the child is wrapped:* A brocade coat worth 1000 piastres, and not one piastre for milk. *She glances round.* Look! There's a carriage, with rich ladies. We ought to get on to that.

In front of a caravansary. Grusha dressed in the brocade coat is seen approaching two elegant ladies. She holds the child in her arms.

GRUSHA: Oh, you ladies want to spend the night here, too? It's awful how crowded it is everywhere! And not a carriage to be found! My coachman simply turned back. I've been walking half a mile on foot. Barefoot, too! My Persian shoes—you know those heels! But why doesn't someone come?

THE ELDER LADY: That innkeeper certainly takes his time. The whole country has lost its manners since those goings-on started in the capital.

The innkeeper appears, a very dignified old man with a long beard, followed by his servant.

THE INNKEEPER: Excuse an old man for keeping you waiting, ladies. My little grandchild was showing me a peach tree in blossom. There on the slope, beyond the cornfields. We're planting fruit trees there, a few cherries. Further west—*pointing*—the ground gets more stony. That's where the farmers graze their sheep. You ought to see the peach blossom, the pink is exquisite.

THE ELDER LADY: You live in a fertile region.

THE INNKEEPER: God has blessed it. How far on is the fruit-blossom further south, my ladies? I take it you come from the south?

THE YOUNGER LADY: I must admit I haven't been paying much attention to the landscape.

THE INNKEEPER *politely:* Of course, the dust. It is advisable to travel slowly on our high roads. Provided, of course, one isn't in too great a hurry.

THE ELDER LADY: Put your scarf round your throat, dearest. The evening breeze seems rather cool here.

THE INNKEEPER: It comes down from the Janga-Tau glaciers, my ladies.

GRUSHA: Yes, I'm afraid my son may catch cold.

THE ELDER LADY: A very spacious caravansary! Shall we go in?

THE INNKEEPER: Oh, the ladies want rooms? But the caravansary is full up, my ladies. And the servants have run off. I very much regret it, but I cannot accommodate another person, not even with references . . .

THE YOUNGER LADY: But we can't spend the night here on the road.

THE ELDER LADY *drily:* How much?

THE INNKEEPER: My ladies, you will understand that in these times, when so many fugitives, no doubt quite respectable people but not popular with the authorities, are looking for shelter, a house has to be particularly careful. Therefore . . .

THE ELDER LADY: My dear man, we aren't fugitives. We're simply moving to our summer residence in the mountains, that's all. It would never occur to us to ask for hospitality if—we needed it all that urgently.

THE INNKEEPER *nodding his head in agreement:* Of course not. I only doubt if the tiny room at my disposal would suit the ladies. I have to charge 60 piastres per person. Are the ladies together?

GRUSHA: In a way. I'm also in need of shelter.

THE YOUNGER LADY: 60 piastres! That's a cut-throat price.

THE INNKEEPER *coldly:* My ladies, I have no desire to cut throats. That's why . . . *He turns to go.*

THE ELDER LADY: Must we talk about throats? Let's go in. *She enters, followed by the servant.*

THE YOUNGER LADY *desperate:* 180 piastres for one room! *Glancing back at Grusha:* But with the child it's impossible! What if it cries?

THE INNKEEPER: The room costs 180, whether it's two persons or three.

THE YOUNGER LADY *changing her attitude to Grusha:* On the other hand, I couldn't bear to think of you on the road, my dear. Do come in. *They enter the caravansary. From the rear on the opposite side of the stage the servant appears with some luggage. Behind him come the elder lady, the younger lady and Grusha with the child.*

THE YOUNGER LADY: 180 piastres! I haven't been so upset since they brought dear Igor home.

THE ELDER LADY: Must you talk about Igor?

THE YOUNGER LADY: Actually, we are four persons. The child is one too, isn't it? *To Grusha:* Couldn't you pay half at least?

GRUSHA: That's impossible. I had to leave in a hurry, you see. And the Adjutant forgot to slip me enough money.

THE ELDER LADY: Perhaps you haven't even got the 60?

GRUSHA: That much I'll pay.

THE YOUNGER LADY: Where are the beds?

THE SERVANT: There aren't any beds. Here are some sacks and blankets. You'll have to arrange them yourselves. Be glad you're not being put in a hole in the earth. Like lots of others. *Exit.*

THE YOUNGER LADY: Did you hear that? I'm going straight to the innkeeper. That man must be flogged.

THE ELDER LADY: Like your husband?

THE YOUNGER LADY: Don't be so cruel! *She weeps.*

THE ELDER LADY: How are we going to arrange something to sleep on?

GRUSHA: I'll see to that. *She puts down the child.* It's always easier when there are several hands. You still have the carriage. *Sweeping the floor.* I was taken completely by surprise. 'My dear Anastasia Katarinovska,' my husband was saying before luncheon, 'do go and lie down for a while. You know how easily you get your migraine.' *She spreads out sacks and makes beds. The ladies, watching her work, exchange glances.* 'Georgi', said I to the Governor, 'I can't lie down when there are sixty for luncheon. And one can't trust the servants. And Michael Georgivich won't eat without me.' *To Michael*: See, Michael? Everything'll be all right, what did I tell you! *She suddenly realizes that the ladies are watching her strangely and whispering.* Well, there we are! At least one doesn't have to lie on the bare floor. I've folded the blankets double.

THE ELDER LADY *imperiously:* You seem to be rather clever at making beds, my dear. Let's have a look at your hands!

GRUSHA *frightened:* What?

THE YOUNGER LADY: You're being asked to show your hands.

Grusha shows the ladies her hands.

THE YOUNGER LADY *triumphant:* Cracked! A servant!

THE ELDER LADY *goes to the door and shouts:* Service!

THE YOUNGER LADY: You're caught! You swindler! Just confess what mischief you're up to!

GRUSHA *confused:* I'm not up to any mischief. I just thought you might take us a little way in your carriage. Please, I ask you, don't make a noise, I'll go on my own.

THE YOUNGER LADY *while the elder lady continues shouting for service:* Yes, you'll go all right, but with the police. For the moment you'll stay. Don't you dare move, you!

GRUSHA: But I was ready to pay the 60 piastres. Here. *She shows her purse.* Look for yourself. I have them. Here are four tens, and here's a five—no, that's another ten, and ten, makes 60. All I want is to get the child on to the carriage. That's the truth.

THE YOUNGER LADY: Aha, so that's what you want. On to the carriage! Now it's come out.

GRUSHA: Madam, I confess, I am from a humble family. Please don't call the police. The child is of noble birth, look at the linen. It's fleeing, like yourself.

THE YOUNGER LADY: Of noble birth! We know that one. The father's a prince, eh?

GRUSHA *to the elder lady, fiercely:* Stop shouting! Have you no heart at all?

THE YOUNGER LADY *to the elder lady:* Look out! She'll attack you! She's dangerous! Help! Murder!

THE SERVANT *entering:* What's going on here?

THE ELDER LADY: This person here has smuggled herself in by playing the lady. She's probably a thief.

THE YOUNGER LADY: And a dangerous one, too. She wanted to murder us. It's a case for the police. Oh God, I can feel my migraine coming on!

THE SERVANT: There aren't any police at the moment. *To Grusha:* Pack up your things, sister, and make yourself scarce.

GRUSHA *angrily picking up the child:* You monsters! And they're already nailing your heads to the wall!

THE SERVANT *pushing her out:* Shut your trap. Or you'll have the Old Man here. And there's no trifling with him.

THE ELDER LADY *to the younger lady:* Just see if she hasn't stolen something already!

While the ladies, right, look feverishly to see whether something has been stolen, the servant and Grusha go out through the door, left.

THE SERVANT: Look before you leap, I say. Another time have a good look at people before you get mixed up with them.

GRUSHA: I thought they'd be more likely to treat their own kind better.

THE SERVANT: Not them! Believe me, nothing's harder than aping a lazy useless person. Once they suspect you can wipe your own arse, or that your hands have ever touched a broom, the game's up. Just wait a minute, I'll get you a corn cake and a few apples.

GRUSHA: Better not. I must get out before the Old Man comes. And if I walk all night I'll be out of danger, I think. *She walks away.*

THE SERVANT *calling after her in a low voice:* At the next crossroads, turn right.

She disappears.

THE SINGER:

As Grusha Vachnadze wandered northwards
She was followed by the Prince's Ironshirts.

THE MUSICIANS

How will the barefooted girl escape the Ironshirts
The bloodhounds, the trappers?
They are hunting even by night.
Pursuers don't get tired.
Butchers sleep little.

Two Ironshirts are trudging along the highway.

THE CORPORAL: Blockhead, you'll never amount to anything. Why? Because your heart's not in it. Your superior sees it in little things. Yesterday when I laid that fat woman, I admit you collared her husband as I commanded. And you did kick him in the stomach. But did you enjoy it like a good soldier? Or did you just do it from a sense of duty? I've kept my eyes on you, blockhead. You're like a hollow reed or a tinkling cymbal. You'll never get promoted. *They walk awhile in silence.* Don't you get the idea I don't notice how insubordinate you are in every way. I forbid you to limp! You do it simply because I sold the horses, and I

sold them because I'd never have got that price again.
I know you: you limp just to show me you don't like
marching. But that won't help you. It'll go against you.
Sing!

THE TWO IRONSHIRTS *singing:*
> O sadly one morning, one morning in May
> I kissed my darling and rode far away.
> Protect her, dear friends, until home from the wars
> I come riding in triumph, alive on my horse.

THE CORPORAL: Louder!

THE TWO IRONSHIRTS:
> When I lie in my grave and my sword turns to rust
> My darling shall bring me a handful of dust.
> For the feet that so gaily ran up to her door
> And the arms that went round her shall please her no
>   more.

They begin to walk again in silence.

THE CORPORAL: A good soldier has his heart and soul in it.
He lets himself be hacked to pieces by his superiors, and
even while dying he's aware of his Corporal nodding approval. For him that's reward enough. That's all he wants.
But *you* won't get a nod. And you'll croak just the same.
Christ, how am I to lay my hands on the Governor's
bastard with an ass like you!

They trudge on.

THE SINGER
> When Grusha Vachnadze came to the River Sirra
> The flight grew too much for her, the helpless child too
>   heavy.

THE MUSICIANS
> The rosy dawn in the cornfields
> Is nothing but cold to the sleepless.
> The gay clatter of the milk cans in the farmyard
> Where the smoke rises is nothing but a threat to the
>   fugitives.
> She who drags the child feels nothing but its weight.

Grusha stops in front of a farm.

GRUSHA: Now you've wetted yourself again, and you know I've no nappies. Michael, we've got to part. This is far enough from the city. They won't want you so badly, little squit, that they'll follow you all this way. The woman looks kind, and just you smell the milk! So farewell, little Michael. I'll forget how you kicked me in the back all night to make me go faster. And you—you forget the meagre fare. It was meant well. I'd love to have kept you, because your nose is so small, but it can't be done. I'd have shown you your first rabbit and—how not to wet yourself, but I must turn back, because my sweetheart the soldier might soon return, and suppose he didn't find me? You can't ask that of me, Michael.

A fat peasant woman carries a milk can to the door. Grusha waits until she has gone in, then gingerly approaches the house. She tiptoes to the door and lays the child on the threshold. Then, hiding behind a tree, she waits until the peasant woman opens the door and sees the bundle.

THE PEASANT WOMAN: Jesus Christ, what's this? Husband!

THE PEASANT: What's up? Let me have my soup.

THE PEASANT WOMAN *to the child:* Where's your mother? Haven't you got one? It's a boy. And the linen is fine; it's from a good family. And they just leave him on our doorstep. Oh, what times we live in!

THE PEASANT: If they think we're going to feed it, they're mistaken. You take it to the priest in the village. That's all we can do.

THE PEASANT WOMAN: What will the priest do with it? It needs a mother. There, it's waking up. Don't you think we could keep it?

THE PEASANT *shouting:* No!

THE PEASANT WOMAN: I could lay it in the corner, next to the armchair. I only need a crib for it. And I can take it into the fields with me. Look how it's smiling! Husband, we have a roof over our heads and we can do it. I won't hear another word.

She carries the child into the house. The peasant follows, protesting.

Grusha steps out from behind the tree, laughs, and hurries away in the opposite direction.

THE SINGER
Why so gay, you, making for home?

THE MUSICIANS
Because with a smile the child
Has won new parents for himself, that's why I'm gay.
Because I am rid of the loved one
That's why I'm happy.

THE SINGER
And why are you sad?

THE MUSICIANS
I'm sad because I'm single and free
Of the little burden in whom a heart was beating:
Like one robbed, like one impoverished I'm going.
Grusha walks for a short while, then meets the two Ironshirts, who hold her up at the point of a lance.

THE CORPORAL: Young lady, you're running into the Armed Forces. Where are you coming from? When are you coming? Are you entertaining illegal relations with the enemy? Where is he hiding? What sort of movements is he making in your rear? What about the hills? What about the valley? How are your stockings fastened?
Grusha stands there frightened.

GRUSHA: They are strongly fastened; you'd better withdraw.

THE CORPORAL: I always withdraw. In that respect I'm reliable. Why are you staring like that at the lance? In the field a soldier never loses control of his lance. That's an order. Learn it by heart, blockhead. Now then, young lady, where are you off to?

GRUSHA: To my intended, one Simon Chachava, of the Palace Guard in Nukha. Wait till I write to him; he'll break your bones for you.

THE CORPORAL: Simon Chachava? Indeed! I know him. He gave me the key so I could keep an eye on you once in a while. Blockhead, we're getting unpopular. We must make her realize we have honourable intentions. Young lady, my apparent flippancy hides a serious nature. So I'll tell you officially: I want a child from you.

Grusha utters a little scream.

Blockhead, she has understood. Ooh, isn't that a sweet fright! 'But first I must take the bread out of the oven, Officer! But first I must change my torn chemise, Colonel!' But joking apart. Listen, young lady, we are looking for a certain child in these parts. Have you heard of a child from the city, of good family, dressed in fine linen?

GRUSHA: No. I've heard nothing.

THE SINGER

Run, kind heart! The killers are coming!
Help the helpless child, helpless girl! And so she runs.

Suddenly, panic-stricken, she turns round and runs. The Ironshirts glance at each other, then follow her, cursing.

THE MUSICIANS

In the bloodiest times
There are still good people.

As Grusha enters the cottage, the peasant woman is bending over the child's crib.

GRUSHA: Hide it! Quick! The Ironshirts are coming! It was I who laid it on your doorstep. But it isn't mine. It's of a noble family.

THE PEASANT WOMAN: Who's coming? What sort of Iron-shirts?

GRUSHA: Don't ask questions. The Ironshirts who are look-ing for it.

THE PEASANT WOMAN: They've no business in my house. But it seems I must have a word with you.

GRUSHA: Take off the fine linen. That will give us away.

THE PEASANT WOMAN: Oh, you and your linen! In this house *I* decide. And don't you mess up my room. But why did you abandon it? That's a sin.

GRUSHA *looking out of the window:* There, they're coming from behind the trees. I shouldn't have run away. That gave them ideas. What on earth shall I do?

THE PEASANT WOMAN *looking out of the window and suddenly starting with fear:* Jesus and Mary! Ironshirts!

GRUSHA: They're after the child!

THE PEASANT WOMAN: But suppose they come in!

GRUSHA: You mustn't give it to them. Say it's yours.

THE PEASANT WOMAN: Yes.

GRUSHA: They'll run it through if you let them have it.

THE PEASANT WOMAN: But suppose they demand it? The money for the harvest is in the house.

GRUSHA: If you let them have it, they'll run it through, here in your room! You've got to say it's yours.

THE PEASANT WOMAN: Yes, but suppose they don't believe me?

GRUSHA: You must speak firmly.

THE PEASANT WOMAN: They'll burn the roof over our head.

GRUSHA: That's why you've got to say it's yours. His name's Michael. I shouldn't have told you that.

The peasant woman nods.

Don't nod your head like that. And don't tremble; they'll notice.

THE PEASANT WOMAN: Yes.

GRUSHA: Stop saying yes. I can't stand it any longer. *She shakes her.* Haven't *you* got a child?

THE PEASANT WOMAN *muttering:* In the war.

GRUSHA: Then perhaps he's an Ironshirt, too, by now? And what if he ran children through? You'd give him a fine piece of your mind! 'Stop waving that lance in my room! Is that what I've reared you for? Go and wash your neck before you speak to your mother.'

THE PEASANT WOMAN: That's true, I wouldn't let him behave like that.

GRUSHA: Promise me you'll say it's yours.

THE PEASANT WOMAN: Yes

GRUSHA: There! They're coming!

There is a knocking at the door. The women don't answer. Enter the Ironshirts. The peasant woman bows deeply.

THE CORPORAL: Well, there she is. What did I tell you? My nose. I smelled her. Young lady, I have a question to ask you: Why did you run away? What did you think I would do to you? I'll bet it was something lewd. Confess!

GRUSHA *while the peasant woman continues to bow:* I'd left the milk on the stove. Then I suddenly remembered it.

THE CORPORAL: I thought it was because you imagined I'd looked at you in a lewd way—as if I were thinking there could be something between us. A lustful glance, know what I mean?

GRUSHA: I didn't see that.

THE CORPORAL: But it could have been, eh? You must admit that. After all, I could be a swine. I'm quite frank with you: I could think of all sorts of things if we were alone. *To the peasant woman:* Haven't you got something to do in the yard? The chickens to feed?

THE PEASANT WOMAN *falling suddenly to her knees:* Soldier, I didn't known anything about it. Please don't set my house on fire.

THE CORPORAL: What are you talking about?

THE PEASANT WOMAN: I have nothing to do with it. She left it on the doorstep, I swear.

THE CORPORAL *suddenly sees the child and whistles:* Ah, there's a little one in the crib! Blockhead, I smell a thousand piastres. Take the old girl out and hold on to her. It looks as though I'll have to do some cross-examining.

The peasant woman lets herself be led out by the soldier, without a word.

Well, there's the child I wanted to have from you. *He walks towards the crib.*

GRUSHA: Officer, it's mine. It's not the one you're after.

THE CORPORAL: I'll just have a look at it. *He bends over the crib. Grusha looks round in despair.*

GRUSHA: It's mine! It's mine!

THE CORPORAL: Nice linen!

Grusha jumps at him to pull him away. He throws her off and again bends over the crib. Looking round in despair, she suddenly sees a big log of wood, seizes it in panic, and hits the Corporal over the head from behind. She quickly picks up the child and dashes off.

THE SINGER

After her escape from the Ironshirts
After twenty-two days of wandering
At the foot of the Janga-Tau glacier
From this moment Grusha Vachnadze decided to be the
    child's mother.

THE MUSICIANS

The helpless girl
Became the mother of the helpless child.

Grusha squats over a half-frozen stream to ladle some water in her hand for the child.

GRUSHA

Nobody wants to take you
So I shall have to take you
There is no-one else but me, my dear
On this black day in a meagre year
Who will not forsake you.

Since I've carried you too long
And with sore feet
Since the milk was too dear
I grew fond of you.
(I wouldn't be without you any more.)

I'll throw your fine little shirt away
And wrap you in rags
I'll wash you and christen you
With glacier water.
(You'll have to bear it.)

She has taken off the child's fine linen and wrapped it in a rag.

THE SINGER

When Grusha Vachnadze, pursued by the Ironshirts
Came to the narrow footbridge of the Eastern slope
She sang the song of the rotten bridge
And risked two lives.

A wind has risen. The bridge on the glacier is visible in the semi-darkness. One rope is broken, and half the bridge is hanging down the precipice. Merchants, two men and a woman, stand undecided before the bridge as Grusha and the child arrive. One man is trying to retrieve a hanging rope with a stick.

THE FIRST MAN: Take your time, young woman. You won't get over that pass anyway.

GRUSHA: But I simply have to get my child over to the east side. To my brother.

THE MERCHANT WOMAN: Have to? What d'you mean by have to? I have to get there, too—because I have to buy two carpets in Atum—carpets a woman had to sell because her husband had to die. But can I do what I have to; can she? Andrei has been fishing for two hours for that rope. And I ask you, how are we to fasten it, even if he gets it?

THE FIRST MAN *listening:* Shush, I think I hear something.

GRUSHA: The bridge is not quite rotten. I think I'll try and cross it.

THE MERCHANT WOMAN: I wouldn't try that even if the devil himself were after me. It's suicide.

THE FIRST MAN *shouting:* Hi!

GRUSHA: Don't shout! *To the merchant woman.* Tell him not to shout.

THE FIRST MAN: But someone down there's calling. Perhaps they've lost their way.

THE MERCHANT WOMAN: And why shouldn't he shout? Is there something wrong with you? Are they after you?

GRUSHA: Well, I'll have to tell you. Ironshirts are after me. I knocked one down.

THE SECOND MAN: Hide our merchandise!

The woman hides a sack behind a rock.

THE FIRST MAN: Why didn't you tell us that at once? *To the other:* If they catch her they'll make mincemeat out of her!

GRUSHA: Get out of my way. I've got to cross that bridge.

THE SECOND MAN: You can't. There's a precipice of two thousand feet.

THE FIRST MAN: Even if we could get the rope it wouldn't make sense. We could hold it with our hands, but then the Ironshirts could get across in the same way.

GRUSHA: Out of my way.

Shouts from a distance: 'Let's get up there!'

THE MERCHANT WOMAN: They're getting near. But you can't take the child across that bridge. It's sure to break. Just look down!

Grusha looks down the precipice. The Ironshirts are heard shouting below.

THE SECOND MAN: Two thousand feet!

GRUSHA: But those men are worse.

THE FIRST MAN: Anyway you can't do it with the child. Risk your own life if they are after you, but not the child's.

THE SECOND MAN: She's even heavier with the child.

THE MERCHANT WOMAN: Perhaps she's really got to go. Give it to me. I'll hide it and you cross the bridge alone.

GRUSHA: I won't. We belong together. *To the child:* Live together, die together. *She sings:*

> If the gulf is deep
> And the rotten bridge sways
> It is not for us, son
> To choose our ways.
>
> The way that I know
> Is the one for your feet
> The bread that I find
> Is all you will eat.
>
> Of every four morsels
> You shall have three.
> I would that I knew
> How big they will be!

I'll try it.

THE MERCHANT WOMAN: That's tempting God.

Shouts from beneath.

GRUSHA: I beg you, throw that stick away, or they'll get the rope and follow me.
She starts off on to the swinging bridge. The merchant woman screams when the bridge looks like breaking. But Grusha walks on and reaches the far side.

THE FIRST MAN: She's done it!

THE MERCHANT WOMAN *who has fallen on her knees and begun to pray, angrily:* But I still think it was a sin.
The Ironshirts appear, the Corporal's head bandaged.

THE CORPORAL: Have you seen a woman with a child?

THE FIRST MAN *while the second throws away his stick:* Yes, there she is! But the bridge won't carry you!

THE CORPORAL: Blockhead, you'll suffer for this!
Grusha, from the far bank, laughs and shows the child to the Ironshirts. She walks on. The bridge is left behind. Wind.

GRUSHA *to the child:* You mustn't mind the wind. It's only a poor wretch, too. It has to push the clouds, and it feels the cold more than any of us. *Snow starts falling.* And the snow isn't the worst, Michael. It covers the little fir trees, so that they won't die in winter. And now I'll sing you a little song. Listen! *She sings:*

> Your father's a thief
> Your mother's a whore:
> All the nice people
> Will love you therefore.
>
> The son of the tiger
> Brings the foals their feed
> The snake-child milk
> To mothers in need.

4

IN THE NORTHERN MOUNTAINS

THE SINGER
Seven days the sister wandered.
Across the glacier, down the hills she wandered.
'When I enter my brother's house', she thought to herself
'He will rise and embrace me'.
'Is that you, sister?' he will say
'I have been expecting you for so long. This here is my
    dear wife.
And this is my farm, come to me by marriage.
With eleven horses and thirty-one cows. Sit down.
Sit down with your child at our table and eat.'
The brother's house was in a lovely valley.
When the sister came to the brother she was ill from her
    wanderings.
The brother rose from the table.
*A fat peasant couple who have just sat down to a meal. Lavrenti
Vachnadze already has a napkin round his neck, as Grusha, pale
and supported by a stableman, enters with the child.*
LAVRENTI: Where do you come from, Grusha?
GRUSHA *feebly:* I've walked across the Janga-Tau Pass,
Lavrenti.
STABLEMAN: I found her in front of the hay barn. She has a
child with her.
THE SISTER-IN-LAW: Go and groom the roan. *Exit stable-
man.*
LAVRENTI: This is my wife, Aniko.
THE SISTER-IN-LAW: We thought you were in service in
Nukha.
GRUSHA *barely able to stand:* Yes, I was there.
THE SISTER-IN-LAW: Wasn't it a good job? We were told it
was a good one.
GRUSHA: The Governor has been killed.

LAVRENTI: Yes, we heard there were riots. Your aunt told us about it. Remember, Aniko?

THE SISTER-IN-LAW: Here, with us, it's quiet. City people always need some kind of excitement. *She walks towards the door and shouts:* Sosso, Sosso, take the flat cake out of the oven, d'you hear? Where are you? *Exit, shouting.*

LAVRENTI *quietly, quickly:* Has it got a father? *As she shakes her head:* I thought so. We must think up something. She's very pious.

THE SISTER-IN-LAW *returning:* These servants! *To Grusha:* You have a child?

GRUSHA: It's mine. *She collapses. Lavrenti helps her up.*

THE SISTER-IN-LAW: Mary and Joseph, she's ill—what are we to do?
Lavrenti tries to lead Grusha to the bench by the stove. Aniko waves her away in horror and points to the sack by the wall.

LAVRENTI *escorting her to the wall:* Sit down, sit down. I think it's just weakness.

THE SISTER-IN-LAW: As long as it's not scarlet fever.

LAVRENTI: Then she'd have spots. I'm sure it's only weakness. Don't worry, Aniko. *To Grusha:* Do you feel better sitting?

THE SISTER-IN-LAW: Is the child hers?

GRUSHA: It's mine.

LAVRENTI: She's on her way to her husband.

THE SISTER-IN-LAW: Really? Your meat's getting cold. *Lavrenti sits down and begins to eat.* Cold food's not good for you. At least the fat parts mustn't get cold; you know your stomach's your weak spot. *To Grusha:* If your husband's not in town, where is he then?

LAVRENTI: She got married on the other side of the mountain, she says.

THE SISTER-IN-LAW: Oh, on the other side. *She also sits down to eat.*

GRUSHA: I think I'll have to lie down somewhere, Lavrenti.

THE SISTER-IN-LAW *goes on questioning her:* If it's consumption we'll all get it. Has your husband a farm?

GRUSHA: He's a soldier.

LAVRENTI: But he's coming into a farm—a small farm from his father.

THE SISTER-IN-LAW: Isn't he in the war? Why not?

GRUSHA *wearily*: Yes, he's in the war.

THE SISTER-IN-LAW: Then why d'you want to go to the farm?

LAVRENTI: When he comes back from the war, he'll come to his farm.

THE SISTER-IN-LAW: But you're going there now?

LAVRENTI: Yes, to wait for him.

THE SISTER-IN-LAW *shrilly*: Sosso, the cake!

GRUSHA *murmurs in fever*: A farm—a soldier—waiting—sit down—eat.

THE SISTER-IN-LAW: That's scarlet fever.

GRUSHA *starting up*: Yes, he has a farm!

LAVRENTI: I think it must be weakness, Aniko. Wouldn't you like to go and look after the cake yourself, my dear?

THE SISTER-IN-LAW: But when will he come back if the war, as they say, has broken out again? *Waddling away, shouting*: Sosso! Where are you? Sosso!

LAVRENTI *getting up quickly and going to Grusha*: You'll get a bed in a moment. She has a good heart. But only after supper.

GRUSHA *holding out the child to him*: Take it. *He takes it, looking anxiously round.*

LAVRENTI: But you can't stay here long. You must realize she's very pious.

Grusha collapses. Lavrenti takes hold of her.

THE SINGER
> The sister was too ill.
> The cowardly brother had to give her shelter.
> The autumn passed, the winter came.
> The winter was long
> The winter was short.
> The people mustn't know.
> The rats mustn't bite
> The spring mustn't come.

Grusha sits bent at the weaving loom in the scullery. She and the child, who squats on the floor, are wrapped in blankets.

GRUSHA *sings while weaving:*

Then the lover started to leave
Then his girl ran pleading after him
Pleading and crying, crying and pleading:
Dearest mine, dearest mine
As you now go into battle
As you now have to fight the enemy
Don't throw yourself into the front line
And don't push with the rear line.
In front is red fire
In the rear is red smoke.
Stay wisely in between
Keep near the standard bearer.
The first ones always die
The last ones are also hit
Those in the centre come home.

Michael, we must be clever. If we make ourselves really small, like cockroaches, our sister-in-law will forget we're in the house. Then we can stay here till the snow melts. And don't cry because of the cold. Being poor and cold as well puts people off.

Enter Lavrenti. He sits down beside Grusha.

LAVRENTI: Why are you two sitting there muffled up like coachmen? Perhaps it's too cold in the room?

GRUSHA *hastily removing her shawl:* It's not too cold, Lavrenti.

LAVRENTI: If it's too cold, you oughtn't to sit here with the child. Aniko would blame herself. *Pause.* I hope the priest didn't question you about the child.

GRUSHA: He did, but I didn't tell him anything.

LAVRENTI: That's good. I wanted to talk to you about Aniko. She has a good heart—but she's very, very sensitive. People only have to mention our farm and she's worried. She takes everything to heart, you know. Our milkmaid once went to church with a hole in her stocking. Ever since then my dear Aniko has always worn two pairs of stockings to church. It's hard to believe, but it's the old family in her. *He listens.* Are you sure there are no rats here? If so, you couldn't stay here. *Sounds of drops from the roof.* What's that dripping?

GRUSHA: Must be a barrel leaking.

LAVRENTI: Yes, it must be a barrel. Now you've already been here six months, haven't you? Was I talking about Aniko? Of course I didn't mention the Ironshirt. She has a weak heart. That's why she doesn't know you can't look for work. And that's why she made those remarks yesterday. *They listen again to the melting snow.* Can you believe it? She's worrying about your soldier. 'Suppose he comes back and doesn't find her!' she says, and lies awake. 'He can't come before the spring,' I tell her. The dear woman! *The drops begin to fall faster.* When d'you think he'll come? What's your idea? *Grusha is silent.* Not before the spring. That's what you think, too? *Grusha is silent.* I see you no longer believe he'll come back. *Grusha does not answer.* But when spring comes and the snow is melting on the passes you must leave here. Because then they can come and look for you. People are already talking about a child with an unmarried mother.

The beat of the falling drops has grown faster and steadier.

Grusha, the snow is melting on the roof and spring is here.

GRUSHA: Yes.

LAVRENTI *eagerly:* Let me tell you what we'll do. You need a place to go to. And because of the child—*he sighs*—you must have a husband, to stop people talking. I've made cautious inquiries about how we can get a husband for you, Grusha, and I've found one. I talked to a woman who has a son, just over the mountain, a little farm. She's willing.

GRUSHA: But I can't marry another man! I must wait for Simon Chachava.

LAVRENTI: Of course. That's all been considered. You don't need a man in bed, but a man on paper. And that's the very man I've found. The son of the woman I spoke to is dying. Isn't that wonderful? He's just at his last gasp. And everything's as we have said: A man just over the mountain! And when you reached him he died, and so you're a widow. What do you say?

GRUSHA: I could do with a stamped up document for Michael.

LAVRENTI: A stamp makes all the difference. Without a stamp even the Shah of Persia couldn't prove he is the Shah. And you'll have a roof over your head.

GRUSHA: How much does she want for it?

LAVRENTI: 400 piastres.

GRUSHA: Where will you find the money?

LAVRENTI *guiltily:* Aniko's milk money.

GRUSHA: No-one will know us over there. I'll do it.

LAVRENTI *gets up:* I'll tell the woman at once. *Exit quickly.*

GRUSHA: Michael, you cause a lot of trouble. I came by you as the pear tree comes by the sparrows. And because a Christian bends down and picks up a crust of bread so it won't go to waste. Michael, I ought to have walked away quickly on that Easter Sunday in Nukha. Now I'm the fool.

THE SINGER

   The bridegroom was lying on his deathbed, when the bride arrived.
   The bridegroom's mother was waiting at the door, bidding them hurry.
   The bride brought along a child, the witness hid it during the wedding.

A space divided by a partition. On one side a bed. Under the mosquito net lies a very sick man. On the other side the mother-in-law rushes in pulling Grusha after her. They are followed by Lavrenti and the child.

THE MOTHER-IN-LAW: Quick! Quick! Or he'll die on us before the wedding. *To Lavrenti:* But I was never told she already had a child.

LAVRENTI: What's it matter? *Pointing towards the dying man:* It's all the same to him in his condition.

THE MOTHER-IN-LAW: Him? But I won't survive the shame. We're honest people. *She begins to weep.* My Yussup doesn't have to marry someone who already has a child.

LAVRENTI: All right, I'll add another 200 piastres. You have it in writing that the farm will go to you; but she has the right to live here for two years.

THE MOTHER-IN-LAW *drying her tears:* It will hardly cover the funeral expenses. I hope she will really lend me a hand with the work. And now what's happened to the monk? He must have slipped out by the kitchen window. When they get wind in the village that Yussup's end is near, they'll all be round our necks. Oh dear! I'll go and get the monk. But he mustn't see the child.

LAVRENTI: I'll take care he doesn't see it. But why a monk? Why not a priest?

THE MOTHER-IN-LAW: Oh, he's just as good. I made one mistake: I paid him half his fee in advance. Now he'll have gone to the tavern. I hope . . . *She runs off.*

LAVRENTI: She saved on the priest, the wretch! She's hired a cheap monk.

GRUSHA: Send Simon Chachava to me if he turns up.

LAVRENTI: Yes. *Glancing at the sick man:* Won't you have a look at him?
Grusha, taking Michael to her, shakes her head.
He's not moving an eyelid. I hope we aren't too late.
They listen. On the opposite side enter neighbours, who look round and take up positions against the walls. They start muttering prayers. Enter the mother-in-law with the monk.

THE MOTHER-IN-LAW *surprised and angry, to the monk:* Now we're for it! *She bows to the guests.* I must ask you to wait a few moments. My son's bride has just arrived from town and we've got to have an emergency wedding. *She goes with the monk into the bedchamber.* I knew you'd spread it about. *To Grusha:* The wedding can start at once. Here's the licence. I and the bride's brother—*Lavrenti tries to hide in the background, after having quickly taken Michael away from Grusha.*

The mother-in law beckons him away from the child—the bride's brother and I are the witnesses.

Grusha has bowed to the monk. They approach the bed: the mother-in-law lifts the mosquito-net: the monk begins babbling the marriage service in Latin. Meanwhile the mother-in-law beckons to Lavrenti to get rid of the child, but Lavrenti, fearing that the child will cry, draws its attention to the ceremony. Grusha glances once at the child, and Lavrenti makes the child wave to her.

THE MONK: Are you prepared to be a faithful, obedient and good wife to this man? And to cleave to him until death you do part?

GRUSHA *looking at the child:* Yes.

THE MONK *to the dying man:* And are you prepared to be a good and loving husband to your wife until death you do part? *As the dying man does not answer, the monk repeats the question, then looks round.*

THE MOTHER-IN-LAW: Of course he is! Didn't you hear him say yes?

THE MONK: All right. We declare this marriage contracted. Now what about Extreme Unction?

THE MOTHER-IN-LAW: Nothing doing! The wedding was quite expensive enough. I must now take care of the mourners. *To Lavrenti:* Did we say 700?

LAVRENTI: 600. *He pays.* Now I don't want to sit and get acquainted with the guests. So farewell, Grusha. And if my widowed sister comes to visit me one day, she'll get a 'welcome' from my wife. Or I'll get disagreeable.

He leaves. The mourners glance after him without interest.

THE MONK: And may one ask whose this child is?

THE MOTHER-IN-LAW: Is there a child? I don't see any child. And you don't see one either—understand? Or else I've seen all kinds of things happening behind the tavern! Come along now.

They move back to the room. After Grusha has put down the child and told it to be quiet, she is introduced to the neighbours.

This is my daughter-in-law. She arrived just in time to find dear Yussup still alive.

ONE OF THE WOMEN: He's been ill now a whole year, hasn't he? When my Vassili was called up he was there to say goodbye.

ANOTHER WOMAN: Such things are terrible for a farm. With the corn ripe on the stalk and the farmer in bed! It will be a blessing for him if he doesn't suffer much longer, I say.

FIRST WOMAN *confidentially:* At first we thought he took to his bed because of military service, you know. And now his end is coming.

THE MOTHER-IN-LAW: Please sit down and have some cakes. *She beckons to Grusha and both women go into the bedroom, where they pick up trays of cakes from the floor. The guests, among them the monk, sit on the floor and begin conversing in subdued voices.*

A VERY OLD PEASANT *to whom the monk has slipped the bottle he has taken from his cassock:* There's a little one, you say! How can Yussup have managed that?

THIRD WOMAN: Anyway, she was lucky to have brought it off in time, with him so sick.

THE MOTHER-IN-LAW: They are gossiping already. And stuffing themselves with the funeral cakes at the same time. And if he doesn't die today, I'll have to bake fresh ones tomorrow.

GRUSHA: I'll bake them.

THE MOTHER-IN-LAW: When some riders passed by last night, and I went out to see who they were, he was lying there like a corpse! That's why I sent for you. It can't take much longer. *She listens.*

THE MONK: Dear wedding guests and mourners! We stand deeply moved in front of a bed of death and marriage, because the bride gets into bed and the groom into the grave. The groom is already washed, and the bride is already hot. For in the marriage-bed lies the last Will, and that makes people randy. Oh, my children, how varied is the fate of man! The one dies to get a roof over his head, and the other marries so that flesh may be turned to dust, from which it was made. Amen.

THE MOTHER-IN-LAW *who had listened:* He's got his own

back. I shouldn't have hired such a cheap one. That's what you'd expect. An expensive one knows how to behave. In Sura there's one who is even in the odour of sanctity; but of course he charges a fortune. A fifty-piastre priest like this one here has no dignity. And as for piety, he has precisely fifty piastres' worth, and no more. And when I fetched him from the tavern he was just finishing a speech and shouting: 'The war is over, beware of the peace!' We must go in.

GRUSHA *giving Michael a cake:* Eat this cake and be a good boy, Michael. We are respectable now.

The two women carry the trays of cakes to the guests. The dying man is sitting up in bed; he puts his head out from under the mosquito-net and watches the two women. Then he sinks back again. The monk takes two bottles from his cassock and offers them to the peasant beside him. Enter three musicians, to whom the monk waves with a grin.

THE MOTHER-IN-LAW *to the musicians:* What have you got your instruments for?

A MUSICIAN: Brother Anastasius here—*pointing at the monk*—told us there was a wedding going on.

THE MOTHER-IN-LAW: What! You brought them? Three more on my neck! Don't you know there's a dying man next door?

THE MONK: That's a tempting task for an artist. They could play a hushed Wedding March or a gay Funeral Dance.

THE MOTHER-IN-LAW: Well, you might as well play. I can't stop you eating, in any case.

The musicians play a musical medley. The women offer cakes.

THE MONK: The trumpet sounds like a whining baby. And you, little drum, what gossip are you spreading abroad?

A PEASANT *beside the monk:* What about the bride shaking a leg?

THE MONK: Shake the legs or rattle the bones?

THE PEASANT *beside the monk, singing:*

When pretty Miss Plushbottom wed
A rich man with no teeth in his head

They enquired, 'Is it fun?'
She replied, 'No, it's none.
Still, there're candles and soon he'll be dead.'
The mother-in-law throws the drunken man out. The music stops.
The guests are embarrassed. Pause.

THE GUESTS *loudly:* Have you heard the latest? The Grand
Duke's back!—But the Princes are against him.—Oh, the
Shah of Persia, they say, has lent him a great army, to
restore order in Grusinia.—How is this possible? After all,
the Shah of Persia is against the Grand Duke!—But against
disorder, too.—In any case, the war's over. Our soldiers
are already coming back.

Grusha drops the tray of cakes.

AN OLD WOMAN *to Grusha:* Are you feeling ill? That's just
excitement about dear Yussup. Sit down and rest awhile,
my dear.

Grusha stands, swaying.

THE GUESTS: Now everything will be as it was. Only the taxes
will go up because we'll have to pay for the war.

GRUSHA *weakly:* Did someone say the soldiers are back?

A MAN: I did.

GRUSHA: That can't be true.

THE MAN *to a woman:* Show her the shawl. We bought it
from a soldier. It's from Persia.

GRUSHA *looking at the shawl:* They are here.

*A long pause. Grusha kneels as if to pick up the cakes. As she does
so she takes the silver cross and chain out of her blouse, kisses it, and
starts praying.*

THE MOTHER-IN-LAW *while the guests silently watch Grusha:*
What's the matter with you? Won't you look after our
guests? What's all this nonsense from the city got to do
with us?

THE GUESTS *resuming their conversation while Grusha remains with
her forehead bent to the ground:* Persian saddles can be bought
from soldiers, but some exchange them for crutches.—
Only one side's bigwigs can win, but the soldiers on
both sides are the losers.—At least the war's over now.

It's something that they can't call you up any more.—*The dying man sits bolt upright in bed. He listens.*—What we need most are two weeks of good weather.—There's hardly a pear on our trees this year.

THE MOTHER-IN-LAW *offering the cakes:* Have some more cake. And enjoy it. There's more to come.

The mother-in-law goes to the bedroom with empty trays. Unaware of the dying man, she bends down to pick up some more cakes, when he begins to talk in a hoarse voice.

YUSSUP: How many more cakes are you going to stuff down their throats? D'you think I can shit money? *The mother-in-law starts, and stares at him aghast, while he puts his head out from behind the mosquito-net.* Did they say the war was over?

FIRST WOMAN *talking kindly to Grusha in the next room:* Has the young woman someone in the war?

THE MAN: That's good news that they're on their way home, eh?

YUSSUP: Don't stare so! Where's the wife you've foisted on me?

Receiving no answer, he climbs out of bed and in his nightshirt staggers past his mother into the other room. Trembling, she follows him with the cake tray.

THE GUESTS *seeing him and shrieking:* Jesus, Mary and Joseph! Yussup!

Everyone leaps up in alarm. The women rush to the door. Grusha, still on her knees, turns round and stares at the man.

YUSSUP: The funeral supper! That's what you'd like! Get out before I kick you out!

The guests stampede from the house.

YUSSUP *grumpily to Grusha:* That puts a spoke in your wheel, eh?

Receiving no answer, he turns round and takes a cake from the tray which his mother holds.

THE SINGER

Oh, confusion! The wife discovers that she has a husband!

By day there's the child, by night there's the man.

The lover is on his way day and night.
The married couple are looking at each other. The
    chamber is narrow.

*Yussup sits naked in a high wooden bathtub. His mother pours
water from a jug. Next door in the bedroom Grusha squats with
Michael, who is playing at mending a straw mat.*

YUSSUP: That's her business, not yours. Where's she hiding
    now?

THE MOTHER-IN-LAW *calling:* Grusha! The peasant wants
    you!

GRUSHA *to Michael:* There are still two holes to mend.

YUSSUP *as Grusha enters:* Scrub my back!

GRUSHA: Can't the peasant do that himself?

YUSSUP: 'Can't the peasant do that himself?' Get the brush!
    To hell with you! Are you the wife or are you a stranger?
    To the mother-in-law: Too cold!

THE MOTHER-IN-LAW: I'll run and get some more hot
    water.

GRUSHA: Let me do it.

YUSSUP: You stay here. *The mother-in-law goes out.* Rub harder.
    And don't make such a fuss. You've seen a naked man be-
    fore. That child of yours can't have come out of thin air.

GRUSHA: The child was not conceived in joy, if that's what
    the peasant means.

YUSSUP *turning and grinning:* A likely story! *Grusha stops scrub-
    bing him and starts back. Enter the mother-in-law.* This is a
    nice thing you've saddled me with here! A cold-fish for
    a wife!

THE MOTHER-IN-LAW: She isn't willing.

YUSSUP: Pour—but go easy! Ow! Go easy, I said. *To Grusha.*
    I'd be surprised if you hadn't been up to something in the
    city. What else would you be here for? But I won't say
    anything about that. I also haven't said anything about the
    bastard you brought into my house. But my patience with
    you is coming to an end. It's against nature. *To the
    mother-in-law:* More! *To Grusha:* And even if your soldier
    does return, you're married.

GRUSHA: Yes.

YUSSUP: But your soldier won't return now. Don't you believe it.

GRUSHA: No.

YUSSUP: You're cheating me. You're my wife and you're not my wife. Where you lie, nothing lies. And yet no other woman can lie there. When I go to work in the mornings I'm dead-tired. When I lie down at night I'm awake as the devil. God has made you a woman, and what d'you do about it? My fields don't bring me in enough to buy myself a woman in town. Besides, it's a long way. Woman hoes the fields and parts her legs. That's what our almanac says. D'you hear?

GRUSHA: Yes. *Quietly.* I don't like cheating you out of it.

YUSSUP: She doesn't like! Pour some more water. *The mother-in-law pours.* Ow!

THE SINGER

> As she sat by the stream to wash the linen
> She saw his image in the water, and his face grew dimmer
> As the months passed by.
> As she raised herself to wring the linen
> She heard his voice from the murmuring maple, and his voice grew fainter
> As the months passed by.
> Excuses and sighs grew more numerous, tears and sweat flowed faster
> As the months passed by, as the child grew up.

Grusha sits by a stream dipping linen into the water. Some distance away a few children are standing. Grusha is talking to Michael.

GRUSHA: You can play with them, Michael. But don't let them order you about because you're the smallest.

Michael nods and joins the children. They start playing.

THE TALLEST BOY: Today we're going to play Heads-off. *To a fat boy:* You're the Prince and you must laugh. *To Michael:* You're the Governor. *To a girl:* You're the Governor's wife and you cry when his head's chopped off. And I do the chopping. *He shows his wooden sword.* With this. First, the Governor's led into the courtyard. The Prince walks ahead. The Governor's wife comes last.

They form a procession. The fat boy goes ahead, and laughs. Then comes Michael, and the tallest boy, and then the girl, who weeps.

MICHAEL *standing still:* Me too chop head off!

THE TALLEST BOY: That's my job. You're the smallest. The Governor's part is easiest. All you do is kneel down and have your head chopped off. That's simple.

MICHAEL: Me too have sword.

THE TALLEST BOY: That's mine. *He gives him a kick.*

THE GIRL *shouting to Grusha:* He doesn't want to do what he's told.

GRUSHA *laughing:* Even ducklings take to water, they say.

THE TALLEST BOY: You can play the Prince if you know how to laugh.

Michael shakes his head.

THE FAT BOY: I'm the best laugher. Let him chop off the head just once. Then you do it, then me.

Reluctantly the tallest boy hands Michael the wooden sword and kneels. The fat boy sits down, smacks his thigh and laughs with all his might. The girl weeps loudly. Michael swings the big sword and chops off the head. In doing so, he topples over.

THE TALLEST BOY: Hi, I'll show you how to do it properly.

Michael runs away, and the children run after him. Grusha laughs, following them with her eyes. On turning round, she sees Simon Chachava standing on the opposite bank. He wears a shabby uniform.

GRUSHA: Simon!

SIMON: Is that Grusha Vachnadze?

GRUSHA: Simon!

SIMON *politely:* A good morning, and good health to the young lady.

GRUSHA *gets up gaily and bows deeply:* A good morning to the soldier. And thank God he has returned in good health.

SIMON: They found better fish than me, so they didn't eat me, said the haddock.

GRUSHA: Courage, said the kitchen boy. Luck, said the hero.

SIMON: And how are things here? Was the winter bearable? Did the neighbour behave?

GRUSHA: The winter was a little rough, the neighbour as usual, Simon.

SIMON: May one ask if a certain person is still in the habit of putting her leg in the water when washing her linen?

GRUSHA: The answer is no. Because of the eyes in the bushes.

SIMON: The young lady is talking about soldiers. Here stands a paymaster.

GRUSHA: Is that worth twenty piastres?

SIMON: And board.

GRUSHA *with tears in her eyes:* Behind the barracks under the date trees.

SIMON: Just there. I see someone has kept her eyes open.

GRUSHA: Someone has.

SIMON: And has not forgotten. *Grusha shakes her head.* And so the door is still on its hinges, as they say. *Grusha looks at him in silence and shakes her head again.* What's that mean? Is something wrong?

GRUSHA: Simon Chachava, I can never go back to Nukha. Something has happened.

SIMON: What has happened?

GRUSHA: It so happened that I knocked down an Ironshirt.

SIMON: Grusha Vachnadze will have had her reasons for that.

GRUSHA: Simon Chachava, my name is also no longer what it was.

SIMON *after a pause:* I don't understand that.

GRUSHA: When do women change their names, Simon? Let me explain it to you: Nothing stands between us. Everything between us has remained as it was. You've got to believe that.

SIMON: How can nothing stand between us and things be changed?

GRUSHA: How can I explain it to you? So fast and with the stream between us? Couldn't you cross that bridge?

SIMON: Perhaps it's no longer necessary.

GRUSHA: It's most necessary. Come over, Simon. Quick!

SIMON: Is the young lady saying that someone has come too late?

Grusha looks up at him in despair, her face streaming with tears. Simon stares before him. He picks up a piece of wood and starts cutting it.

THE SINGER

So many words are said, so many words are left unsaid.
The soldier has come. Whence he comes he doesn't say.
Hear what he thought but didn't say:
The battle began at dawn, grew bloody at noon.
The first fell before me, the second behind me, the third at my side.
I trod on the first, I abandoned the second, the captain sabred the third.
My one brother died by steel, my other brother died by smoke.
My neck was burnt by fire, my hands froze in my gloves, my toes in my socks.
For food I had aspen buds, for drink I had maple brew, for bed I had stones in water.

SIMON: I see a cap in the grass. Is there a little one already?

GRUSHA: There is, Simon. How could I hide it? But please don't let it worry you. It's not mine.

SIMON: They say: Once the wind begins to blow, it blows through every crack. The woman need say no more.

Grusha lowers her head and says no more.

THE SINGER

There was great yearning but there was no waiting.
The oath is broken. Why was not disclosed.
Hear what she thought, but didn't say:
While you fought in the battle, soldier
The bloody battle, the bitter battle
I found a child who was helpless
And hadn't the heart to do away with it.
I had to care for what otherwise would have come to harm

I had to bend down on the floor for breadcrumbs
I had to tear myself to pieces for what was not mine
But alien.
Someone must be the helper.
Because the little tree needs its water
The little lamb loses its way when the herdsman is asleep
And the bleating remains unheard.

SIMON: Give me back the cross I gave you. Or better, throw
it in the stream.
He turns to go.
GRUSHA: Simon Chachava, don't go away. It isn't mine, it
isn't mine! *She hears the children calling.* What is it, children?
VOICES: Soldiers have come!—They are taking Michael
away!
*Grusha stands aghast as two Ironshirts, with Michael between
them, come towards her.*
IRONSHIRT: Are you Grusha? *She nods.* Is that your child?
GRUSHA: Yes. *Simon goes off.* Simon!
IRONSHIRT: We have official orders to take this child, found
in your charge, back to the city. There is suspicion that it is
Michael Abashvili, son and heir of the late Governor Georgi
Abashvili, and his wife, Natella Abashvili. Here is the
document and the seal.
They lead the child away.
GRUSHA *running after them and shouting:* Leave it here, please!
It's mine!
THE SINGER
The Ironshirts took the child away, the precious child.
The unhappy girl followed them to the city, the danger-
ous place.
The real mother demanded the child back. The foster
mother faced her trial.
Who will try the case, on whom will the child be be-
stowed?
Who will be the Judge? A good one, a bad one?
The city was in flames. On the Judgment Seat sat Azdak.

5

THE STORY OF THE JUDGE

THE SINGER

Listen now to the story of the Judge:

How he turned Judge, how he passed judgment, what
kind of Judge he is.

On the Easter Sunday of the great revolt, when the
Grand Duke was overthrown

And his Governor Abashvili, father of our child, lost his
head

The village clerk Azdak found a fugitive in the woods and
hid him in his hut.

*Azdak, in rags and tipsy, helps a fugitive dressed as a beggar into
his hut.*

AZDAK: Don't snort. You're not a horse. And it won't do you
any good with the police if you run like a dirty nose in
April. Stop, I tell you. *He catches the fugitive, who has trotted
into the hut as though he would go through the walls.* Sit down and
feed: here's a piece of cheese. *From under some rags in a chest
he fishes out some cheese, and the fugitive greedily begins to eat.*
Haven't had anything for some time, eh? *The fugitive groans.*
Why did you run so fast, you arse-hole? The police
wouldn't even have seen you!

THE FUGITIVE: Had to.

AZDAK: Blue funk? *The fugitive stares, uncomprehending.* Got the
squitters? Afraid? Don't slobber like a Grand Duke or a
sow. I can't stand it. It's well-born stinkers we've got to put
up with as God made them. Not the likes of you. I once
heard of a Senior Judge who farted at a public dinner. Just
to show his independence. Watching you eat like that really
gives me the most awful ideas! Why don't you say something? *Sharply.* Let's have a look at your hand. Can't you
hear? Show me your hand. *The fugitive slowly puts out his
hand.* White! So you're no beggar at all! A fraud! A swindle

on legs! And here am I hiding you from the police as though you were a decent human being! Why run like that if you're a landowner? Because that's what you are. Don't try to deny it. I see it in your guilty face. *He gets up.* Get out of here! *The fugitive looks uncertainly at him.* What are you waiting for, you peasant-flogger?

THE FUGITIVE: Am hunted. Ask for undivided attention. Make proposition.

AZDAK: What do you want to make? A proposition? Well, if that isn't the height of insolence! He making a proposition! The bitten man scratches his fingers bloody, and the leech makes a proposition. Get out, I tell you!

THE FUGITIVE: Understand point of view. Persuasion. Will pay 100,000 piastres for one night. How's that?

AZDAK: What? Do you think you can buy me? And for 100,000 piastres? A third-rate farm. Let's say 150,000. Got it?

THE FUGITIVE: Not on me, of course. Will be sent. Hope, don't doubt.

AZDAK: Doubt profoundly! Get out!
The fugitive gets up and trots to the door. A voice from off-stage.

VOICE: Azdak!
The fugitive turns, trots to the opposite corner and stands still.

AZDAK *shouting:* I'm not in. *He walks to the door.* Is that you spying around here again, Shauva?

POLICEMAN SHAUVA *outside, reproachfully:* You've snared another rabbit, Azdak. You promised me it wouldn't happen again.

AZDAK *severely:* Shauva, don't talk about things you don't understand. The rabbit is a dangerous and destructive animal. It devours plants, especially what they call weeds. So it must be exterminated.

SHAUVA: Azdak, don't be so hard on me. I'll lose my job if I don't arrest you. I know you have a good heart.

AZDAK: I *don't* have a good heart! How often am I to tell you I'm a man of intellect?

SHAUVA *slyly:* I know, Azdak. You're a superior person. You say so yourself. I'm a Christian and I've no education. So I ask you: if one of the Prince's rabbits is stolen, and I'm a policeman, what am I to do with the offender?

AZDAK: Shauva, Shauva, shame on you! There you stand asking me a question. Nothing is more tempting than a question. Suppose you were a woman—let's say Nunovna, that bad girl—and you showed me your thigh—Nunovna's thigh, that is—and you asked me: what shall I do with my thigh? It itches. Is she as innocent as she pretends? No. I catch a rabbit, you catch a man. Man is made in God's image. Not so a rabbit, you know that. I'm a rabbit-eater; but you're a man-eater, Shauva. And God will pass judgment on you. Shauva, go home and repent. No, stop! There's something . . . *He looks at the fugitive, who stands trembling in the corner.* No, it's nothing after all. Go home and repent. *He slams the door behind Shauva. To the fugitive:* Now you're surprised, eh? Surprised I didn't hand you over? But I couldn't hand over even a bedbug to that beast of a policeman! It goes against my grain. Don't tremble at the sight of a policeman. So old and yet so cowardly! Finish your cheese, but eat it like a poor man, or else they'll still catch you. Do I even have to tell you how a poor man behaves? *He makes him sit down, and then gives him back the cheese.* The box is the table. Put your elbows on the table, and now surround the plate with your arms as though you expected the cheese to be snatched from you at any moment. What right have you to be safe? Now hold the knife as if it were a small sickle; and don't look so greedily at your cheese, look at it mournfully—because it's already disappearing—like all good things. *Azdak watches him.* They're after you. That speaks in your favour. But how can I be sure they're not mistaken about you? In Tiflis they once hanged a landowner, a Turk. He could prove he quartered his peasants instead of merely cutting them in half, as is the custom. And he squeezed twice the usual amount of taxes out of them. His zeal was above all suspicion, and yet they hanged him like a common criminal. Why? Because he was

a Turk—something he couldn't do much about. An in-
justice! He got on to the gallows like Pontius Pilate into
the Creed. In a word, I don't trust you.

THE SINGER
> Thus Azdak gave shelter to the old beggar
> Only to find out that he was that murderer, the Grand
> Duke.
> And he was ashamed of himself, he accused himself and
> ordered the policeman
> To take him to Nukha, to Court, to be judged.

*In the Court of Justice three Ironshirts sit drinking. From a pillar
hangs a man in judge's robes. Enger Azdak, in chains, dragging
Shauwa behind him.*

AZDAK *shouting:* I have helped the Grand Duke, the Grand
Thief, the Grand Murderer, to escape! In the name of
Justice, I demand to be judged severely in a public trial!

THE FIRST IRONSHIRT: Who is this queer bird?

SHAUVA: That's our clerk, Azdak.

AZDAK: I am despicable, treacherous, branded! Tell them,
flatfoot, how I insisted on being put in chains and brought
to the capital. Because I sheltered the Grand Duke, the
Grand Swindler, by mistake. As I realized only afterwards
when I found this document in my hut. *The Ironshirts study
the document. To Shauva:* They can't read. Point out that the
branded man is accusing himself. Tell them how I forced
you to walk with me through half the night, to get everything cleared up.

SHAUVA: And all by threats. That wasn't nice of you, Azdak.

AZDAK: Shauva, shut your trap. You don't understand. A
new age has come, which will thunder over you. You're
finished. The police are being wiped out, pfft! Everything
is being investigated, brought into the open. In which
case a man prefers to give himself up. Why? Because he
won't escape the mob. Tell them how I've been shouting
all along Shoemaker Street! *He acts with expansive gestures,
looking sideways at the Ironshirts.* 'Out of ignorance I let the

Grand Swindler escape. Tear me to pieces, brothers!' So as
to get in first.

THE FIRST IRONSHIRT: And what was their answer?

SHAUVA: They comforted him in Butcher Street, and laughed
themselves sick in Shoemaker Street. That's all.

AZDAK: But here with you it's different, I know you're men
of iron. Brothers, where is the Judge? I must be tried.

THE FIRST IRONSHIRT *pointing at the hanged man:* Here's the
Judge. And stop 'brothering' us. That's rather a sore spot
this evening.

AZDAK: 'Here's the Judge.' That's an answer never heard in
Grusinia before. Citizens, where's His Excellency the
Governor? *Pointing at the gallows:* Here's His Excellency,
stranger. Where's the Chief Tax Collector? Where's the
official Recruiting Officer? The Patriarch? The Chief of
Police? Here, here, here—all here. Brothers, that's what I
expected from you.

THE SECOND IRONSHIRT: Stop! What did you expect, you
bird?

AZDAK: What happened in Persia, brothers. What happened
there.

THE SECOND IRONSHIRT: And what did happen in Persia?

AZDAK: Forty years ago. Everyone hanged. Viziers, tax-
collectors. My grandfather, a remarkable man, saw it all.
For three whole days. Everywhere.

THE SECOND IRONSHIRT: And who reigned after the Vizier
was hanged?

AZDAK: A peasant.

THE SECOND IRONSHIRT: And who commanded the army?

AZDAK: A soldier, soldier.

THE SECOND IRONSHIRT: And who paid the wages?

ADAZK: A dyer. A dyer paid the wages.

THE SECOND IRONSHIRT: Wasn't it a carpet weaver perhaps?

THE FIRST IRONSHIRT: And why did all this happen, you
Persian?

AZDAK: 'Why did all this happen?' Must there be a special

reason? Why do you scratch yourself, brother? War! Too long a war! And no justice! My grandfather brought back a song that tells what it was all about. I and my friend the policeman will sing it for you. *To Shauva:* And hold on to the rope, that's part of it. *He sings, with Shauva holding the rope.*

> Why don't our sons bleed any longer, why don't our daughters weep any more?
> Why do only the calves in the slaughterhouse have any blood, why only willows on Lake Urmi tears?
> The Grand King must have a new province, the peasant must relinquish his savings.
> In order to capture the roof of the world, the cottage roofs have to be torn down.
> Our men are scattered in all directions, so that the great ones can eat at home.
> The soldiers kill each other, the marshals salute each other.
> The widow's tax money has to be fingered to see if it's good, the swords break.
> The battle has been lost, but the helmets have been paid for.
> Is that right? Is that right?

SHAUVA: Yes, yes, yes, yes, yes, that's right.

AZDAK: Do you want to hear the whole thing?

The first Ironshirt nods.

THE SECOND IRONSHIRT *to Shauva:* Did he teach you that song?

SHAUVA: Yes. Only my voice isn't good.

THE SECOND IRONSHIRT: No. *To Azdak:* Go on singing.

AZDAK: The second verse is about the peace. *He sings:*

> The offices are jammed, the officials are working in the streets.
> The rivers overflow their banks and lay waste the fields.
> Those incapable of letting down their own trousers rule countries.
> Those who can't count up to four devour eight courses.

The corn farmers look round for buyers, but see only the
    starving.
The weavers go home from their looms in rags.
Is that right? Is that right?

SHAUVA: Yes, yes, yes, yes, yes, that's right.

AZDAK:
    That's why our sons bleed no longer, our daughters weep
        no more.
    That's why only the calves in the slaughterhouse have
        any blood.
    And the willows in the morning on Lake Urmi have any
        tears.

THE FIRST IRONSHIRT *after a pause:* Are you going to sing
    that song here in town?

AZDAK: Of course. What's wrong with it?

THE FIRST IRONSHIRT: Do you see the sky getting red?
    Turning round, Azdak sees the sky reddened by fire. That's in the
    outer town. This morning when Prince Kazbeki had Gover-
    nor Abashvili beheaded our carpet weavers also caught the
    'Persian disease'. They asked if Prince Kazbeki isn't eating
    too many courses. And this afternoon they strung up the
    town judge. But we beat them to pulp for two piastres per
    weaver, you understand?

AZDAK *after a pause:* I understand.
    *He glances shyly round and, creeping away, sits down in a corner, his
    head in his hands.*

THE FIRST IRONSHIRT *to the third, after they have all had a
    drink:* Just wait and see what'll happen next.
    *The first and second Ironshirts walk towards Azdak and block his
    exit.*

SHAUVA: I don't think he's a really bad character, gentlemen.
    He poaches a few chickens here and there, and perhaps an
    odd rabbit.

THE SECOND IRONSHIRT *approaching Azdak:* You've come
    here to fish in troubled waters, eh?

AZDAK *looking up:* I don't know why I've come here.

THE SECOND IRONSHIRT: Do you happen to be in with the

carpet weavers? *Azdak shakes his head.* And what about this song?

AZDAK: From my grandfather. A stupid, ignorant man.

THE SECOND IRONSHIRT: Right. And what about the dyer who paid the wages?

AZDAK: That was in Persia.

THE FIRST IRONSHIRT: And what about denouncing yourself for not having hanged the Grand Duke with your own hands?

AZDAK: Didn't I tell you that I let him escape?

SHAUVA: I swear to it. He let him escape.

The Ironshirts drag Azdak screaming to the gallows. Then they let him loose and burst out laughing. Azdak joins in the laughter, laughing loudest. They then unchain him. They all start drinking. Enter the fat prince with a young man.

THE FIRST IRONSHIRT *to Azdak:* There you have your new age.

More laughter.

THE FAT PRINCE: And what is there to laugh about here, my friends? Permit me a serious word. Yesterday morning the Princes of Grusinia overthrew the Grand Duke's warthirsty government and did away with his governors. Unfortunately the Grand Duke himself escaped. In this fateful hour our carpet weavers, these eternal troublemakers, had the audacity to incite a rebellion and hang our universally beloved city Judge, our dear Illa Orbeliani. Tuttut. My friends, we need peace, peace, peace in Grusinia. And justice. Here I bring you my dear nephew, Bizergan Kazbeki. He's to be the new Judge, a talented fellow. I say: the people must decide.

THE FIRST IRONSHIRT: Does this mean we elect the Judge?

THE FAT PRINCE: Precisely. The people propose a talented fellow. Confer, my friends. *The Ironshirts confer.* Don't worry, little fox. The job's yours. And once we've run the Grand Duke to earth we won't have to kiss the rabble's arse any more.

THE IRONSHIRTS *to each other:* They've got the jitters because they still haven't caught the Grand Duke.—We've this clerk to thank for that. He let him get away.—They're not sure of things yet. So they say: 'My friends!' And: 'The people must decide!'—Now he even wants justice for Grusinia!—But fun's fun as long as it lasts.—We'll ask the clerk; he knows all about justice. Hey, scoundrel . . .

AZDAK: You mean me?

THE FIRST IRONSHIRT *continues:* Would you like to have the nephew as Judge?

AZDAK: You asking me? You're not really asking me that, are you?

THE SECOND IRONSHIRT: Why not? Anything for a laugh!

AZDAK: I take it you want him put to the test? Am I right? Have you a crook on hand? An experienced one? So the candidate can show how good he is?

THE THIRD IRONSHIRT: Let me see. We have the Governor's tarts' two doctors down there. Let's use them.

AZDAK: Stop! That's no good! You can't take real crooks till we're sure of the Judge being appointed. He may be an ass, but he must be appointed or else the law is violated. The law is a very sensitive organ. Like the spleen. Once attacked with fists, death occurs. You can hang those two. Why not? You won't have violated the law, because no Judge was present. Judgment must always be passed with complete solemnity—because it's such rot. Suppose a Judge throws a woman into clink for having stolen a corncake for her child. And he isn't wearing his robes. Or he's scratching himself while passing sentence so that more than a third of his body is exposed—in which case he'd have to scratch his thigh— then the sentence he passes is a disgrace and the law is violated. It would be easier for a Judge's robe and a Judge's hat to pass sentence than for a man without all that paraphernalia. If you don't look out, the law goes up in smoke. You don't taste wine by offering it to a dog. Why not? Because the wine would be gone.

THE FIRST IRONSHIRT: So what do you suggest, you hair-splitter?

AZDAK: I'll be the defendant. I even know what sort. *Azdak whispers to them.*

THE FIRST IRONSHIRT: You? *All burst out laughing.*

THE FAT PRINCE: What have you decided?

THE FIRST IRONSHIRT: We've decided to have a rehearsal. Our good friend will act as defendant, and here's the Judge's seat for the candidate.

THE FAT PRINCE: That's unusual. But why not? *To the nephew:* A mere formality, little fox. What did they teach you? Who gets there first? The slow runner or the fast one?

THE NEPHEW: The silent one, Uncle Arsen.

The nephew sits in the Judge's seat, the fat prince standing behind him. The Ironshirts sit on the steps. Enter Azdak, imitating the unmistakeable gait of the Grand Duke.

AZDAK: Is there anyone here who knows me? I am the Grand Duke.

THE FAT PRINCE: What is he?

THE SECOND IRONSHIRT: The Grand Duke. He really does know him.

THE FAT PRINCE: Good.

THE FIRST IRONSHIRT: Get on with the proceedings.

AZDAK: Listen! I'm accused of war-mongering. Ridiculous! Am saying: ridiculous! Is that enough? If not, have brought lawyers along. About 500. *He points behind him, pretending to be surrounded by lawyers.* Requisition all available seats for lawyers. *The Ironshirts laugh; the fat prince joins in.*

THE NEPHEW *to the Ironshirts:* Do you want me to try this case? I must admit I find it rather unusual. From the point of view of taste, I mean.

THE FIRST IRONSHIRT: Go on.

THE FAT PRINCE *smiling:* Let him have it, little fox!

THE NEPHEW: All right. People of Grusinia versus Grand Duke. What have you to say, defendant?

AZDAK: Any amount. Of course, have myself read war lost. Started war at the time on advice of patriots like Uncle

Kazbeki. Demand Uncle Kazbeki as witness. *The Ironshirts laugh.*

THE FAT PRINCE *to the Ironshirts, affably:* Quite a card, eh?

THE NEPHEW: Motion overruled. You're being accused not of declaring war, which every ruler has to do once in a while, but of conducting it badly.

AZDAK: Rot! Didn't conduct it at all! Had it conducted. Had it conducted by Princes. Made a mess of it, of course.

THE NEPHEW: Do you deny having been Commander in Chief?

AZDAK: Not at all. Always was Commander in Chief. Even at birth ticked off wet-nurse; dismissed turds promptly in potty. Got used to command. Always commanded officials to rob my cash-box. Officers flog soldiers only on my command. Landlords sleep with peasant's wives only when strictly commanded by me. Uncle Kazbeki here grew stomach only on my command.

THE IRONSHIRTS *clapping:* He's good! Up the Grand Duke!

THE FAT PRINCE: Answer him, little fox! I'm with you!

THE NEPHEW: I shall answer him according to the dignity of the law. Defendant, preserve the dignity of the law.

AZDAK: Agreed. Command you proceed with the trial.

THE NEPHEW: It's not your business to command me. So you claim the Princes forced you to declare war. Then how can you claim they made a mess of it?

AZDAK: Didn't send enough troops. Embezzled funds. Brought sick horses. During attack found drunk in whorehouse. Propose Uncle Kaz as witness. *The Ironshirts laugh.*

THE NEPHEW: Are you making the outrageous claim that the Princes of this country did not fight?

AZDAK: No. Princes fought. Fought for war contracts.

THE FAT PRINCE *jumping up:* That's too much! This man talks like a carpet weaver!

AZDAK: Really? Only telling the truth!

THE FAT PRINCE: Hang him! Hang him!

THE FIRST IRONSHIRT: Keep quiet. Get on, Excellency.

THE NEPHEW: Quiet! Now pass sentence. Must be hanged.

Hanged by the neck. Having lost war. Sentence passed. No appeal.

THE FAT PRINCE *hysterically:* Away with him! Away with him! Away with him!

AZDAK: Young man, seriously advise not to fall publicly into jerky, clipped manner of speech. Can't be employed as watchdog if howl like wolf. Got it?

THE FAT PRINCE: Hang him!

AZDAK: If people realize Princes talk same language as Grand Dukes, may even hang Grand Dukes and Princes. By the way, sentence quashed. Reason: war lost, but not for Princes. Princes have won *their* war. Got themselves paid 3,863,000 piastres for horses not delivered.

THE FAT PRINCE: Hang him!

AZDAK: 8,240,000 piastres for food supplies not produced.

THE FAT PRINCE: Hang him!

AZDAK: Are therefore victors. War lost only for Grusinia, which is not present in this Court.

THE FAT PRINCE: I think that's enough, my friends. *To Azdak:* You can withdraw, gaol-bird. *To the Ironshirts:* I think you can now ratify the new Judge's appointment, my friends.

THE FIRST IRONSHIRT: Yes, we can do that. Take down the Judge's robe. *One of the Ironshirts climbs on the back of another and pulls the robe off the hanged man.* And now—to the nephew— you be off so that we can put the right arse on the right seat. *To Azdak:* Step forward, you, and sit on the Judge's seat. *Azdak hesitates.* Sit down up there, man. *Azdak is thrust on to the seat by the Ironshirts.* The Judge was always a rascal. Now the rascal shall be the Judge. *The Judge's robe is placed round his shoulders, the wicker from a bottle on his head.* Look! There's a Judge for you!

THE SINGER

Now there was civil war in the land. The rulers were unsafe.

Now Azdak was made a Judge by the Ironshirts.

Now Azdak remained a Judge for two years.

THE SINGER WITH HIS MUSICIANS
> Great houses turn to ashes
>   And blood runs down the street.
> Rats come out of the sewers
>   And maggots out of the meat.
> The thug and the blasphemer
>   Lounge by the altar-stone:
> Now, now, now Azdak
>   Sits on the Judgment throne.

Azdak sits on the Judge's seat peeling an apple. Shauva sweeps out the hall. On one side an invalid in a wheelchair, the accused doctor and a man in rags with a limp; opposite, a young man accused of blackmail. An Ironshirt stands on guard holding the Ironshirts' banner.

AZDAK: In view of the large number of cases, the Court today will hear two cases simultaneously. Before I open the proceedings, a short announcement: I receive—*he stretches out his hand; only the blackmailer produces some money and hands it to him*—I reserve for myself the right to punish one of these parties here—*he glances at the invalid*—for contempt of court. You—*to the doctor*—are a doctor, and you—*to the invalid*—are bringing a complaint against him. Is the doctor responsible for your condition?

THE INVALID: Yes. I had a stroke because of him.

AZDAK: That sounds like professional negligence.

THE INVALID: More than negligence. I gave this man money to study. So far he hasn't paid me back one penny. And when I heard he was treating a patient free, I had a stroke.

AZDAK: Rightly. *To the limping man.* And you, what do you want here?

THE LIMPING MAN: I'm the patient, your Worship.

AZDAK: He treated your leg?

THE LIMPING MAN: Not the right one. My rheumatism was in the left leg, and he operated on my right. That's why I'm limping now.

AZDAK: And you got that free?

THE INVALID: A 500-piastre operation free! For nothing! For a God-Bless-You! And I paid this man's studies! *To the doctor:* Did you learn to operate for nothing at school?

THE DOCTOR *to Azdak:* Your Worship, it is actually the custom to demand the fee before the operation, as the patient is more willing to pay before an operation than after. Which is only human. In this case I was convinced, when I started the operation, that my servant had already received the fee. In this I was mistaken.

THE INVALID: He was mistaken! A good doctor doesn't make mistakes. He examines before he operates.

AZDAK: That's right. *To Shauva:* Public Prosecutor, what's the other case about?

SHAUVA *busily sweeping:* Blackmail.

THE BLACKMAILER: High Court of Justice, I'm innocent. I only wanted to find out from the landowner in question if he really had raped his niece. He kindly informed me that this was not the case, and gave me the money only so that I could let my uncle study music.

AZDAK: Ah ha! *To the doctor:* You on the other hand can't produce any extenuating circumstances in your defence?

THE DOCTOR: Except that to err is human.

AZDAK: And you know that in money matters a good doctor is conscious of his responsibility? I once heard of a doctor who made a thousand piastres out of one sprained finger: he discovered it had something to do with the circulation of the blood, which a less good doctor would have overlooked. On another occasion, by careful treatment, he turned a mediocre gall bladder into a gold mine. You have no excuse, Doctor. The corn merchant Uxu made his son study medicine to get some knowledge of trade—our medical schools are that good. *To the blackmailer:* What's the name of the landowner?

SHAUVA: He doesn't want it to be known.

AZDAK: In that case I will pass judgment. The Court considers the blackmail proved. And you—*to the invalid—* are sentenced to a fine of 1000 piastres. If you get a second stroke the doctor will have to treat you free and if necessary amputate. *To the limping man:* As compensation, you will receive a bottle of embrocation. *To the blackmailer:* You are sentenced to hand over half the proceeds of your deal to the Public Prosecutor, to keep the landowner's name secret. You are advised, moreover, to study medicine. You seem well suited to that profession. And you, Doctor, are acquitted because of an inexcusable professional mistake. The next cases!

THE SINGER WITH HIS MUSICIANS
    Beware of willing Judges
      For Truth is a black cat
  In a windowless room at midnight
    And Justice a blind bat.
  A third and shrugging party
    Alone can right our wrong.
  This, this, this, Azdak
    Does for a mere song.

Enter Azdak from the caravansary on the highway, followed by the old, bearded innkeeper. The Judge's seat is carried by a manservant and Shauva. An Ironshirt with a banner takes up position.

AZDAK: Put it here. Then at least we can get some air and a little breeze from the lemon grove over there. It's good for Justice to do it in the open. The wind blows her skirts up and you can see what's underneath. Shauva, we have eaten too much. These rounds of inspection are very exhausting. *To the innkeeper:* So it's about your daughter-in-law?

THE INNKEEPER: Your Worship, it's about the family honour. I wish to bring an action on behalf of my son, who's gone on business across the mountain. This is the offending stableman, and here's my unfortunate daughter-in-law.
Enter the daughter-in-law, a voluptuous wench. She is veiled.

AZDAK *sitting down:* I receive. *Sighing, the innkeeper hands him some money.* Good. Now the formalities are disposed of. This is a case of rape?

THE INNKEEPER: Your Worship, I surprised this rascal in the stable in the act of laying our Ludovica in the straw.

AZDAK: Quite right, the stable. Beautiful horses. I particularly like the little roan.

THE INNKEEPER: The first thing I did of course was to berate Ludovica on behalf of my son.

AZDAK *seriously:* I said I liked the little roan.

THE INNKEEPER *coldly:* Really?—Ludovica admitted that the stableman took her against her will.

AZDAK: Take off your veil, Ludovica. *She does so.* Ludovica, you please the Court. Tell us how it happened.

LUDOVICA *as though well rehearsed:* When I entered the stable to look at the new foal, the stableman said to me of his own accord: 'It's hot today' and laid his hand on my left breast. I said to him: 'Don't do that!' But he continued to handle me indecently, which provoked my anger. Before I realized his sinful intentions, he became intimate with me. It had already happened when my father-in-law entered and accidentally trod on me.

THE INNKEEPER *explaining:* On behalf of my son.

AZDAK *to the stableman:* Do you admit that you started it?

THE STABLEMAN: Yes.

AZDAK: Ludovica, do you like to eat sweet things?

LUDOVICA: Yes, sunflower seeds.

AZDAK: Do you like sitting a long time in the tub?

LUDOVICA: Half an hour or so.

AZDAK: Public Prosecutor, just drop your knife on the floor. *Shauva does so.* Ludovica, go and pick up the Public Prosecutor's knife.

Ludovica, hips swaying, goes and picks up the knife.

Azdak points at her. Do you see that? The way it sways? The criminal element has been discovered. The rape has been proved. By eating too much, especially sweet things, by lying too long in warm water, by laziness and too soft a skin, you have raped the poor man. Do you imagine you can go around with a bottom like that and get away with it in Court? This is a case of deliberate assault with a dangerous weapon. You are sentenced to hand over to the Court the little roan which your father liked to ride on behalf of

his son. And now, Ludovica, come with me to the stable
so that the Court may investigage the scene of the crime.

*Azdak is carried on his Judge's seat by Ironshirts from place to
place on the Grusinian highway. Behind him come Shauva dragging
the gallows and the stableman leading the little roan.*

THE SINGER WITH HIS MUSICIANS
    No more did the Lower Orders
        Tremble in their shoes
    At the bellows of their Betters
        At Come-Here's and *Listen-You's.*
    His balances were crooked
        But they shouted in the streets:—
    'Good, good, good is Azdak
        And the measure that he metes!'

    He took them from Wealthy Peter
        To give to Penniless Paul
    Sealed his illegal judgments
        With a waxen tear, and all
    The rag-tag-and-bobtail
        Ran crying up and down:—
    'Cheer, cheer, cheer for Azdak
        The darling of the town!'

The little group slowly withdraws.

    To love your next-door neighbour
        Approach him with an axe
    For prayers and saws and sermons
        Are unconvincing facts.
    What miracles of preaching
        A good sharp blade can do:
    So, so, so, so Azdak
        Makes miracles come true.

*Azdak's Judge's seat is in a tavern. Three farmers stand before
Azdak. Shauva brings him wine. In a corner stands an old peasant
woman. In the open doorway, and outside, stand villagers and
spectators. An Ironshirt stands guard with a banner.*

AZDAK: The Public Prosecutor opens the proceedings.

SHAUVA: It's about a cow. For five weeks the defendant has had a cow in her stable, the property of farmer Suru. She was also found to be in the possession of a stolen ham. And cows belonging to farmer Shutoff were killed after he had asked the defendant to pay the rent for a field.

THE FARMERS: It's about my ham, Your Worship.—It's about my cow, Your Worship.—It's about my field, Your Worship.

AZDAK: Granny, what have you got to say to all this?

THE OLD WOMAN: Your Worship, one night towards morning, five weeks ago, there was a knock at my door, and outside stood a bearded man with a cow. He said, 'Dear woman, I am the miracle-working St Banditus. And because your son has been killed in the war, I bring you this cow as a keepsake. Take good care of it!'

THE FARMERS: The robber Irakli, Your Worship!—Her brother-in-law, Your Worship! The cattle thief, the incendiary!—He must be beheaded!

Outside a woman screams. The crowd grows restless and retreats. Enter the bandit Irakli, with a huge axe.

THE FARMERS: Irakli! *They cross themselves.*

THE BANDIT: A very good evening, dear friends! A glass of wine!

AZDAK: Public Prosecutor, a jug of wine for the guest. And who are you?

THE BANDIT: I'm a wandering hermit, Your Worship. And thank you for the kind gift. *He empties the glass which Shauva has brought.* Same again!

AZDAK: I'm Azdak. *He gets up and bows. The bandit also bows.* The Court welcomes the stranger hermit. Go on with your story, Granny.

THE OLD WOMAN: Your Worship, that first night I didn't know that St Banditus could work miracles, it was only the cow. But one night a few days later the farmer's servants came to take the cow away from me. Then they turned round in front of my door and went off without the cow.

And on their heads sprouted bumps big as a fist. Then I knew that St Banditus had changed their hearts and turned them into friendly people.

The bandit roars with laughter.

THE FIRST FARMER: I know what changed them.

AZDAK: That's good. You can tell us later. Continue.

THE OLD WOMAN: Your Worship, the next one to become a good man was farmer Shutoff—a devil, as everyone knows. But St Banditus brought it about that Shutoff let me off paying the rent for the field.

THE SECOND FARMER: Because my cows were killed in the field.

The bandit laughs.

THE OLD WOMAN *answering Azdak's sign to continue:* And then one morning the ham came flying in at my window. It hit me in the small of the back. I've been lame ever since. Look, Your Worship. *She limps a few steps. The bandit laughs.* I ask Your Worship: when was a poor old body ever given a ham except by a miracle?

The bandit starts sobbing.

AZDAK *rising from his seat:* Granny, that's a question that strikes straight at the Court's heart. Be so kind as to sit down here.

Hesitating, the old woman sits on the Judge's seat. Azdak sits on the floor, glass in hand.

> Little mother, I almost called you Mother Grusinia, the woebegone
> The bereaved one, whose sons are in the war.
> Who is beaten with fists, but full of hope.
> Who weeps when she is given a cow
> And is surprised when she is not beaten.
> Little mother, pass merciful sentence on us, the damned!

He bellows to the farmers.

Admit that you don't believe in miracles, you atheists! Each of you is sentenced to pay 500 piastres! For your lack of faith. Get out!

The farmers creep out.

And you, little mother, and you—*to the bandit*—pious man, drink a jug of wine with the Public Prosecutor and Azdak!

THE SINGER WITH HIS MUSICIANS
    To feed the starving people
        He broke the laws like bread
    There on the seat of justice
        With the gallows over his head
    For more than seven hundred
        Days he calmed their wails
    Well, well, well, did Azdak
        Measure with false scales.

    Two summers and two winters
        A poor man judged the poor
    And on the wreck of justice
        He brought them safe to shore
    For he spoke in the mob language
        That the mob understands.
    I, I, I, cried Azdak
        Take bribes from empty hands.

THE SINGER
    Then the era of disorder was over, the Grand Duke
        returned
    The Governor's wife returned, a Judgment was held.
    Many people died, the suburbs burned anew, and fear
        seized Azdak.

Azdak's Judge's seat stands again in the Court of Justice. Azdak sits on the ground mending a shoe and talking to Shauva. Noises outside. Above a wall the fat prince's head is carried by on a lance.

AZDAK: Shauva, your days of slavery are numbered, perhaps even the minutes. For a long time I have held you on the iron curb of reason, and it has made your mouth bloody. I have lashed you with arguments founded on reason, and ill-treated you with logic. You are by nature a weak creature, and if one slyly throws you an argument, you have to devour it; you can't resist. By nature you are compelled to lick the hand of a superior being, but superior beings can be very different. And now comes your liberation, and you will soon be able to follow your inclinations, which are low. You will be able to follow your unerring instinct, which teaches you to plant your heavy boot on the faces of men. Gone is the era of confusion and disorder, and the great times which I found described in the Song of Chaos have not yet come. Let us now sing that song together in memory of those wonderful days. Sit down and don't violate the music. Don't be afraid. It sounds all right. It has a popular refrain.

He sings

> Sister, hide your face; brother, take your knife, the times are out of joint.
>
> The noblemen are full of complaints, the simple folk full of joy.
>
> The city says: let us drive the strong ones out of our midst.
>
> Storm the government buildings, destroy the lists of the serfs.
>
> Now the masters' noses are put to the grindstone. Those who never saw the day have emerged.
>
> The poor-boxes of ebony are broken, the precious sesame wood is used for beds.
>
> He who lacked bread now possesses barns; he who lived on the corn of charity, now measures it out himself.

SHAUVA: Oh, oh, oh, oh.

AZDAK:

> Where are you, General? Please, please, please, restore order.
>
> The son of the nobleman can no longer be recognized; the child of the mistress becomes the son of her slave.
>
> The councillors are taking shelter in the barn; he who was barely allowed to sleep on the wall now lolls in bed.
>
> He who once rowed a boat now owns ships; when their owner looks for them, they are no longer his.
>
> Five men are sent out by their master. They say: go yourself, we have arrived.

SHAUVA: Oh, oh, oh, oh.

AZDAK:

Where are you, General? Please, please, please restore order!

Yes, so it might have been, if order had been much longer neglected. But now the Grand Duke, whose life I saved like a fool, has returned to the Capital. And the Persians have lent him an army to restore order. The outer town is already in flames. Go and get me the Big Book I like to sit on. *Shauva brings the book from the Judge's seat. Azdak opens it.* This is the Statute Book and I've always used it, as you can confirm.

SHAUVA: Yes, to sit on.

AZDAK: Now I'd better look and see what they can do to me, because I've always allowed the have-nots to get away with everything. And I'll have to pay for it dearly. I helped to put Poverty on to its rickety legs, so they'll hang me for drunkenness. I peeped into the rich man's pocket, which is considered bad taste. And I can't hide anywhere, for all the world knows me, since I have helped the world.

SHAUVA: Someone's coming!

AZDAK *in a panic walks trembling to the seat:* The game is up! But I'll give no man the pleasure of seeing human greatness. I'll beg on my knees for mercy. Spittle will slobber down my chin. The fear of death is upon me.

Enter Natella Abashvili, the Governor's wife, followed by the Adjutant and an Ironshirt.

THE GOVERNOR'S WIFE: What kind of man is that, Shalva?

AZDAK: A willing one, Your Excellency, a man ready to oblige.

THE ADJUTANT: Natella Abashvili, wife of the late Governor, has just returned and is looking for her three-year-old son, Michael. She has been informed that the child was abducted to the mountains by a former servant.

AZDAK: It will be brought back, Your Highness, at your service.

THE ADJUTANT: They say that the person in question is passing it off as her own child.

AZDAK: She will be beheaded, Your Highness, at your service.

THE ADJUTANT: That's all.

THE GOVERNOR'S WIFE *leaving:* I don't like that man.

AZDAK *following her to the door, and bowing:* Everything will be arranged, Your Highness, at your service.

6

THE CHALK CIRCLE

THE SINGER
  Now listen to the story of the trial concerning the child of
    the Governor Abashvili
  To establish the true mother
  By the famous test of the Chalk Circle.
  The courtyard of the lawcourts in Nukha. Ironshirts lead Michael in, then go across the stage and out at the back. One Ironshirt holds Grusha back under the doorway with his lance until the child has been taken away. Then she is admitted. She is accompanied by the former Governor's cook. Distant noises and a fire-red sky.

GRUSHA: He's so good, he can wash himself already.

THE COOK: You're lucky. This is not a real Judge; this is Azdak. He's a drunk and doesn't understand anything. And the biggest thieves have been acquitted by him, because he mixes everything up and because the rich never offer him big enough bribes. The likes of us get off lightly sometimes.

GRUSHA: I need some luck today.

THE COOK: Touch wood. *She crosses herself.* I think I'd better say a quick prayer that the Judge will be drunk.
  Her lips move in prayer, while Grusha looks round in vain for the child.

THE COOK: What I can't understand is why you want to hold on to it at any price, if it's not yours. In these days.

GRUSHA: It's mine. I've brought it up.

THE COOK: But didn't you ever wonder what would happen when she returned?

GRUSHA: At first I thought I'd give it back to her. Then I thought she wouldn't return.

THE COOK: And a borrowed coat keeps one warm, too, eh? *Grusha nods.* I'll swear anything you like, because you're a decent person. *Memorizes aloud:* I had him in my care for five piastres, and on Thursday evening, when the riots started, Grusha came to fetch him. *She sees the soldier, Chachava, approaching.* But you have done Simon great wrong. I've talked to him. He can't understand it.

GRUSHA *unaware of Simon's presence:* I can't be bothered with that man just now, if he doesn't understand anything.

THE COOK: He has understood that the child is not yours; but that you're married and won't be free until death parts you —he can't understand that.
Grusha sees Simon and greets him.

SIMON *gloomily:* I wanted to tell the woman that I am ready to swear I am the father of the child.

GRUSHA *low:* That's right, Simon.

SIMON: At the same time, I would like to say that I am hereby not bound to anything; nor the woman, either.

THE COOK: That's unnecessary. She's married. You know that.

SIMON: That's her business and doesn't need rubbing in.
Enter two Ironshirts.

THE IRONSHIRTS: Where's the Judge?—Has anyone seen the Judge?

GRUSHA *who has turned away and covered her face:* Stand in front of me. I shouldn't have come to Nukha. If I run into the Ironshirt, the one I hit over the head . . .
The Ironshirt who has brought in the child steps forward.

THE IRONSHIRT: The Judge isn't here.
The two Ironshirts go on searching.

THE COOK: I hope something hasn't happened to him. With any other Judge you'd have less chance than a chicken has teeth.
Enter another Ironshirt.

THE IRONSHIRT *who had inquired for the Judge, to the other Iron-shirt:* There are only two old people and a child here. The Judge has bolted.

THE OTHER IRONSHIRT: Go on searching!

The first two Ironshirts exit quickly. The third remains behind. Grusha lets out a scream. The Ironshirt turns round. He is the Corporal, and has a large scar right across his face.

THE IRONSHIRT *in the gateway:* What's the matter, Shotta? Do you know her?

THE CORPORAL *after a long stare:* No.

THE IRONSHIRT: She's the one who's supposed to have stolen the Abashvili child. If you know anything about it, Shotta, you can make a packet of money.

Exit the Corporal, cursing.

THE COOK: Was it him? *Grusha nods.* I think he'll keep his mouth shut, otherwise he'll have to admit he was after the child.

GRUSHA *relieved:* I'd almost forgotten I'd saved the child from them . . .

Enter the Governor's wife, followed by the Adjutant and two lawyers.

THE GOVERNOR'S WIFE: Thank God! At least the common people aren't here. I can't stand their smell, it always gives me migraine.

THE FIRST LAWYER: Madam, I must ask you to be as careful as possible in everything you say, until we have another Judge.

THE GOVERNOR'S WIFE: But I didn't say anything, Illo Shuboladze. I love the people—with their simple, straight-forward ways. It's just their smell that brings on my migraine.

THE SECOND LAWYER: There will hardly be any spectators. Most of the population is behind locked doors because of the riots in the outer town.

THE GOVERNOR'S WIFE *looking at Grusha:* Is that the creature?

THE FIRST LAWYER: I beg you, most gracious Natella

Abashvili, to abstain from all invective until it is absolutely certain that the Grand Duke has appointed a new Judge and we have got rid of the present one, who is about the lowest ever seen in a Judge's robe. And things seem to be on the move, as you will see.

Ironshirts enter the courtyard.

THE COOK: Her Ladyship wouldn't hesitate to pull your hair out if she didn't know that Azdak is for the poor people. He goes by the face.

Two Ironshirts begin by fastening a rope to the pillar. Azdak, in chains, is led in, followed by Shauwa, also in chains. The three farmers bring up the rear.

ONE IRONSHIRT: Trying to run away, eh? *He beats Azdak.*

ONE FARMER: Pull the Judge's robe off before we string him up!

Ironshirts and farmers pull the robe off Azdak. His torn underwear becomes visible. Then someone kicks him.

AN IRONSHIRT *pushing him on to someone else:* Anyone want a bundle of Justice? Here it is!

Accompanied by shouts of 'It's all yours!' and 'I don't want it!' they hurl Azdak back and forth until he collapses. Then he is hauled up and dragged under the noose.

THE GOVERNOR'S WIFE *who, during the 'ball-game', has been clapping her hands hysterically:* I disliked that man from the moment I first saw him.

AZDAK *covered in blood, panting:* I can't see. Give me a rag.

THE OTHER IRONSHIRT: What is it you want to see?

AZDAK: You, you dogs! *He wipes the blood out of his eyes with his shirt.* Good morning, dogs! How are you, dogs? How's the dog world? Does it stink good? Have you got another boot to lick? Are you back at each other's throats, dogs?

Enter a dust-covered rider accompanied by a corporal. He takes some documents from a leather case and looks through them. He interrupts.

THE RIDER: Stop! I bring a despatch from the Grand Duke, containing the latest appointments.

THE CORPORAL *bellows:* Atten - shun!

All jump to attention.

THE RIDER: Of the new Judge it says: We appoint a man whom we have to thank for the saving of a life of the utmost importance to the country. A certain Azdak in Nukha. Which is he?

SHAUVA *pointing:* That's him on the gallows, Your Excellency.

THE CORPORAL *bellowing:* What's going on here?

THE IRONSHIRT: I ask to be allowed to report that His Worship has already been His Worship. He was declared the enemy of the Grand Duke only on these farmers' denunciation.

THE CORPORAL *pointing at the farmers:* March them off! *They are marched off, bowing incessantly.* See to it that His Worship is exposed to no more indignities.

Exit the rider with the corporal.

THE COOK *to Shauva:* She clapped her hands! I hope he saw it!

THE FIRST LAWYER: This is a catastrophe.

Azdak has fainted. Coming to, he is dressed again in a Judge's robe. He walks away, swaying, from the group of Ironshirts.

THE IRONSHIRTS: Don't take it amiss, Your Worship. What are Your Worship's wishes?

AZDAK: Nothing, fellow dogs. An occasional boot to lick. *To Shauva:* I pardon you. *He is unchained.* Fetch me some of the red wine. The sweetest. *Exit Shauva.* Get out of here, I've got to judge a case. *The Ironshirts go. Shauva returns with a jug of wine. Azdak takes deep gulps.* Get me something for my backside. *Shauva brings the Statute Book and puts it on the Judge's seat. Azdak sits on it.* I receive! *The faces of the prosecutors, among whom a worried council has been held, show smiles of relief. They whisper.*

THE COOK: Oh dear!

SIMON: 'A well can't be filled with dew!' they say.

THE LAWYERS *approaching Azdak, who stands up expectantly:* An absolutely ridiculous case, Your Worship. The accused has abducted the child and refuses to hand it over.

AZDAK *stretching out his hand, and glancing at Grusha:* A most attractive person. *He receives more money.* I open the proceedings and demand the absolute truth. *To Grusha:* Especially from you.

THE FIRST LAWYER: High Court of Justice! Blood, as the saying goes, is thicker than water. This old proverb . . .

AZDAK: The Court wants to know the lawyer's fee.

THE FIRST LAWYER *surprised:* I beg your pardon? *Azdak rubs his thumb and index finger.* Oh, I see. 500 piastres, Your Worship, is the answer to the Court's somewhat unusual question.

AZDAK: Did you hear? The question is unusual. I ask it because I listen to you in a quite different way if I know you are good.

THE FIRST LAWYER *bowing:* Thank you, Your Worship. High Court of Justice! Of all bonds the bonds of blood are the strongest. Mother and child—is there a more intimate relationship? Can one tear a child from its mother? High Court of Justice! She has conceived it in the holy ecstasies of love. She has carried it in her womb. She has fed it with her blood. She has borne it with pain. High Court of Justice! It has been observed, Your Worship, how even the wild tigress, robbed of her young, roams restless through the mountains, reduced to a shadow. Nature herself . . .

AZDAK *interrupting, to Grusha:* What's your answer to all this and anything else the lawyer might have to say?

GRUSHA: He's mine.

AZDAK: Is that all? I hope you can prove it. In any case, I advise you to tell me why you think the child should be given to you.

GRUSHA: I've brought him up according to my best knowledge and conscience. I always found him something to eat. Most of the time he had a roof over his head. And I went to all sorts of trouble for him. I had expenses, too. I didn't think of my own comfort. I brought up the child to be friendly with everyone. And from the beginning I taught him to work as well as he could. But he's still very small.

THE FIRST LAWYER: Your Worship, it is significant that the person herself doesn't claim any bond of blood between herself and this child.

AZDAK: The Court takes note.

THE FIRST LAWYER: Thank you, Your Worship. Please permit a woman who has suffered much—who has already lost her husband and now also has to fear the loss of her child—to address a few words to you. Her Highness, Natella Abashvili...

THE GOVERNOR'S WIFE *quietly:* A most cruel fate, sir, forces me to ask you to return my beloved child. It's not for me to describe to you the tortures of a bereaved mother's soul, the anxiety, the sleepless nights, the...

THE SECOND LAWYER *exploding:* It's outrageous the way this woman is treated. She's not allowed to enter her husband's palace. The revenue of her estates is blocked. She is told cold-bloodedly that it's tied to the heir. She can't do anything without the child. She can't even pay her lawyers. *To the first lawyer who, desperate about this outburst, makes frantic gestures to stop him speaking:* Dear Illo Shuboladze, why shouldn't it be divulged now that it's the Abashvili estates that are at stake?

THE FIRST LAWYER: Please, Honoured Sandro Oboladze! We had agreed... *To Azdak:* Of course it is correct that the trial will also decide whether our noble client will obtain the right to dispose of the large Abashvili estates. I say 'also' on purpose, because in the foreground stands the human tragedy of a mother, as Natella Abashvili has rightly explained at the beginning of her moving statement. Even if Michael Abashvili were *not* the heir to the estates, he would still be the dearly beloved child of my client.

AZDAK: Stop! The Court is touched by the mention of the estates. It's a proof of human feeling.

THE SECOND LAWYER: Thanks, Your Worship. Dear Illo Shuboladze, in any case we can prove that the person who took possession of the child is not the child's mother. Permit me to lay before the Court the bare facts. By an unfortunate chain of circumstances, the child, Michael Abashvili, was left behind while his mother was making her escape. Grusha, the Palace kitchenmaid, was present on this Easter Sunday and was observed busying herself with the child . . .

THE COOK: All her mistress was thinking about was what kind of dresses she would take along.

THE SECOND LAWYER *unmoved:* Almost a year later Grusha turned up in a mountain village with a child, and there entered into matrimony with . . .

AZDAK: How did you get into that mountain village?

GRUSHA: On foot, Your Worship. And he was mine.

SIMON: I am the father, Your Worship.

THE COOK: I had him in my care for five piastres, Your Worship.

THE SECOND LAWYER: This man is engaged to Grusha, High Court of Justice, and for this reason his testimony is not reliable.

AZDAK: Are you the man she married in the mountain village?

SIMON: No, Your Worship, she married a peasant.

AZDAK *winking at Grusha:* Why? *Pointing at Simon:* Isn't he any good in bed? Tell the truth.

GRUSHA: We didn't get that far. I married because of the child, so that he should have a roof over his head. *Pointing at Simon.* He was in the war, Your Worship.

AZDAK: And now he wants you again, eh?

SIMON: I want to state in evidence . . .

GRUSHA *angrily:* I am no longer free, Your Worship.

AZDAK: And the child, you claim, is the result of whoring? *Grusha does not answer.* I'm going to ask you a question: What kind of child is it? Is it one of those ragged streeturchins? Or is it a child from a well-to-do family?

GRUSHA *angrily:* It's an ordinary child.

AZDAK: I mean, did he have fine features from the beginning?

GRUSHA: He had a nose in his face.

AZDAK: He had a nose in his face. I consider that answer of yours to be important. They say of me that once, before passing judgment, I went out and sniffed at a rosebush. Tricks of this kind are necessary nowadays. I'll cut things short now, and listen no longer to your lies. *To Grusha:* Especially yours. *To the group of defendants:* I can imagine what you've cooked up between you to cheat me. I know you. You're swindlers.

GRUSHA *suddenly:* I can quite understand your wanting to cut it short, having seen what you received!

AZDAK: Shut up! Did I receive anything from you?

GRUSHA *while the cook tries to restrain her:* Because I haven't got anything.

AZDAK: Quite true. I never get a thing from starvelings. I might just as well starve myself. You want justice, but do you want to pay for it? When you go to the butcher you know you have to pay. But to the Judge you go as though to a funeral supper.

SIMON *loudly:* 'When the horse was shod, the horsefly stretched out its leg', as the saying is.

AZDAK *eagerly accepting the challenge:* 'Better a treasure in the sewer than a stone in the mountain stream.'

SIMON: ' "A fine day. Let's go fishing," said the angler to the worm.'

AZDAK: ' "I'm my own master," said the servant, and cut off his foot.'

SIMON: ' "I love you like a father," said the Czar to the peasant, and had the Czarevitch's head chopped off.'

AZDAK: 'The fool's worst enemy is himself.'

SIMON: But 'a fart has no nose'.

AZDAK: Fined ten piastres for indecent language in Court. That'll teach you what Justice is.

GRUSHA: That's a fine kind of Justice. You jump on us because we don't talk so refined as that lot with their lawyers.

AZDAK: Exactly. The likes of you are too stupid. It's only right that you should get it in the neck.

GRUSHA: Because you want to pass the child on to her. She who is too refined even to know how to change its nappies! You don't know any more about Justice than I do, that's clear.

AZDAK: There's something in that. I'm an ignorant man. I haven't even a decent pair of trousers under my robe. See for yourself. With me, everything goes on food and drink. I was educated in a convent school. Come to think of it, I'll fine you ten piastres, too. For contempt of Court. What's more, you're a very silly girl to turn me against you, instead of making eyes at me and wagging your backside a bit to keep me in a tood temper. Twenty piastres!

GRUSHA: Even if it were thirty, I'd tell you what I think of your justice, you drunken onion! How dare you talk to me as though you were the cracked Isaiah on the church window! When they pulled you out of your mother, it wasn't planned that you'd rap her over the knuckles for pinching a little bowl of corn from somewhere! Aren't you ashamed of yourself when you see how afraid I am of you? But you've let yourself become their servant. So that their houses are not taken away, because they've stolen them. Since when do houses belong to bed-bugs? But you're on the look-out, otherwise they couldn't drag our men into their wars. You bribe-taker!

Azdak gets up. He begins to beam. With a little hammer he knocks on the table half-heartedly as if to get silence. But as Grusha's scolding continues, he only beats time with it.

I've no respect for you. No more than for a thief or a murderer with a knife, who does what he wants. You can take the child away from me, a hundred against one, but I tell you one thing: for a profession like yours, they ought to choose only bloodsuckers and men who rape children. As a punishment. To make them sit in judgment over their fellow men, which is worse than swinging from the gallows.

AZDAK *sitting down:* Now it will be thirty! And I won't go on brawling with you as though we were in a tavern. What would happen to my dignity as a Judge? I've lost all interest in your case. Where's the couple who wanted a divorce? *To Shauva:* Bring them in. This case is adjourned for fifteen minutes.

THE FIRST LAWYER *to the Governor's wife:* Without producing any more evidence, Madam, we have the verdict in the bag.

THE COOK *to Grusha:* You've gone and spoiled your chances with him. You won't get the child now.

Enter a very old couple.

THE GOVERNOR'S WIFE: Shalva, my smelling salts!

AZDAK: I receive. *The old couple do not understand.* I hear you want to be divorced. How long have you been living together?

THE OLD WOMAN: Forty years, Your Worship.

AZDAK: And why d'you want a divorce?

THE OLD MAN: We don't like each other, Your Worship.

AZDAK: Since when?

THE OLD WOMAN: Oh, from the very beginning, Your Worship.

AZDAK: I'll consider your case and deliver my verdict when I'm finished with the other one. *Shauva leads them into the background.* I need the child. *He beckons Grusha towards him and bends not unkindly towards her.* I've noticed that you have a soft spot for justice. I don't believe he's your child, but if he were yours, woman, wouldn't you want him to be rich? You'd only have to say he isn't yours and at once he'd have a palace, scores of horses in his stable, scores of beggars on his doorstep, scores of soldiers in his service, and scores of petitioners in his courtyard. Now, what d'you say? Don't you want him to be rich?

Grusha is silent.

THE SINGER: Listen now to what the angry girl thought, but didn't say. *He sings:*

He who wears the shoes of gold
Tramples on the weak and old
Does evil all day long
And mocks at wrong.

O to carry as one's own
Heavy is the heart of stone.
The power to do ill
Wears out the will.

Hunger he will dread
Not those who go unfed:
Fear the fall of night
But not the light.

AZDAK: I think I understand you, woman.

GRUSHA: I won't give him away. I've brought him up, and he knows me.

Enter Shauva with the child.

THE GOVERNOR'S WIFE: It's in rags!

GRUSHA: That's not true. I wasn't given the time to put on his good shirt.

THE GOVERNOR'S WIFE: It's been in a pig-sty.

GRUSHA *furious:* I'm no pig, but there are others who are. Where did you leave your child?

THE GOVERNOR'S WIFE: I'll let you have it, you vulgar person. *She is about to throw herself on Grusha, but is restrained by her lawyers.* She's a criminal! She must be flogged! Right away!

THE SECOND LAWYER *holding his hand over her mouth:* Most gracious Natella Abashvili, you promised . . . Your Worship, the plaintiff's nerves . . .

AZDAK: Plaintiff and defendant! The Court has listened to your case, and has come to no decision as to who the real mother of this child is. I as Judge have the duty of choosing a mother for the child. I'll make a test. Shauva, get a piece of chalk and draw a circle on the floor. *Shauva does so.* Now place the child in the centre. *Shauva puts Michael, who smiles at Grusha, in the centre of the circle.* Plaintiff and defendant, stand near the circle, both of you. *The Governor's wife and Grusha step up to the circle.* Now each of you take the child by a hand. The true mother is she who has the strength to pull the child out of the circle, towards herself.

THE SECOND LAWYER *quickly:* High Court of Justice, I protest! I object that the fate of the great Abashvili estates, which are bound up with the child as the heir, should be made dependent on such a doubtful wrestling match. Moreover, my client does not command the same physical strength as this person, who is accustomed to physical work.

AZDAK: She looks pretty well fed to me. Pull!

The Governor's wife pulls the child out of the circle to her side. Grusha has let it go and stands aghast.

THE FIRST LAWYER *congratulating the Governor's wife:* What did I say! The bonds of blood!

AZDAK *to Grusha:* What's the matter with you? You didn't pull!

GRUSHA: I didn't hold on to him. *She runs to Azdak.* Your Worship, I take back everything I said against you. I ask your forgiveness. If I could just keep him until he can speak properly. He knows only a few words.

AZDAK: Don't influence the Court! I bet you know only twenty yourself. All right, I'll do the test once more, to make certain.

The two women take up positions again.

AZDAK: Pull!

Again Grusha lets go of the child.

GRUSHA *in despair:* I've brought him up! Am I to tear him to pieces? I can't do it!

AZDAK *rising:* And in this manner the Court has established the true mother. *To Grusha:* Take your child and be off with it. I advise you not to stay in town with him. *To the Governor's wife:* And you disappear before I fine you for fraud. Your estates fall to the city. A playground for children will be made out of them. They need one, and I have decided it shall be called after me—The Garden of Azdak.

The Governor's wife has fainted and is carried out by the Adjutant. Her lawyers have preceded her. Grusha stands motionless. Shauva leads the child towards her.

AZDAK: Now I'll take off this Judge's robe—it has become

too hot for me. I'm not cut out for a hero. But I invite you all to a little farewell dance, outside on the meadow. Oh, I had almost forgotten something in my excitement. I haven't signed the decree for divorce.

Using the Judge's seat as a table, he writes something on a piece of paper and prepares to leave. Dance music has started.

SHAUVA *having read what is on the paper:* But that's not right. You haven't divorced the old couple. You've divorced Grusha from her husband.

AZDAK: Have I divorced the wrong ones? I'm sorry, but it'll have to stand. I never retract anything. If I did, there'd be no law and order. *To the old couple:* Instead, I'll invite you to my feast. You won't mind dancing with each other. *To Grusha and Simon:* I've still got 40 piastres coming from you.

SIMON *pulling out his purse:* That's cheap, Your Worship. And many thanks.

AZDAK *pocketing the money:* I'll need it.

GRUSHA: So we'd better leave town tonight, eh, Michael? *About to take the child on her back. To Simon:* You like him?

SIMON *taking the child on his back:* With my respects, I like him.

GRUSHA: And now I can tell you: I took him because on that Easter Sunday I got engaged to you. And so it is a child of love. Michael, let's dance.

She dances with Michael. Simon dances with the cook. The old couple dance with each other. Azdak stands lost in thought. The dancers soon hide him from view. Occasionally he is seen again, but less and less as more couples enter and join the dance.

THE SINGER

And after this evening Azdak disappeared and was never seen again.

But the people of Grusinia did not forget him and often remembered

His time of Judgment as a brief

Golden Age that was almost just.

The dancing couples dance out. Azdak has disappeared.

But you, who have listened to the story of the Chalk
    Circle
Take note of the meaning of the ancient song:
That what there is shall belong to those who are good for
    it, thus
The children to the maternal, that they thrive;
The carriages to good drivers, that they are driven well;
And the valley to the waterers, that it shall bear fruit.